# Qualitative and Mixed Methods Data Analysis Using Dedoose

Sara Miller McCune founded SAGE Publishing in 1965 to support the dissemination of usable knowledge and educate a global community. SAGE publishes more than 1000 journals and over 800 new books each year, spanning a wide range of subject areas. Our growing selection of library products includes archives, data, case studies and video. SAGE remains majority owned by our founder and after her lifetime will become owned by a charitable trust that secures the company's continued independence.

Los Angeles | London | New Delhi | Singapore | Washington DC | Melbourne

# Qualitative and Mixed Methods Data Analysis Using Dedoose

## A Practical Approach for Research Across the Social Sciences

Michelle Salmona
*Institute for Mixed Methods Research*

Eli Lieber
*University of California, Los Angeles*

Dan Kaczynski
*University of Canberra*

**Foreword by Lyn Richards**
**Closing Remarks by Thomas S. Weisner**

Los Angeles | London | New Delhi
Singapore | Washington DC | Melbourne

FOR INFORMATION:

SAGE Publications, Inc.
2455 Teller Road
Thousand Oaks, California 91320
E-mail: order@sagepub.com

SAGE Publications Ltd.
1 Oliver's Yard
55 City Road
London, EC1Y 1SP
United Kingdom

SAGE Publications India Pvt. Ltd.
B 1/I 1 Mohan Cooperative Industrial Area
Mathura Road, New Delhi 110 044
India

SAGE Publications Asia-Pacific Pte. Ltd.
18 Cross Street #10-10/11/12
China Square Central
Singapore 048423

*Library of Congress Control Number: 2019947870*

ISBN 978-1-5063-9781-8

Acquisitions Editor: Leah Fargotstein
Editorial Assistant: Claire Laminen
Production Editor: Rebecca Lee
Copy Editor: QuADS Prepress Pvt. Ltd.
Typesetter: Hurix Digital
Proofreader: Larry Baker
Indexer: Naomi Linzer
Cover Designer: Lysa Becker
Marketing Manager: Shari Countryman

19 20 21 22 23 10 9 8 7 6 5 4 3 2 1

# Brief Contents

# Detailed Contents

# Foreword

·······················································································

There's no point in designing software if researchers can't use it, and use it *well*, for *useful* research. And there's no point in writing user guides and introductory texts to help them use it if it won't help them to do what they are trying to do. (This challenge is tougher if they are not quite sure what they were trying to do!) But there is also no point in software developers telling researchers that they should be trying to do what this particular software supports. These are lessons learned long ago as researchers and software developers began creating tools to help embattled qualitative researchers do justice to their rich, unruly data.

More than a quarter of a century ago, I coauthored a paper titled "Computing in Qualitative Analysis: A Healthy Development?" (Richards & Richards, 1991). A decade after the first heady days of qualitative computing, I wasn't at all sure that this revolution was unequivocally good for research and researchers. Yes, they could do much more with their data, but there were valid concerns about the ways technology was skewing method. Qualitative computing was developing alongside and in clear connection with the increased acceptance of (various versions of) qualitative method, in disciplines that had hitherto derided small samples and messy data. Researchers with no qualitative training were discovering the excitement of unstructured data and increasingly relying on software to do the analysis.

It's been a long revolution, and in many ways a disappointing one. Most of the challenges met in the 1990s by developers, users, and teachers exist today. Most of the howlers we hit at the help desks in the early years are heard today, and we still bite back the honest answer. (Q: "Will your software analyze my data?" A: "No, and it won't write your thesis either." Q: "I've coded all my data, what do I do next?" A: "If you don't know why you were coding, jump off the roof.") All the qualitative software developers learned fast that in this context, a user guide was not enough to help researchers approach and skillfully use software tools for their research purposes. So a new category of methods books was born, explaining a particular research software package within the context of the research goals and challenges a user is (probably) bringing to it.

This book is the latest in that fine tradition, and it takes a welcome new approach to the problem of combining three purposes: (1) methodological discussion (here the emphasis is on mixed qualitative and quantitative studies), (2) user guide instruction (for Dedoose), and (3) real examples of projects (from published evaluation studies).

Writing simultaneously for all three purposes is enormously difficult as each requires a different sort of writing and a continuity of content. Inevitably when combined they tend to produce a sort of spaghetti heap of tangled threads. In this book, the decision has been made for a more lasagne-like approach. Each of the later sections offers three layers: a section on methods, then software instruction, and finally stand-alone case studies. This structure should assist readers in accessing the help they need—and skipping material they are not ready for.

In particular, the detailed case study reports, highly valuable for the confident but possibly alarming for the novice, are separately presented so that they can be revisited later. (But do revisit them.)

The challenge of teaching research in the context of software is to resist all the time the pull of the software's tools. This book starts in the right place—since its aim is to get the researcher working in software, its first message is that the analytic strategies must drive the use of the software, rather than have the capabilities of the software drive the analytic choices. We confront the "Foundations of Mixed Methods Research" before we meet Dedoose (with a case study) and address the challenges of teamwork before we do it with software and meet another case study—and so on through to the tasks of reporting to different audiences. Along the way, you'll meet some topics little discussed—such as the emergence of cloud technologies—and some thorny problems—such as intercoder reliability issues, a highly controversial topic dealt here with care.

It won't suffice for all intended audiences. The authors are writing for anyone who will listen—as they cheerfully summarize, "academics, teachers, graduate students, evaluators, doctoral students, program administrators, and investigators in a wide range of disciplines planning to use Dedoose." They also are offering to "introduce the necessary methodological skills to use Dedoose properly as a social science researcher." That's a big ask, and it's inevitable that the book will leave some of those audiences unsatisfied. But that is of course a good thing—there's no claim that from this book you can learn all you need to know of method and also how to use the software or that you should stop here. Researchers will use it at different stages—some after thorough immersion in social science methods, some as an entry to the software package, others when confronted with already piling up data. It has to provide enough methodological material to direct the reader methodologically, but it must stick to the primary goal of walking the user into the software. To shift the analogy, it's a shrink-wrap job—the parts of the book have to be as large as needed and as small as possible.

Finally, to return to my theme about software design and researcher purpose, there's no point in designing software if users can't rigorously and convincingly report out of it—and report appropriately to their multiple audiences. (Among the horror stories of my own experience was a short-lived beta version of an unnamed product whose marketing branch had bound it to an output tool designed for market research presentations. Qualitative researchers were to be presented with an output that was not editable!!) The final sections of this book, on sharing data by open access, and reporting via cloud computing, are among its most significant—so read on!

*Lyn Richards, Melbourne, 2019*

**Lyn Richards** was a reader in Sociology at La Trobe University until her research needed software. With Tom Richards, she became codeveloper of NUD*IST and NVivo, and cofounder and director of QSR International. She authored many user guides and more on methods and using software, and she trained researchers and trainers in 14 countries. She left that maelstrom in 2005 for research teaching at RMIT University and firmly hands requests for NVivo training to friends she has trained. She has authored 10 books, if you count books (like this one) that are part methods, part manual—and passionately believes researchers need more such works. She is currently at work on the fourth edition of *Handling Qualitative Data* (London, UK: SAGE), a text that assumes you'll use (some) software and advises and warns at every stage about how to manage your relationship with it.

## REFERENCE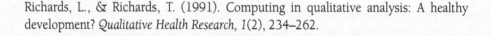

Richards, L., & Richards, T. (1991). Computing in qualitative analysis: A healthy development? *Qualitative Health Research, 1*(2), 234–262.

# Preface

∙∙∙∙∙∙∙∙∙∙∙∙∙∙∙∙∙∙∙∙∙∙∙∙∙∙∙∙∙∙∙∙∙∙∙∙∙∙∙∙∙∙∙∙∙∙∙∙∙∙∙∙∙∙∙∙∙∙∙∙∙∙

This book provides a detailed framework for preparing and doing qualitative and mixed methods data analysis using Dedoose. The reader will be able to integrate mixed methods research design with the many features of Dedoose, while extending skills in mixed methods research.

Research methods and the types of data we use today are continually evolving. Dedoose's collaborative, platform-independent, and accessible technologies continue to develop in response to the changing needs of researchers and research teams. Those mastering this book will be prepared for future cloud-based methodological and technological advances.

The authors represent the leadership team of the Institute for Mixed Methods Research (immrglobal.org), where the vision includes leading in the improvement and expansion of mixed methods research and evaluation practice beyond exclusive traditional quantitative and qualitative methods—ultimately developing new ways of designing, conducting, and communicating high-quality social science research.

This book is about an emerging paradigm of technology use in mixed methods data management and analysis. The use of cloud-based tools is a new and growing area. Dedoose was built by researchers for researchers, and it continues to advance cutting-edge approaches to analysis. Readers of this book will advance their skills in mixed methods analysis and reporting and learn how Dedoose can provide them with tools that promote success.

This book is provided as a teaching resource for graduate-level research courses in the social sciences. It focuses on advanced analysis with mixed methods research. Case studies throughout the book are written by prominent social science researchers. Each case study has questions designed to help the readers develop their thinking about their own research. The case studies offer an inside look at the research design and analysis process showing how top-notch researchers are getting the job done. Activities are also presented in a number of chapters to help the readers master difficult concepts.

This brings us to our mascot Bruce, the Dedoose Moose.

Throughout the book, Bruce's Tips highlight best practices for the reader from both a methodological and a technological use point of view.

Bruce joined the Dedoose team a few years back during a hike in the forest. Bruce quickly won over the research team with his perceptive insights into meaning making. When asked his views on human social problems, Bruce just gave a happy moose smile and asked, "How much grass can a moose munch if a moose could munch grass?" Well, we are still reflecting on this, so for now Bruce is patiently waiting for our answer.

Since Bruce joined the Dedoose team, he has had plenty of time to find his way through the application. He will be sharing his tips with you throughout this text to help you use Dedoose in the best way possible.

Visit **http://www.dedoose.com/** and **http://www.immrglobal.org/** for additional resources, including videos, user guides, FAQs, articles, case studies, and more to help you use Dedoose for your research.

# Acknowledgments

•••••••••••••••••••••••••••••••••••••••••••••••••••••••••••••

We wish to express our sincere appreciation to our partners and children who both supported and tolerated us expending energy and time on this project.

We also wish to thank the Dedoose team for helping us with the technical aspects of this book. We recognize the creativity and vision of the Dedoose chief technical architect, Jason Taylor, and his team. In particular, we would like to recognize Jose Gamez for his huge role behind the scenes in helping us with technical support in this book. Dedoose is a testament to what can be produced after endless hours of work and conversations between academic researchers and brilliant programmers about research needs and technical possibilities. As Dedoose is in the business of building tools and supporting a user community, it was very generous of the staff to share their time and energy with us, to assist in producing this book.

We would like to thank the following reviewers for their comments and suggestions on how to strengthen the book:

- Lucia Alcalá, California State University Fullerton

- Stuart Allen, Robert Morris University

- Vanessa L. Bond, University of Hartford's The Hartt School

- Liesette Brunson, Université du Québec à Montréal

- Sheryl L. Chatfield, College of Public Health at Kent State University

- Anjali J. Forber-Pratt, Vanderbilt University

- Lisa Foster, Liberty University

- Tabitha Hart, San José State University

- Julie Kugel, Loma Linda University

- Cristina Redko, Wright State University Boonshoft School of Medicine

- Shaunna Smith, Texas State University

- Rebecca Stephenson, Loyola Marymount University

- Mary Shepard Wong, Azusa Pacific University

Finally, many thanks to our case study authors. This was a big project with many moving parts, and they are all driven by passion and constant wonder about how mixed methods research can be strengthened and improved.

We hope our efforts here are a useful contribution to the body of knowledge in the social sciences.

# Glossary: Dedoose Common Terms

●●●●●●●●●●●●●●●●●●●●●●●●●●●●●●●●●●●●●●●●●●●●●●●●●●●

Key terms will be used throughout this text to describe various application functions of Dedoose. The following is a listing of many of these key common terms. You may find it convenient to refer back to this list as you become increasingly familiar with key features in Dedoose.

## Code/Tag

The application of codes to excerpts: The themes/concepts that are used by you to label any meanings, patterns, connections, or relationships you find in sections of documents or other media files.

## Code Weighting/Rating

The application of specified weighting/rating scales associated with code application.

## Data Security

Dedoose Data Security Protocols: Dedoose systems rely on a custom-built solution for the transfer of daily database backup files, which are transferred to three geo-redundant locations. These three servers are HIPPA (Health Insurance Portability and Accountability Act) compliant, and this security is sufficient to pass scrutiny of most institutional review board/ethics reviews.

Dedoose also allows end users to carry out a simple project export for local storage. From a project home dashboard via the "Export Data" feature, users can easily export an encrypted and password-protected copy of their project. This export can be loaded to a new project or provided to others if a user wishes to share a snapshot of their project at a particular time. Users have always had the capability to export all of their data for local use and storage by exporting all project excerpts with the default export settings, but this project export feature makes this action much more straightforward.

## Descriptors

These are the actual data for each unit of analysis or participant in a project. If you imagine the spreadsheet with titles for each column, descriptors are the rows of information describing each unit. Refer to Section 6.2 for a detailed discussion about descriptors.

## Descriptor Field

Descriptors Fields are used in Dedoose from a quantitative perspective when referring to data, for example, demographic or categorical variables such as age-group, gender, or a happiness score. Descriptor fields can be text, number, option list (with a set of values defined, e.g., for a gender field the values might be a dichotomous choice of male or female), or a range of dates. If you imagine a spreadsheet of information, descriptor fields are the titles of each column. Note that it is recommended in Dedoose to maximize the use of option list–type fields as these are where the investigator has the most control over how variation in work within the excerpting and tagging process can be displayed visually or focused on via filtering.

## Descriptor Sets

These are containers in Dedoose that hold sets of descriptor fields and descriptors. Dedoose uses sets because you can have multiple sets in a study. For example, one might be about children and families, another might be about schools and how they differ, and another might be about neighborhoods.

## Excerpt

This is a chunk of a media file that contains something important and meaningful about your research questions—much of qualitative and mixed methods analysis focuses on the content in excerpts.

## Media

Media are your data sources. These are the transcripts, stories, notes, video streams, audio streams, images, and the like, which are the core qualitative data in a Dedoose project. Refer to Chapter 3 for more detailed discussions on data sources used in Dedoose.

## Security Center: Account Information and Settings

Managing access to projects. Add users in the Project Security tab, if you want to add them to the project.

- Invite user—new user will be responsible for payment
- Create user—project administrator will be responsible for payment

## Security Workspace and Working With Team Members

One of Dedoose's strengths is the possibility for multiple members of a research team to work simultaneously, in real time, from any Internet-connected device.

Collaboration is important in Dedoose, as is maximizing data protection. User access and the privileges assigned to each user regarding their ability to affect project data are all managed through a Dedoose project's Security Center. Note that these are project-specific settings and providing access privileges to a user on one of your projects has no impact on other projects you or others may be working on.

The Security Workspace can be used by project administrators to set up new Dedoose user accounts to be linked to a project and control user privileges through the activation of access groups and then the assignment of project users to appropriate groups. The Security Workspace can be accessed by clicking the security tab in the Dedoose main menu bar.

## Training Center

The Dedoose Training Center is designed to assist research teams in building and maintaining interrater reliability for both coding and code weighting/rating. Training sessions ("tests") are specified based on the coding and/or rating of an "expert" coder/rater. Creating a training session is as simple as selecting the codes to include in the "test," the selection of previously coded/rated excerpts to constitute the test, and then specifying a name and description for the test. "Trainees" access the session and are prompted to apply codes or weights to the set of excerpt making up the session. During the exercise, the trainee is blind to the work that was done by the expert. On session completion, results present Cohen's kappa coefficient for code application and Pearson's correlation coefficient for code weighting/ratings overall and for each individual code as indexes of the interrater reliability as well as details of where the "trainee" and "expert" agreed or disagreed. See more on the Training Center in Chapter 4.

## Workspace

These are the different areas in Dedoose where all the work gets done, including the Home Dashboard, Codes, Media, Excerpts, Descriptors, Analyze, Memos, Training, Security, Data Set, and Projects.

*Three researchers at a professional development roundtable find a magic app containing a genie, who grants them each one wish. The first researcher wishes to leave the training event and return to their university immediately. The second researcher wishes the same. The third researcher says, "I'm lonely. I wish my friends were back here to help me dig deeper into data analysis." Lucky you, with this book you have what you need to do just that.*

# About the Authors

**Michelle Salmona** is the president, and co-founder, of the Institute for Mixed Methods Research (IMMR) and an adjunct associate professor at the University of Canberra, Australia. With a background as a project management professional and a senior fellow of the Higher Education Academy, UK, she is a specialist in research design, methods, and analysis. She is a cofounder of IMMR, building global collaborations for grant development and customized training and consultancy services for individuals and groups engaged in mixed methods and qualitative analysis.

Michelle works as an international consultant in program evaluation, research design, and mixed methods and qualitative data analysis using data applications. Her research focus is to better understand how to support doctoral success and strengthen the research process and to build data-driven decision-making capacity in the corporate world. Her particular interests relate to the relationship between digital tools and doctoral success. Her recent research includes exploring the changing practices of qualitative research during the dissertation phase of doctoral studies and investigates how we bring learning into the use of technology during the research process. Michelle is currently working on projects with researchers from education, information systems, business communication, leadership, and finance.

**Eli Lieber** has spent more than 20 years at the University of California, Los Angeles (UCLA), focusing on the advancement of thinking about and strategically implementing qualitative and mixed methods approaches in social science research. His recent work has focused on the continued development of mixed methods strategies. He is particularly interested in what we do with all the data we gather, how we integrate data, and how evolving technologies can make our research and evaluation more efficient and effective.

As for next steps, Eli (vice president and co-founder of IMMR) is looking forward to continuing his work with his IMMR colleagues—a truly diverse group of individuals from around the world. He believes that the IMMR mission will be an ongoing service to building methodological capacity, relationship building, engagement and communication regarding evolving mixed methods work, and bringing the deep experience of IMMR associates into the service of those employing these practices. He is optimistic about how strong mixed methods research can benefit the social sciences through engaging with colleagues directly, with groups at larger institutions and professional organizations, and through the forging of strategic partnerships.

**Dan Kaczynski** is a senior research fellow at the IMMR. He is currently appointed as a professor supervising doctoral candidates at the University of Canberra, Australia, and is Professor Emeritus at Central Michigan University. His research interests are in advanced technological innovations in qualitative and mixed methods data analysis in the social sciences in the United States and Australia.

Dan is actively engaged as a program evaluation consultant and has more than 20 years of consulting experience conducting state, national, and international evaluations. He has held leadership roles in program administration and has been a research center director with extensive experience as principal investigator of more than $35 million in grant awards. His work has been shared professionally with more than 230 professional presentations nationally and internationally. He has written more than 40 published research articles and coauthored six books and book chapters. In addition, he has supervised over 100 doctoral dissertations and professional specialist theses.

# Foundations of Mixed Methods Research

# CHAPTER 1

# Using Mixed Methods and Dedoose

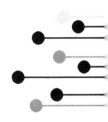

## 1.1   About This Book

Conducting social science research and program evaluations is about solving problems. Whatever the focus of the work, challenges may be best solved by taking particular perspectives that dictate the methods to be employed. Design issues to be considered include the target population, the data to be gathered, how one might interact with and transform these data, what analyses are to be conducted, and how best to reach the intended audience.

Deciding to employ a particular methodological approach must be guided by the central research question(s). This central point of a study is also referred to as the focus of the study, and the researcher must determine what types of data will best support an inquiry into the central point. Will the research goal(s) be best served with qualitative or quantitative data, or both? Once the data are gathered, the researcher must consider what strategies to use to analyze these data: for example, exclusively qualitative or quantitative, or comingled and analyzed from a mixed methods perspective. When considering a mixed methods approach, the researcher must keep in mind that this mixing can take place in different ways at different stages of a project. Finally, in what form will the researcher prepare the study findings to assure credibility and utility for the target audience(s)?

This book is structured into three parts, each addressing a key overarching theme in mixed methods research using technology. Part I, Foundations of Mixed Methods Research, discusses the foundational principles of mixed methods research, including qualitative and quantitative research and challenges for mixing, framing the purpose and focus of a study, and successfully adopting digital tools with an introduction to Dedoose. Part II, Data Interaction and Analysis, discusses collaboration and describes a more in-depth look at Dedoose, including data transformation and integration. Part III, Reporting Credible Results and Sharing Findings, discusses challenges and strategies for reporting meaningful findings and sharing data with a larger audience. Within these three themes, key areas are covered such as developing a mixed methods design; implementation of the mixed methods design; approaches to sampling, data gathering, synthesis, and analysis; and sharing your findings.

As illustrated in Figure 1.1, qualitative and mixed methods data analysis using a data application such as Dedoose requires an interaction with all three parts of

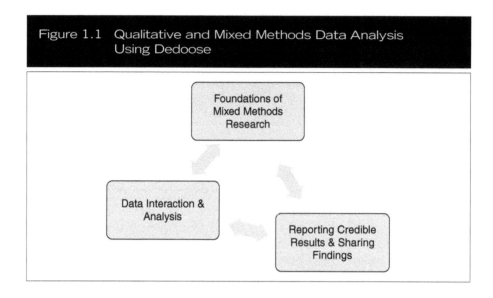

**Figure 1.1** Qualitative and Mixed Methods Data Analysis Using Dedoose

this book. The goal of this book is to provide connections between the research process and computer-aided data management, analysis, and visualization using Dedoose. Specifically, proven analytic strategies for qualitative and mixed methods work as illustrated by various case studies. The book is written for a broad audience of academics, teachers, graduate students, evaluators, doctoral students, program administrators, and investigators in a wide range of disciplines planning to use Dedoose.

Throughout this book, the importance of engaging in well-considered research design thinking to complement researcher technological skill building is emphasized. To begin this broader discussion, essential steps in thinking through a research design are highlighted. That is, a study typically begins with a core topic often expressed with key words. Next, the social problem is framed so as to demonstrate the importance of the proposed research. From there research design thinking wrestles with the methodological complexity of a central focus and key research questions. A well-known remark attributed to Albert Einstein highlights the importance of this upfront thinking:

> If I had an hour to solve a problem and my life depended on the solution, I would spend the first 55 minutes determining the proper question to ask, for once I know the proper question, I could solve the problem in less than five minutes.

This book also introduces the necessary methodological skills to use Dedoose properly as a social science researcher. These skills and empirical practices promote sound, high-quality mixed methods work. In the coming chapters, look for examples in how Dedoose functionality and features facilitate the "mixing" that is purported to enhance the quality and complexity of your mixed methods study/work/results. Accordingly, this book provides some review of research foundations, design, and practical examples to establish the clear building blocks on why and how to use Dedoose effectively.

Part I, Foundations of Mixed Methods Research, is covered in Chapters 1 to 3, where foundational principles of mixed methods research, successfully adopting digital tools, and an introduction to Dedoose are discussed.

## 1.2   Mixed Methods and Mixed Paradigms

If qualitative research is defined as working with words and images, and quantitative research as working with numbers, then a superficial definition of mixed methods is the working with both words and numbers. Researchers recognize that social science inquiry involves much more than simply working with words and numbers. Today, researchers work with all kinds of data, including images, social media, audio recordings, and video files, and increasingly appreciate recent advances in applications of mixed methods research, which is evolving to mean so much more. This book takes a very general perspective in defining mixed methods and strives to be as inclusive as possible to the range of perspectives taken by others. When seeking to address a research question, researchers commonly apply a particular level of analysis that, in the past, may have been represented in purely qualitative or purely quantitative terms. When a single paradigm was used, the analysis of data was restricted to that paradigm. This practice did not allow for mixing of research methods.

Where the authors accept that all methods have limitations, those seeking to "mix" methods recognize that an understanding of the phenomena under study may be better represented by the application of multiple methods of inquiry. Where such an approach is taken, in any of many forms, the general intention is to capitalize on the strengths of various methods with the hopes of acquiring more comprehensive understandings of that inherent complexity faced when exploring natural phenomena in context.

As mixed methods research practices have grown, so too has the importance of recognizing the challenges of mixing paradigms. For the purposes of discussion in this book, the term *paradigm* is intended to represent the research methods of a qualitative or quantitative study along with the distinct philosophical worldviews of each. For example, a qualitative paradigm would encompass accepted data gathering and analysis procedures. In addition, the qualitative paradigm would philosophically integrate an appropriate qualitative theoretical orientation to the study. Refer to Patton (2015, Chapter 3) for an examination of 16 different qualitative theoretical approaches. Further discussions regarding philosophical integration may be found in a range of research methods textbooks, including Creswell and Poth (2017), Denzin and Lincoln (2013), O'Reilly and Kiyimba (2015), and Somekh and Lewin (2012). Of importance to this discussion is acknowledging and respecting that qualitative and quantitative approaches represent distinctly different field research methods and philosophical foundations. Toward that end, this book is intended as a guide to mixing these two paradigms.

### 1.2.1 Mixed Methods Considerations

Given the emphasis on mixed methods data analysis in this book, upcoming chapters explore the key characteristics of both qualitative and quantitative paradigms, including the use of data and data management techniques. Furthermore, this book explores the integration of mixed approaches within social science. Of greatest importance to this distinction is that any mixing demands thoughtful design decisions toward generating high-quality inquiry that anticipates identifying insights that are greater than what might have been achieved where only a single perspective was employed.

A key consideration here is that the researcher must justify up front the need to conduct a mixed methods study. Mixed methods is not an easy shortcut taken by the researchers because they cannot make up their mind if their study is qualitative or quantitative. "Oh, it is all too complicated, I will just throw it all together and do mixed methods." Rather, there must be a clear rationale for using a mixed methods design from the outset.

### 1.2.2 Combining Paradigms

It is important to acknowledge that a strong collection of either quantitative or qualitative data with only a token amount of data from the other paradigm does not justify a mixed methods design. Simply having a bit of extra data from the opposite paradigm is not sufficient to claim the use of mixed methodology. A mixed methods study must comprise a well-designed qualitative study and a well-designed quantitative study with clearly written justification supporting the use of a mixed methods design.

The purpose and focus, or central point, of the study will determine if mixed methods research is the appropriate choice for your study rather than the types of available data. Refer to Section 2.2, Framing the Purpose and Focus (Chapter 2), for further discussions on framing the purpose and focus. Appropriate mixed methods research questions must be constructed based on this research design thinking. From here, this book is intended to assist you with designing and conducting a mixed methods study using Dedoose.

There is a rich body of research literature to draw on that can assist with guiding the mixing process for research design decisions (Creswell, 2017; Hesse-Biber, 2010b; Mertens, 2017; Onwuegbuzie, Slate, Leech, & Collins, 2009; Tashakkori & Teddlie, 2003). A few of the more common mixing approaches include sequential, concurrent, and nested. Nested is also referred to as embedded. Each of these approaches offers variations to positioning the qualitative and quantitative stages. Figure 1.2 shows these three variations of mixing research. All three variations begin with the same social problem and conclude with the results drawn from credible mixed research evidence. It is the middle part where the mixing process varies. The concurrent approach involves both quantitative and qualitative field research methods conducted simultaneously. The sequential approach involves either quantitative or qualitative field research methods conducted in order. Note

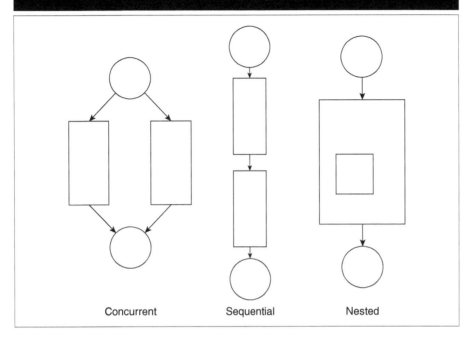

Figure 1.2 Common Mixing Approaches

Concurrent    Sequential    Nested

that positioning which is first and which is second requires thoughtful consideration. A nested approach is unique in that either quantitative or qualitative field research is chosen as primary, and the secondary approach is nested within the primary. Choosing which is primary and which is secondary must be based on the overall study requirements of the research design and appropriately justified. As noted by Hesse-Biber (2010b), mixing practices have previously favored primary quantitative methodologies. Mixing today, however, has become more accepting of qualitative designs that are primary or equal. An example of this shift would be a nested mixed methods design with quantitative inquiry embedded within a larger qualitative project.

## 1.3  Using Cloud Technology to Support Mixed Methods Research

Cloud-based services and tools such as Dropbox, Google Drive, Google Hangouts, SurveyMonkey, Qualtrics, Skype, Pamela, WeChat, WhatsApp, and Viber are now widely adopted and are making the online sharing of resources, gathering of data, manipulation of documents and other information, and communication far more efficient and accessible. Many of these listed apps are commonly used by researchers today. Over the next few years, there will continue to be version updates full of new functions and new apps providing functionality beyond what exists today. Consider what steps you might take to prepare yourselves for the future. What does the changing app environment mean for you and your research? Does it make a difference if you are working alone or working in a team?

While there is a rich history in the literature on technology adoption, very little of this work has focused systematically on how end users choose to adopt and then make use of technology when conducting social science research. From a general perspective, there are widely held views that individuals show varying levels of predisposition to adopt technology (Crook, 1994; Rogers, 1962; Schiffman, 1991). However, where serious concern is raised about quality and methodological rigor, as in academic work, researchers must be similarly concerned about whether the use of any technology is appropriate. Keeping in mind the barriers to technology adoption that are discussed in Chapter 2, and when and how technology is brought into the investigative process, work must include salient reflection on the nature of the question being addressed, the nature of the data, and the technological expertise of those responsible for "driving" the process where technology is in play.

For the anthropologist studying the use of technology in human cultural development, the notion of working in the cloud opens boundless possibilities for sharing and connectivity. The shared work setting also portrays an ongoing struggle for researchers as technologies advance. In many respects, getting one type of computer to talk to a different type continues to be challenging. Researchers require an intuitive work environment that transcends proprietary products, equipment, and communication platforms. A cloud-based work environment has proven to effectively respond to this problem. In particular, finding the best way for qualitative and quantitative data to interact in a mixed methods design is increasingly of vital importance. Technology continues to rapidly evolve in response to the problem of great inefficiencies in research data management and integration.

## 1.4   What Is Dedoose?

This book is about Dedoose, so what is Dedoose? Dedoose is a web-based application that allows you to organize and analyze research data, no matter what form those data take. Whether your research data are qualitative (text, audio, images, or video), quantitative (spreadsheets, surveys, test scores, ratings, or demographics), or a mixture of both, Dedoose's design is flexible enough for you and your team to manage these data and apply whatever methodologies you choose. Dedoose supports both traditional qualitative approaches and mixed methods approaches to data interaction and analysis in a secure, collaborative environment. As an application, Dedoose can assist you with your data analysis—however, like all qualitative and mixed methods data applications, it will not do the analysis for you. The researchers drives the analysis process, not the data application.

## 1.4.1 Relational Database

Dedoose is a web-based application that is built as a relational database. You can connect your mixed methods data by using codes, code weights, descriptors, and memos. This allows you to manage your project and build, and track, a web of connections between various aspects of your database.

Basically, a relational database allows data to live in natural forms within an application. An example is text imported as .docx or .txt files. The Dedoose relational database also supports spreadsheets as .xls or .csv files, video as .mp4 files, audio as .mp3 files, and images as .jpg files. The key benefit to allowing different forms of data to live in natural formats within a single application is maximized efficiency. For example, when you paste an image into a document, the result is a single file with two different forms of data—image and text. Your use of this file is limited by what you can do with each form of data. However, through a set of relationships these different types of data are connected in Dedoose as a relational database so that all the information can be efficiently used for visualization and analysis.

## 1.4.2 Research and Evaluation Data Applications

The acronyms QDAS (qualitative data analysis software) and CAQDAS (computer-assisted qualitative data analysis software) have been in common use for many years (Gilbert, Jackson, & di Gregorio, 2013; Richards, 2015; Silver & Lewins, 2014). This book adopts the use of research and evaluation data applications (REDA), which has more recently been introduced as an acronym to broaden the use of technological tools by welcoming more mixed methods data handling than what QDAS or CAQDAS has traditionally represented.

Consider the implications for REDA such as Dedoose, which are emerging as new cloud-based applications for data analysis. This acronym supports the adoption of strategies that promote quality technological integration and improved mixed methods practices by exploring how researchers, educators, and evaluators adopt advances in technology.

REDA implies an ability to not only manage your data but also analyze it. Examples of REDA therefore include Google Sheets, SurveyMonkey, and Dedoose. Given ongoing technological advances in REDA, ongoing researcher skill building is encouraged. Furthermore, teachers and trainers should stimulate students to think outside the box when adopting new features in REDA.

## 1.5   Dedoose: A Historical Journey

Looking back at the history of technologies for qualitative and mixed methods research, consider the tasks in which scholars were engaged, the tools available at the time, and how they attempted to capitalize on these tools and their functionality. Prior to the commonplace use of personal computers, paper, pen/pencil, typewriters, and hand calculators were the "tools" of the day.

Anthropologists and other social scientists engaged in text analysis were noted for their use of colored pens/pencils and margin notes to mark up their text files as they identified and explored patterns that emerged from their data. The first highlighter was invented in 1963, then sticky notes in 1968, adding other tools to the arsenal of investigators looking to mark up their documents. To this point, the work was all manual, and there are endless stories of the painstaking sorting, exploring, and resorting that took place as researchers would organize their documents across dining room tables searching for the patterns around which they would tell their stories.

Following the availability of mainframe computers in the 1950s, the later 1970s ushered in the personal computer. For the first time, individuals could afford to purchase these digital tools and the associated productivity software that was of particular value to academic audiences. In the early 1980s, software for the management and interaction with qualitative data was being developed to essentially digitize the work carried out by anthropologists previously done with paper and pencil. These software packages allowed for more rapid movement through qualitative data management and analysis. Coding activities particularly benefitted from rapid technological advances in the excerpting process and subsequent pattern exploration and retrieval processes, especially when individuals were dealing with larger data sets.

During the 1980s, academic early adopters of technology for qualitative and mixed methods research were commonly confronted with methodological tensions when using software packages. Due to demanding learning curves, these early software packages were often found gathering dust on an academic office shelf as researchers reverted to traditional manual data management and analysis practices. Setting aside the time to learn the software and to integrate training into established research methods courses was often overwhelming and costly. Academic early adopters, such as ourselves, who persevered with early software adoption began to organize training support groups and conference training events. From these early adoption efforts, social science disciplines increasingly acknowledged the benefits to incorporating technology into social science methodological research and teaching practices.

Dedoose was developed at the University of California, Los Angeles (UCLA), Fieldwork and Qualitative Data Research Laboratory. The lab served as a methodological consulting service in qualitative and mixed methods research. There were pockets of individuals and teams attempting to make use of traditional qualitative data analysis software, but many were abandoning these tools due to cost and complexity. These frustrations prompted the development of macros for word processor software that allowed for basic coding and excerpt retrieval without the need for purchasing or learning other software (Ryan, 1993). When you consider what most people are doing most of the time with their qualitative data, exploring and tagging content for later retrieval, this relatively simple solution met 100% of the needs for many who were supported by the lab.

However, as researchers and evaluation teams began adopting more mixed methods approaches, the data being collected became increasingly complex and research demanded the use of other tools to manage, integrate, and analyze. As this methodological evolution (some would argue rebirth) took place, it was common to see the use of word processors (with their code and retrieve macros), statistical software to carry out the more traditional quantitative data analysis, and spreadsheet software to help integrate various forms of data and to build visual displays for manuscripts and presentations. Moreover, research teams were increasingly crossing disciplinary boundaries and collaborating with other teams working on different computer platforms in locations spread across the country and the globe. The challenges faced with file sharing, platform compatibility, and version control cannot be understated, and so as more complex data sets were being generated by geographically distributed teams, the work became increasingly inefficient.

In 1999, Salesforce emerged as one of the first applications to be delivered via the Internet. Cloud technologies provide a platform on which a wide range of applications can be built and delivered along with a powerful and rapidly advancing set of tools for the development of these applications. In 2003, EthnoNotes first became widely available for the collaborative, cross platform, management, analysis, and visualization of qualitative and mixed methods research data (Lieber, Weisner, & Presley, 2003). While initially built on a more traditional relational database software package, EthnoNotes was fully transformed into a pure web application in 2006 and later re-engineered and rebranded as Dedoose in 2010. Dedoose now serves qualitative and mixed methods researchers and research teams as an application (REDA) for managing, interacting with, sharing, analyzing, and visualizing qualitative and mixed methods research data.

Visit **http://www.dedoose.com/** and **http://www.immrglobal.org/** for additional resources, including videos, user guides, FAQs, articles, case studies, and more to help you use Dedoose for your research.

# CHAPTER 2

# Adopting Dedoose

In this chapter, we examine the barriers to adopting technology in both qualitative data analysis and mixed methods research. Exploring these barriers to successful adoption of digital tools will help you get the most from your research when using Dedoose. Furthermore, the more we understand the research process, the better we can support emerging researchers and evaluators toward successfully working with technology in their qualitative and mixed methods data analysis.

This chapter is divided into four sections: The first section discusses the successful adoption of digital tools; the second section considers the methodological framing of your purpose and focus; the third section shows you how to get started in Dedoose; and the final section builds on the barriers discussion with an example applying the *Five-Level QDA®* method with Dedoose.

## 2.1 Successful Adoption of Digital Tools

The dramatic growth in the use of digital tools in the research design process is changing how researchers and evaluators perform their analysis. Researchers are progressively expanding the adoption of digital tools in the gathering, management, analysis, interpretation, and presentation of data. This increasing adoption of technology has been cited as a major contribution to greater acceptance and credibility of qualitative research (Bazeley, 2013; Davidson & di Gregorio, 2012; Richards, 2015).

The use of digital tools during analysis involves the researcher letting go and immersing into the analytic process through the tool. At this point, the tool becomes a gateway into what Schram (2006) refers to as the inductive and deductive ebb and flow of inquiry. To the casual observer, qualitative and mixed methods research may look easy from the outside when a single paradigm is being used. In practice, though, the complexity of methods and combinations of theoretical orientations require a high level of understanding to produce robust research with commensurate quality, not just for researchers uncomfortable with technology. The researcher begins with complicated data and then applies techniques that result in making the data even more complicated. A key, potential, advantage of any digital tool is that it can easily support the researcher's efforts to pursue and interpret new paths of inquiry. This, however, is dependent on the researcher remaining in control of the analytic process.

Although digital tools may make the research process rigid, they may actually have the opposite effect. For example, using memos as bookmarks to help capture the researcher's thoughts involving interpretive investigation can help document the ebb and flow of the research inquiry. When the time arises to pursue those paths that were written and set aside, the task may be daunting due to time constraints or the growing complexity of data management. Digital tools, however, facilitate the researcher pursuing these paths by allowing previous work to be saved swiftly and securely and to be easily retrieved. The researcher is able to flow and shift between lines of inquiry and revisit the data instantly using the digital tool. This nimble functionality provides the researcher with the option to start over at any point exploring new paths of interpretation without the fear of losing previous work.

## 2.1.1 Trusting a Digital Tool

Numerous advantages to using digital tools have been discussed in the literature such as data management, increased flexibility, more transparent data analysis, systemized analysis procedures, and rigorous documentation of a visible audit trail (Gibbs, Friese, & Mangabeira, 2002; Patton, 2015; Salmona & Kaczynski, 2016; St. John & Johnson, 2000). When using a digital tool, there are a wide range of commands that can be easily employed, often without consciously examining each step. The researcher's thoughts are commonly centered on the main task of writing. In the same way, the researcher is critically engaged in analysis that combines several complex skills. Proficiency in using any tool allows the analysis process to progress with minimal intellectual qualms and emotional apprehensions related to the intrusion of technology. In this sense, the researcher trusts that the tool is doing what it is intended to do.

The interplay of complex analysis processes when the researcher engages with digital tools is, as yet, not fully understood. Previously, concern existed that the integration of technology into traditional analysis had the potential to threaten the distinctive nature of mixed methods and qualitative research (Gibbs et al., 2002; Welsh, 2002). Presently, as the researcher explores multiple paths of inquiry using digital tools, substantial benefits are accepted. Digital tools offer the researcher a stable platform to better understand complexity by creating a manageable and flexible working environment that enhances immersion and grounding in the data. As innovative analysis techniques evolve from technology-based practice, the researcher may discover that the digital tool is working in ways that have not yet been considered. As a result, researchers and evaluators must consider and contend with inevitable changes to traditional methodologies and practices. The question before you is, "How can you harness and regulate the use of digital tools in analysis and best position yourself to manage the challenges of design and methodological changes?" It is hoped that this book will help you answer this question.

## 2.1.2 Building Successful Skills

Now that you have considered the growing role of technology in research, let's talk about how you can be more successful in using technology. In our earlier work (Salmona & Kaczynski, 2016), we identified two barriers to successful adoption of technology in data analysis that apply to any researcher who is directly interacting with their data, not just those researchers unfamiliar with technology. The following discussion provides a brief overview of the first barrier and then expands into a discussion about the second barrier as researchers and evaluators become clearer about their own approach and methodological thinking.

Using an analytic lens framed by elements of the technology acceptance model (TAM) theory (Davis, 1986, 1989), Salmona and Kaczynski (2016) describe the barriers users often face when deciding to adopt and appropriately make use of technology (see Figure 2.1). These barriers are (a) perceiving the technology as easy to learn and useful and (b) methodological transparency, where the researcher can conceptualize the research and understands that the technology is simply a tool to assist in the research. When adopting technology to appropriately make use of technology in research, it is very important for the potential user to thoroughly consider the barriers commonly faced during this decision-making process.

Key issues regarding the use of technology and better understanding include perceived transparency (Gilbert, 2000; Janz, 2015; Moravcsik, 2014; Wickham & Woods, 2005) and methodological rigor (Barbour, 2001; Blismas & Dainty, 2003; Coffey, Holbrook, & Atkinson, 1996). Viewing the adoption process through these two barriers provides a valuable framework for individuals to use when considering the adoption of technology for qualitative or mixed methods research.

**Figure 2.1   Barriers to Successful Technology Adoption**

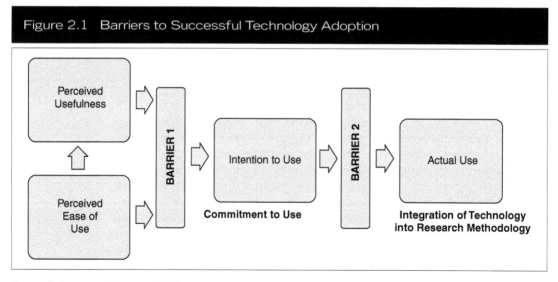

*Source:* Salmona and Kaczynski (2016).

We believe that with a clearer understanding about your own characteristics and perceptions of technology, and those of anyone else with whom you may be working, you will be able to make wise decisions about any tools you bring into your work and successfully use these digital tools.

### 2.1.3 Strategies for Successful Adoption of Dedoose

Before moving ahead, find a comfy chair and pause to reflect about where you fit into this discussion. Are you an innovator, early adopter, majority user, or, perhaps, a laggard (Rogers, 2003)? The laggards find technology disruptive and confusing, and they think about how it might interfere with their research design thinking, becoming isolated and disengaged from technological adoption. Their decision is clear; they are not going to adopt technology in their research. The other extreme of innovators and early adopters are strongly committed to the benefits of using technology, and creativity helps them engage in their research design thinking. The middle ground between these two extremes is where the majority of users sit. This group of researchers has the greatest potential to successfully adopt a digital tool without giving up methodological control of their inquiry, as they neither outright reject adoption, nor enthusiastically leap to adoption without much thought about potential costs and benefits.

How secure, comfortable, optimistic, and "innovative" do you feel when trying a new digital tool for research? To be successful with a new tool, you need to think about the two barriers discussed in the previous section and consider several questions:

- Is the digital tool easy to use and do you think it is useful?

- How are you thinking about your methodology?

- Are you confident about your methodological skills?

- Do you think you know what to do, if the work did not use a digital tool?

- What steps are you taking to integrate your methodological awareness with your developing technical skills?

It is well-known that qualitative data analysis software has been used for decades in both research and educational settings. Indeed, di Gregorio and Davidson (2008) suggest that the use of such software applications will become a standard in qualitative research. Yet researchers continue to discuss methodological concerns about the adoption and use of such technology.

Once you have made the decision about whether to adopt digital tools, it is time to think about the first barrier: Is the package easy to learn and use? Shop around and test-drive the wide range of available applications and software programs. Most packages will offer you a free trial. Take advantage of this opportunity by creating a test project for playing with a number of different packages. Are you comfortable with the technological functions, and can you do what you want to do? Is the tool convenient and accessible? What is the learning curve's trajectory? How long will it take you to master the software so that you can use it successfully in your work? Reflection can help users capitalize on the benefits of technology while confronting and overcoming barriers to adoption (di Gregorio, 2012; Moylan, Derr, & Lindhorst, 2015).

The next step is to think about the second barrier of methodological transparency. Consider the methodological decisions that you have made supporting the research design of your study. Remember that you are the investigator and it is your job to determine the direction of inquiry and drive the research process. Do you have a clearly articulated and documented approach? Have you justified what you are doing and the purpose of your mixed methods research? Learn, know, embrace, and trust your methodological framework before you begin using digital tools.

---

**EXERCISE**

Have a conversation with a colleague, fellow student, or friend about your research. How are you using tools for real work that is being designed at the same time?

---

From our research, we now know that if you think a digital tool is easy to use and you perceive the tool to be useful, you are more likely to use it successfully (Salmona & Kaczynski, 2016). Once you have negotiated this first barrier, you are on your way to be successful with your chosen digital tool. To address the second barrier, strive to be methodologically confident and aware throughout your study. That is to say, allow your research focus to define your path of inquiry, not the technological functions of the tool.

## 2.2  Framing the Purpose and Focus

When starting any social science inquiry, and before using any digital tools, careful detailed research design thinking is required. This is a critical step to ensure that your study is successful. Before you jump ahead into promoting a solution to the social problem or identifying sources of data, you must reflect on your connection to this topic. You have come to this research idea for a reason. Your role as a social science researcher in this study has a purpose. Do you have an agenda? What do you hope to achieve? Now is the time to articulate and write down the intentions behind your inquiry, which will include goals, expectations, and rationale.

As Patton (2015) explains, "Purpose is the controlling force in research" (p. 248). A well-articulated purpose statement supports each decision regarding a study design. Fieldwork decisions such as setting, sample population, data gathering, and analysis all flow from your research purpose. Different purposes typically view a social problem from unique vantage points, so every study has a unique purpose. Matching a study's design to the purpose of the study is therefore essential in promoting quality and credibility. This upfront thinking also helps avoid prematurely jumping into crafting research questions.

Looking at what a purpose statement is not can be very helpful in identifying what it is. A purpose statement is not any of the following:

- A continuation of the social problem discussion

- A literature review

- A description of fieldwork methods

- A hypothesis statement

- A focus or central research question statement

- Reflections on your role as a researcher

- An abstract

You have an agenda behind your choice of topic and the social problem(s) related to this topic. Explain this agenda by writing a well-crafted purpose statement. As you do this, think about the following:

- Where do I want my path of inquiry to take me?

- What is the central point to my research?

Answering these questions will help you get started on crafting your purpose statement. Purpose statements are typically about one to two pages in length and follow your discussion of the social problem. This purpose narrative must aid your audience in making sense of and figuring out what you are up to. Your goal is to be transparent by offering some insights into your design-based research thinking. Explain your perspective that is shaping how you define this social problem. You are sharing the underlying agenda to what this study is about. Key words that you are using to describe this thinking would likely be sprinkled throughout the purpose statement. An important benefit to writing this purpose statement is that it helps you make your study unique and stand apart from a vast body of related social science research.

**EXERCISE**

Write your purpose statement. Have a conversation with a colleague, a fellow student, or a friend about your purpose statement. Is it easy to understand and follow? Have you clearly made an argument about why your research matters? Is the "So what?" factor clearly described?

A focus statement often follows the purpose statement discussion. The focus statement is one or two sentences that drive to the heart of what the study is about. This step may also be referred to as a central research question (Creswell, 2017). Regardless of the terminology, this statement shapes every design decision you will make for your study. As such, it is essential to the overall quality of a study to distill this statement about the study into a single sentence or two that are not changed or revised as the study proceeds. If the focus is changed, the study is changed.

**EXERCISE**

Write your focus statement. Have a conversation with a colleague, a fellow student, or a friend about your purpose statement. Is it easy to understand and follow?

As you refine your focus statement, think beyond the barriers to technological adoption discussed earlier in Section 2.1. Try to identify possible methodological barriers and clarify possible challenges you may face. Writing memos is a very useful technique to compartmentalize your challenges and an effective approach for coming up with systematic responses to these challenges. Refer to Section 3.3 "Memos as Data" for further details.

 dedoose

## 2.3  Dedoose: Starting Your Project

So now, you are ready to begin using REDA and you choose to use Dedoose—good choice. The following steps show you how to create an account, create a project, and to prepare data for import into your new project. Chapter 3 will then discuss in more detail the gathering of data for a research study.

### 2.3.1 Creating an Account in Dedoose

It is easy to sign up for an account at Dedoose. Just follow these steps:

1. Click on the red Sign Up button at the top of any page of Dedoose (**www.dedoose.com**).

2. Fill in the two required fields on the form (email address and your desired username).

3. There are optional fields for promo codes, referrals, and comments.

4. When you have completed the form, click Submit.

Once signed up to Dedoose, you will immediately receive your temporary password. You can then log in and create a permanent password by going to the *Account Space*. While you are there, have a look around the billing area. You will also receive a confirmation email with additional helpful information.

To log into Dedoose, do the following:

1. Click the Log In tab in the upper right corner of the Dedoose home page.

2. Enter your username and password.

3. If you want to avoid having to reenter that information, check the Remember Me box in the lower right corner.

4. Click login or hit the hard return key.

Returning users will see the Home Dashboard for the project you most recently visited. To access a different project, or to create a new project, click the Projects tab in the Main Menu bar.

**BRUCE'S TIP #1**

Free Access to Dedoose

Your first month using Dedoose is FREE. At the end of your free 30 days, you will be asked for payment. For current pricing options and to sign up, see the Dedoose website: **https://www.dedoose.com/home/pricing**.

- Change your pricing plan at any time via Dedoose Support at support@ dedoose.com.

- If you are a student, ask about the student discount.

- For individual accounts, you are only charged for monthly cycles when you log into your account.

## 2.3.2 Creating a Dedoose Project

When you set up an account in Dedoose, you are given a demo project for playing with and exploring features, so you can find those of most value in your work. As a first-time user, you will see your Demo Project in the Home Dashboard when you first log in. Once there, you will see mixed methods data from a study of literacy development. Keep in mind, this demo is specific to your account.

Try deleting, editing, or making any other changes to acclimate yourself to the Dedoose workspaces.

Dedoose is not platform specific or browser specific, so you can use it in any browser on a PC or a Mac. You can also download the Desktop App—see instructions by following the link on the log-in page. Mobile users can use the Puffin Browser as this supports the use of Flash, although Dedoose still recommends using the Desktop App on a dedicated computer with a mouse.

The Project Workspace allows users with appropriate access privileges to do the following:

- Create/add new projects by entering the Project Workspace and clicking the "Create Project" button in the lower right corner

- Switch the active project—when logging into Dedoose, by default, you will be entering the most recently accessed project. However, note that periodic system maintenance will take you to your first project (most commonly your demo project). If this occurs, simply enter your Project Workspace to load the project you wish to access

- Work with a newly created project or load any project you have authorized access to

- Rename, copy, or delete a selected project

Please note that renaming, copying, and deleting a project can only be done if you are the creator of the project.

 **BRUCE'S TIP #2**

Naming Your Project

When you name your project, add a description and decide if you need an additional level of security. If you decide to apply the added layer of encryption, be certain to note your password, as Dedoose cannot help you recover it if forgotten. NOTE: Most users do not need this exceptional added level of encryption. In addition, cross-document and cross-excerpt searching are disabled for encrypted project as our system has no way of interpreting the encrypted data without the key.

Once you have created your new project, the next time you log in, Dedoose will load that project instead of the Demo project. If you create additional projects, you will go to whichever project you accessed most recently.

### 2.3.3 Saving and Storing a Dedoose Project

Digital tools such as REDA are recommended to assist in two areas: (1) data management and (2) data analysis. Researchers must think about how they will systematically manage their data during their research. Data management includes developing a clear structure around the data to be gathered for both storage and backup. We recommend having a complete set of raw data stored separately to any REDA as a backup. No matter how diligently you back up your data, having a complete clean copy stored on multiple media, such as a university server and a DVD or thumb drive secured in a bank vault, can lead to fewer sleepless nights while you are conducting your research.

**BRUCE'S TIP #3**

Copy Your Project

Make a copy of a Dedoose project for storage, personal reference, safe keeping, and exploring and experimenting with your data without affecting the original project. It is always good to regularly export a backup of your project and store it on a secure server. Creating a copy of your project can be beneficial for testing project-wide changes or for taking a snapshot of your analysis progress. Since you are only charged to access the system, not for the number of projects, do not be afraid to take advantage and make copies liberally.

**To copy a project**

1. Click the Projects tab.
2. Highlight a project.
3. Click Copy Project.
4. Click Change.
5. Type your username at the top.
6. Click it when it appears.
7. Click Submit twice.

### 2.3.4 Managing Users in a Dedoose Project

Collaborating in Dedoose may require your team to have separate roles or be limited to a specific type of work at any given time. These roles can be defined in Dedoose through the Security Group system.

The Security tab allows you to invite other users and assign them specific permissions in your project. By default, the only user group available in Dedoose is the Full Access group. So before adding any users to the project, you may want to add a specific permission level:

1. Click the Security tab.

2. Click Add Group.

3. Click the permission level you would like to add.

4. Title the group.

5. Click Submit.

Some popular security groups include the following:

- *Full Access:* This group allows members to view, create, modify, and delete any object in the project. Furthermore, only members of this group can access the Security Center.

- *Standard Assistant:* This group allows members to create or import resources and create and code/tag excerpts. They can only view tags, descriptor fields, and descriptors, and they are not given access to the Security Center. Furthermore, they can only edit or delete excerpts that they created themselves.

- *Project-Wide Assistant:* Members of this group have the same privileges as those in the Full Access group, except for the ability to enter the project Security Center.

- *Isolated User:* Members of this group have the ability to create items but only view their own work.

- *Guest Access:* Members of this group can fully explore the data but are unable to edit or effect any change to the project.

Once you've added your chosen security group(s), you can follow these steps to add (invite) a user to a group:

1. Click the Security tab.

2. Click Add User.

3. Select the permission level.

4. Click Use Selected Group.

5. Input the user's email.

6. Click Submit.

7. Click Yes.

**BRUCE'S TIP #4**

Good Security Practices

Roles in your project can be directly translated to security groups in Dedoose. We suggest creating a list of your colleagues who will be working in Dedoose, identifying their roles, creating security groups in Dedoose for each role, and adding each user to the appropriate group. For more information on Dedoose's security groups, see **https://www.dedoose.com/blog/ access-groups-and-you**.

## 2.3.5 Preparing Data for Import

Dedoose makes it easy for you to import existing media files for your qualitative data, regardless of whether they are stored as spreadsheets, text, PDFs, images, audio, or video. These data may be field notes, observations, interview or focus-group transcripts, manuscripts, pasted images, audio streams, photographs, video streams, hyperlinks, survey data—anything that you can store as a text, spreadsheet, audio, or video file (.doc, .docx, .rtf, .txt, .pdf, .xls, .xlsx, .csv, .tif, .jpg, .png, .gif, .mp3, .mp4, .wma, and .m4a).

Before importing any data, it is good to take some time to prepare your data for import. Take care with transcripts as these data may come back from a transcriber in table format. It only takes a moment to copy the transcription and paste as text into

**BRUCE'S TIP #5**

Always Better to Work With De-Identified Data

It is important that your data (media) are complete and any sensitive identifying information has been removed or changed before importing your data into Dedoose.

Note: To learn about our recommendations on how best to prepare your data for import, please see the "Working With Media" section of the user guide.

another Word document to get rid of the formatting—this makes the text much easier to work with in any data application. Also, when working with online documents—for example, newspaper articles—copy the text and paste into a Word document rather than scan and save as PDF, as it is easier to work with text rather than images.

To import your files, start from the Project Workspace dashboard and click the Import Data icon in the upper left panel. You will then see a pop-up menu where you will indicate the type of data you are importing. Locate the files and submit. You can also import data in other Workspaces. If you select multiple text files, you will see a Success pop-up that indicates that your documents have been uploaded.

1. Click the Home tab.

2. Click Import Data.

3. Select the file type you are importing.

4. Click Submit.

5. Select your file(s).

6. Click Open.

**BRUCE'S TIP #6**

Naming Your Documents

When naming documents, it is useful to implement a systematic and informative convention throughout your project that works for, and makes sense to, you. Examples of document naming conventions:

- "435MFGModerate" could represents cases with
  - ID (number)
  - Gender (male or female)
  - Type (focus group, interview, observations)
  - Socioeconomic status (low, moderate, high)
- 2017.06.Int_Resp43 OR 2017.04.Obs1_Org1

There is no correct way to do this, but coming up with a file naming convention that works for you and your team can be very powerful. Consistency is the key.

When importing audio and video files, you will first see a progress bar and then get a pop-up after the import indicating that the file has been added and is being processed in the background. You can continue to work elsewhere in

Dedoose while this occurs, and when the file finishes processing, you will get a pop-up notifying you of its completion. Finally, please keep in mind that the process of video files can take some time depending on the queue on the Dedoose servers for processing these routines.

Within Dedoose, it is possible to edit documents; however, we recommend that you do this prior to import to ensure that you can keep a complete, clean copy of all your data elsewhere in a secure environment.

## 2.3.6 Auto Linking Qualitative and Quantitative Data in Dedoose

Dedoose's analytics can really help with linking your qualitative and quantitative data, allowing you to view code application distributions across groups, general quantitative statistics, and more. Note that this will only help you in studies with data that lend themselves to this type of analysis. While this process can be handled manually by going through the media files and linking them to the appropriate descriptors, with a little preparation you can use the auto link function in Dedoose to perform the task almost instantly.

Descriptor auto linking allows you to link media (your qualitative data) to any other quantitative data that includes the document title. When you have a smaller number of participants, this process is easy to do manually; however, with larger data sets, it is best to use descriptor auto linking. Figure 2.2 shows a portion of an Excel sheet displaying the media titles in our Dedoose project together with some associated descriptor data.

**BRUCE'S TIP #7**

Auto Linking Qualitative and Quantitative Data in Dedoose

Steps to follow in Dedoose:

1. Add a title column to your spreadsheet.
2. Add the title of your documents to the empty cell for each row, making sure to include the title exactly as it appears in Dedoose.
3. Import the file.
4. Click the Descriptors tab.
5. Click Auto Link.
6. Select the Title field.
7. Click Continue.

Figure 2.2   Descriptor Data With Associated Media Titles

| | A | B | C | D |
|---|---|---|---|---|
| 1 | Title | ID | TC First Name | Home Language |
| 2 | 1.15_post.docx | | 1.15 Martin | Spanish |
| 3 | 4.20_pre.docx | | 4.2 Reynaldo | Bilingual |
| 4 | 2.23_pre.docx | | 2.23 Jayson | Bilingual |
| 5 | 2.23_post.docx | | 2.23 Jayson | Bilingual |
| 6 | 2.18_pre.docx | | 2.18 Omar | Spanish |
| 7 | 2.18_post.docx | | 2.18 Omar | Spanish |
| 8 | 1.15_pre.docx | | 1.15 Martin | Spanish |
| 9 | 1.20_pre.docx | | 1.2 Juan | Spanish |
| 10 | 4.22_Post.docx | | 4.22 Aisa | English |
| 11 | 4.21_post.docx | | 4.21 Mayra | Bilingual |
| 12 | 4.22_pre.docx | | 4.22 Aisa | English |

Figure 2.3   Descriptor × Descriptor × Code Chart

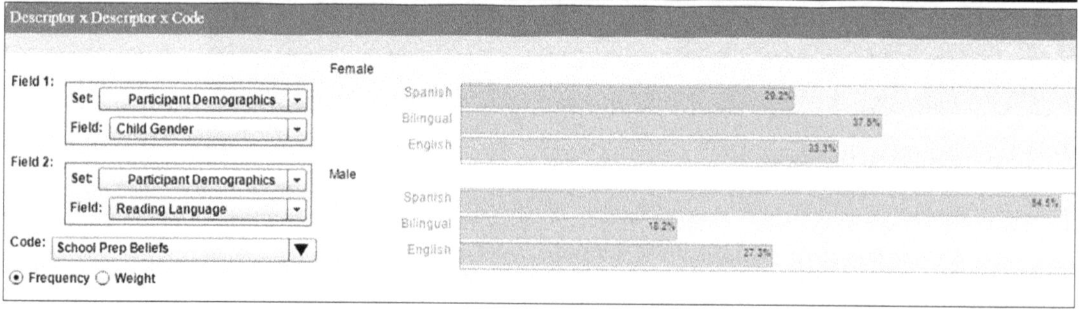

Once the links are generated and you have completed your qualitative data coding, the Analyze workspace can show you different visualizations, or snapshots, of your data such as the code application distributions. Figure 2.3 shows the distribution of the code "School Prep Beliefs" across the subgroups created by the descriptor fields: Child Gender and Reading Language. In this example, the visual shows the reading language separately for females and males of any data coded at School Prep Beliefs.

Auto linking can be a great time-saving tool, as long as everything has been prepared correctly. By using the steps above, you can complete any necessary linking quickly. In addition, while auto linking need not be a step for your particular project, diligent data preparation, in general, will result in reduced work in the later stages of a project. Explore auto linking as a way to make the transition from raw data to a populated Dedoose project as seamless as possible.

## 2.4 Case Study: Using the *Five-Level QDA*® Method With Dedoose

Having read this chapter, you have some ideas about beginning your data analysis and starting to work with Dedoose. You are in a position to start challenging yourself about what data you can actually use in your study design and how you are going to start your Dedoose project. Spend some time thinking about your position in relation to the two barriers to successful adoption of a data application. What are your upcoming challenges to being successful?

This case study now introduces you to the *Five-Level QDA*® method and how you can use it with Dedoose. The method argues that "translating" analytic tasks into software tools, and data applications, is best served when done thoughtfully, and those with lots of experience no longer need to think about the process. So for new users or users picking up new tools, the *Five-Level QDA* method can make the process transparent by documenting the thinking process via Analytic Planning Worksheets, which have been designed for the purpose. This forces this more thoughtful translation from concept to tool.

Earlier, we introduced you to the acronym REDA. In this case study, the ubiquitous acronym CAQDAS is used, referring to traditional computer-based software. Dedoose is a cloud-based application rather than a traditional software and is referred to as REDA.

---

**THINK ABOUT, AND ANSWER, THESE QUESTIONS AS YOU READ THE CASE STUDY**

1. Complete a self-assessment for yourself about using Dedoose. Refer to the discussion of first barrier and the following case study to complete this assessment:
   a. Do you see it as easy to use and useful?
   b. Are you through the first barrier?
   c. What is holding you back?

2. How confident do you feel about your methodology? Are you ready to start using Dedoose? What can you do to strengthen your research design? Refer to the discussion of the second barrier and look for ideas in the following case study.

3. How will you translate your research design into using Dedoose for your data analysis?

---

# Using the *Five-Level QDA*® Method With Dedoose: Examples From a Critical Discourse Analysis Project

## Christina Silver & Nicholas H. Woolf

This case study illustrates our *Five-Level QDA*® method (**https://www.fivelevelqda .com**) using Dedoose. In our combined 40 years of teaching and using CAQDAS packages, we have observed the challenges faced by new researchers and new users of CAQDAS in quickly learning to use these programs as powerfully as experts (Silver & Woolf, 2015). We developed the *Five-Level QDA* method as a way of describing what experts have learned to do over a long period of time and practice. In this case study, we provide an abbreviated summary of the principles of the method and illustrate how it can be used in Dedoose to fulfill a few analytic tasks in a real-world research project. We do not intend these examples to provide skills that can be directly transferred to quite different analytic tasks in quite different research projects but rather to demonstrate what the process involves and why it is applicable in all CAQDAS packages, qualitative methodologies, and styles of qualitative research. A full exposition of the method with numerous and varied worked examples that does intend to impart transferable skills appears in our textbooks (Woolf & Silver, 2018).

In any complex or ill-structured field, expertise is developed through long practice in a wide variety of situations, after which it becomes automatized, or unconscious, and the process becomes difficult to describe (Jonassen, 1997; Spiro, Coulson, Feltovich, & Anderson, 1988; Sternberg, 2014). Qualitative data analysis is an example of such a field. Our experience has been that the reaction of long-time qualitative researchers and expert CAQDAS users and teachers when presented with the *Five-Level QDA* principles is "Yes—that describes what I do but haven't been quite able to put it into words." The method lays out these principles and provides a systematic way of putting them into practice, with the intention that the procedures gradually become less and less necessary as the skills of powerfully harnessing CAQDAS packages become unconscious. However, many of our students report that they plan to continue with the full-blown procedures as a helpful way of documenting and later auditing the progress of their projects.

We first provide an overview of the principles, then illustrate how three analytic tasks in a Critical Discourse analysis can be accomplished in Dedoose using the method. We then illustrate the *Five-Level QDA* principle that there is no one correct way to harness a CAQDAS package by showing how the flexibility of Dedoose allows alternative ways of fulfilling two of the tasks if the context of the tasks is different. The case study concludes by discussing the nature of expertise in CAQDAS programs as facility in moving among emergent, algorithmic, and heuristic mind-sets.

## 2.4.1 The *Five-Level QDA* Principles

We have tried to understand what inhibits researchers from quickly learning to harness CAQDAS packages powerfully, and our conclusion lies in the distinction between strategies and tactics. Strategies—*what we plan to do*—and tactics—*how we plan to do it*—are distinct, yet they are commonly treated as synonyms or near-synonyms. For example, a well-known author writes, "An alternative search strategy is to select a sample of journals and to search for articles . . . this tactic was employed" (Bryman, 2006, p. 101). Conflating strategies and tactics in this way unconsciously leads to combining the QDA methodology and the use of the CAQDAS package's features as a single process of *what we plan to do and how we plan to do it.* A consequence is that the features of the software, which are concrete, readily understandable, and straightforward to put into practice, tend to drive the qualitative analysis process, which is much harder for new researchers to put into practice. The primary principle of the *Five-Level QDA* method is to ensure that this does not occur by *first* becoming clear about what you plan to do and *then* to be clear about how you plan to do it—in other words, for the analytic strategies to drive the use of the software, rather than the capabilities of the software to drive the analytic choices.

An additional element is the contradiction between the nature of the strategies and the tactics. Analytic strategies are, to varying degrees, iterative and emergent, with unique strategies evolving from moment to moment as the analysis unfolds. But the nature of computer software is cut and dried, operated with predetermined step-by-step software operations in which it is natural to assume, but improperly in our view, that the software features must be learned and used in the "correct" way in every analysis. The manner in which the researcher recognizes and manages this contradiction leads to the way in which the software is harnessed.

There is more than one way to manage a contradiction, and it is beyond the scope of this case study to distinguish the different ways and their implications for the use of CAQDAS. In brief, either denying or ignoring the contradiction, or compromising with a blended process that is somewhat emergent and somewhat procedural, leads to the software tactics driving the analytic strategies to some degree, with detrimental effects to the quality of the analysis (for further discussion, see Woolf & Silver, 2018). We have concluded from our observation of experienced CAQDAS users, as well as reflection on our own research practice, that powerful use results from transcending the contradiction. This means considering analytic strategies and software tactics as independent and separate within a larger context of the five-level process, so that the contrast between the nature of the strategies and the tactics remains unproblematic. The key to the method is then a process of *translation* between the strategies and the tactics.

Figure C2.4-1 illustrates the *Five-Level QDA* process. In brief, the first two levels are the levels of analytic strategies. At Level 1 are the guiding methodology and objectives or research questions. At Level 2 is the analytic plan to fulfill these objectives consistent with the methodology, including a conceptual framework of the data analysis and the identification of specific, detailed analytic tasks. In the *Five-Level QDA* method, *analytic tasks* have a special significance. They are well-defined tasks written at a level of detail that is most effective for translating into individual software operations. Extensive explanation about, and guidance

## Figure C2.4-1 The *Five-Level QDA* Process

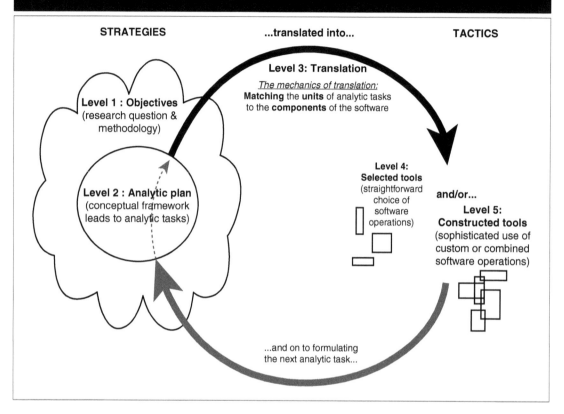

in, writing analytic tasks and several appendices of examples are provided in our textbook (Woolf & Silver, 2018).

Level 3 is the critical level of *translation* between an *analytic task*, identified at Strategy Levels 1 and 2, and the two levels of software tactics, Levels 4 and 5 (see Figure C2.4-1). Translation comes intuitively to an experienced CAQDAS user who has completed many research projects. They just "know" the most helpful way to harness the software for a particular task, even though they may not think of what they do as a process of "translation." To learn this process efficiently, it is helpful to understand that a translation process is indeed what is occurring. For learning purposes, we have unpacked five steps of translation that explicate what experts accomplish unconsciously.

In brief, this involves learning to write an analytic task at the most helpful level of detail, identifying the units and purpose of the task, selecting possible "components" of the software to represent the units of the task, and then selecting the best choice of software component to operate on in order to fulfill the task. The selection of a component is always based on the context of the analytic task within the project, which means *what has been accomplished so far* and *what is anticipated to happen next*. The outcome of this process is the most appropriate software operation for the analytic task, either a *selected tool*—a straightforward choice of a software operation—or a *constructed tool*—a more sophisticated use of custom or combined software operations (see Figure C2.4-1; for further explanation and illustration of the five steps of translation, see Woolf & Silver, 2018, Chapter 6).

## 2.4.2 The Components of Dedoose

The *Five-Level QDA* method does not concern itself with the "features" of the software but rather with its "components." Every software package has a set of components—roughly speaking, the things in the program that can be acted on. However, software designers generally present their software on the screen as a set of "features," each feature being a combination of a component and an action. This allows the user to interact with the software at a higher level without needing to think about which components are being acted on when using one of the features of the program. CAQDAS experts have intuitively learned that to harness this type of software in the most flexible way for many different qualitative methodologies, it is more helpful to interact with the software at a lower level of its organization, in terms of its underlying components.

### Table C2.4-1 Dedoose Components

| Component | Definition |
|---|---|
| media | A data file displayed in the Dedoose-project |
| descriptor-value | A factual characteristic about the units in an analysis (e.g., respondents, organizations, events, artifacts, etc.) that can be linked to media |
| excerpt | A defined segment of data that is not linked to anything else in the Dedoose-project |
| code | A named concept that can be linked to other components for analytic or housekeeping purposes |
| coded-excerpt | An excerpt linked to one or more codes |
| weighted-excerpt | A coded-excerpt linked to one or more codes that have been assigned a numeric value |
| memo | A piece of writing that can be stand-alone or linked to other components |
| memo-group | A collection of memos |
| chart | A visualization of the relationship between other components |

To give an idea of what we mean by the components of software, Table C2.4-1 lists and defines the nine components we focus on when teaching Dedoose using the *Five-Level QDA* method. It is beyond the scope of this case study to identify the sets of actions that can be taken on each component, although this information would be needed with the *Five-Level QDA* method to make the appropriate choices of components and then to either select or construct tools to fulfill the particular analytic task.

## 2.4.3 Translation in Action: An Example From a Discourse Analysis

We now demonstrate three analytic tasks from a study of the speeches of former U.K. prime minister, Tony Blair. This project explored Blair's rhetoric while he was the prime minister compared with after he left office. The purpose was to understand whether the aspects of his rhetoric related solely to his promulgation of the New Labour movement or whether they were more deeply entrenched and continued after he left office. The analysis centered on Blair's use of 15 keywords, called "New Labour Keywords," as they appeared in speeches made in the 5 years after he left office. The project is described in greater detail in the Case Study Appendix.

In the *Five-Level QDA* method, we move through a project in a series of *analysis phases*, each consisting of a cluster of analytic tasks. The analysis phase discussed here is *Interrogate the distribution of New Labour Keywords by year*. This analysis phase has three analytic tasks. We use *Analytic Planning Worksheets* to plan, manage, and document each analysis phase and its associated tasks. These worksheets spell out the five steps of translation for each task that result in either a *selected* or a *constructed tool* at Level 5. The Case Study Appendix displays the full Analytic Planning Worksheet for the three tasks demonstrated below in Dedoose. Table C2.4-2 summarizes the translation of these three tasks.

### 2.4.3.1 Task (a): Categorize Speeches According to Year of Delivery

To be able to interrogate the distribution of New Labour Keywords by year, the first task was to categorize the speeches according to the year in which they were delivered. The first row of Table C2.4-2 summarizes this analytic task. The middle column summarizes the conclusion of the translation process (described in more detail in the Case Study Appendix). The final column documents the decision to accomplish the task by linking each media to a descriptor-value representing each year between 2007 and 2011, a straightforward capability of Dedoose that we therefore refer to as a *selected tool*. This can be done manually in Dedoose or by importing the information from a spreadsheet. The result is illustrated in Dedoose in Figure C2.4-2.

## 2.4.3.2 Task (b): Capture the Occurrence of New Labour Keywords Across All Speeches

The second task in Table C2.4-2 was to count the number of times Blair used each New Labour Keyword across all the speeches. At the time of writing, Dedoose did not have a word frequency tool, or a tool that allows words to be found across media and automatically linked to codes. We therefore needed a *constructed tool*, a step-by-step way of accomplishing the task documented in the final column and illustrated in Dedoose in Figure C2.4-3.

### Table C2.4-2  Summary of the Translation of Three Analytic Tasks

| Level 2: ANALYTIC TASKS | Level 3: SUMMARY OUTCOME OF TRANSLATION PROCESS (for details see Case Study Appendix, Figure C2.4-9) | Level 4: SELECTED TOOL or Level 5: CONSTRUCTED TOOL |
|---|---|---|
| (a) Categorize speeches according to year of delivery | *Speeches* to be represented by MEDIA and *Year* to be represented by DESCRIPTOR-VALUE | **Selected tool**<br>In the Descriptor Tab create a Set Field for Year of Delivery with values for each Year within a Descriptor Set. Link each DESCRIPTOR-VALUE to the relevant media |
| (b) Capture the occurrence of New Labour Keywords across all speeches | *New Labour Keywords* to be represented by CODE (resulting in linked CODED-EXCERPTS)<br>Additional component for writing/visualizing purpose of task: CHART | **Constructed tool**<br>• Create one code to represent each New Labour Keyword<br>• Open the first media<br>• Use the search tool to find the first New Labour Keyword<br>• Navigate to each hit and link just the whole word to the relevant code<br>• Repeat for all New Labour Keywords in this media<br>• Repeat for all other media<br>• In the Analyze Tab choose the Code Application Chart (under Code Charts). |
| (c) Compare the frequency of New Labour Keywords by year of delivery | **UNITS:**<br>*New Labour Keywords* to be represented by CODE (and linked CODED-EXCERPTS)<br>*Year* to be represented by DESCRIPTOR-VALUE<br>Additional components from writing/visualizing purpose of task: CHART | **Selected tool**<br>In the Analyze Tab choose the Descriptor x Code Count Table |

## Figure C2.4-2 Descriptor Values Applied to Media in Dedoose to Capture Year of Speech Delivery

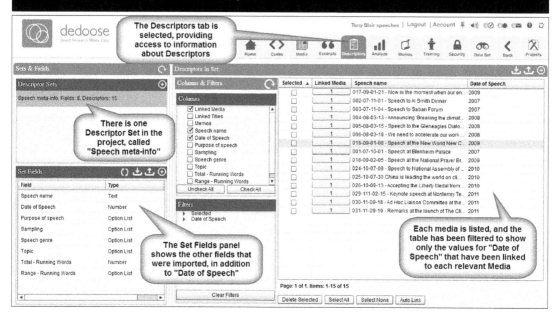

## Figure C2.4-3 Using the Text Search Tool to Code and Count New Labour Keywords Across Speeches

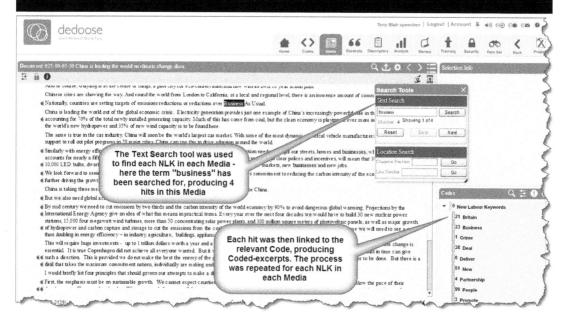

Coding each instance of each New Labour Keyword across all 15 speeches took about 3 hours. However, as noted in the Reflections section of the Worksheet (see Case Study Appendix, Figure C2.4-9), the process entailed viewing each instance in context, which led to the realization that Blair was using these words in sometimes very different contexts. It was therefore an analytically important process of familiarization, and as a result, it was decided to alter what had been planned for the next phase of analysis. Changing direction like this is characteristic of the iterative and emergent nature of qualitative data analysis, and documenting the progress of the analysis using successive Analytic Planning Worksheets means that these decisions can be systematically captured.

After the coding was completed, the occurrence of New Labour Keywords across all speeches could be visualized in several ways. As shown in Figure C2.4-4, the default view in the codes tab displays the list of codes down the left, a code count × media display top right, and a code × descriptor display bottom right. In addition, the code applications chart in the Analyze Tab shows a more detailed overview—the count for each New Labour Keyword by each media in a table from which comparisons can more easily be visualized (see Figure C2.4-5).

### 2.4.3.3 Task (c): Compare the Frequency of New Labour Keywords by Year of Speech Delivery

The final task in this phase was to compare the frequency of New Labour Keywords by year of speech delivery. Having already grouped media by year using

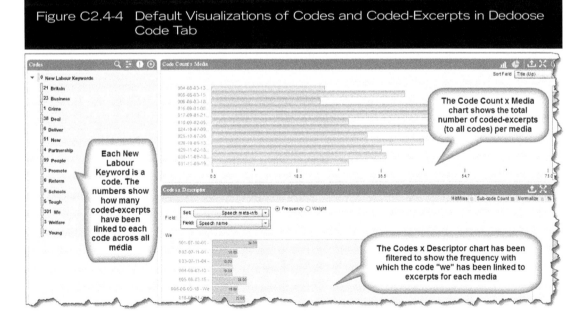

Figure C2.4-4   Default Visualizations of Codes and Coded-Excerpts in Dedoose Code Tab

## Figure C2.4-5   Code Application Chart Showing Distribution of New Labour Keywords in Each Speech

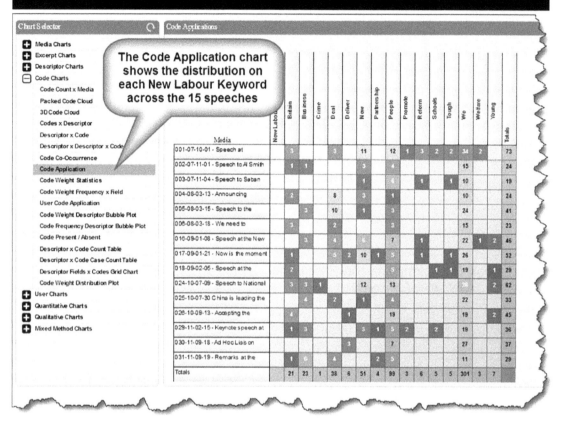

descriptor-values in Task (a), and then captured the occurrence of each New Labour Keyword across all speeches in Task (b), this new task was straightforward because Dedoose has a chart specifically designed to display the number of coded-excerpts in relation to descriptor-values. Task (c) could therefore be accomplished with a *selected tool*, documented in the final column of Table C2.4-2 and illustrated in Dedoose in Figure C2.4-6.

Fulfilling Task (c) using the descriptor × code Count Table completed this phase of analysis and allowed us to visualize and then interpret the distribution of New Labour Keyword in Blair's speeches according to year of delivery.

### 2.4.4 Alternative Choices

An important principle of the *Five-Level QDA* method is that there is no single "correct" way to harness the software. The best choice always depends on the

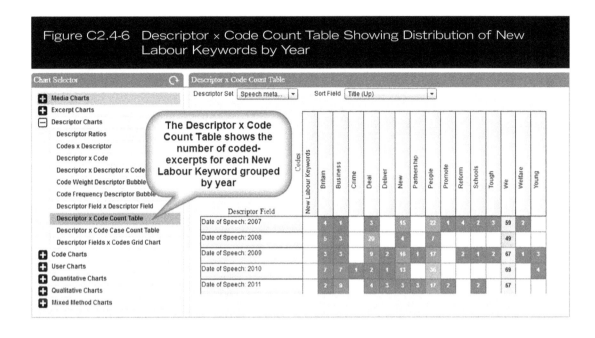

**Figure C2.4-6** Descriptor × Code Count Table Showing Distribution of New Labour Keywords by Year

context of the specific analytic task. In the *Five-Level QDA* method, context includes three aspects: (1) what has been accomplished so far, (2) the units and purpose of the current analytic task, and (3) what is currently anticipated will come next. The five steps of translation and the Analytic Planning Worksheet provide a process for first identifying candidate components to act on to fulfill a task and then a process for selecting the best choice in the particular context. All three aspects of context are used to select the choice of component, and our textbooks provide many illustrations of this process that can be easily applied to Dedoose (Woolf & Silver, 2018).

Dedoose is a flexible application, and an individual analytic task can often be fulfilled in more than one way. This is indicated by the list of *possible components* in Case Study Appendix, Figure C2.4-9, for each analytic task. A key principle of the *Five-Level QDA* method is that there is no right or wrong way to use the software, but rather an appropriate way in the context of the analysis phase and individual analytic task. To illustrate the importance of the context of analytic tasks in choosing appropriate components, we briefly discuss an alternative way of fulfilling Task (c).

Task (a) was fulfilled using descriptor-values to represent year of delivery, because they are specifically designed for the purpose of assigning factual characteristics to individual or groups of media. However, codes could also have been to fulfill this task. We could have created a code for each year of delivery and linked it to an extract that covered the whole of each media relating to each year. This would have been a more appropriate way to fulfill this task if all the speeches were contained within one media, as may have been the case had they been downloaded from an online archive or database rather than as individual files from Blair's website. In terms of Dedoose features, this may not have been the most efficient way of capturing the factual characteristics about each speech, and with only 15 speeches, it would have been straightforward and not very time-consuming to split the data in order to create one media per speech. However, if this project had included hundreds of speeches, a not uncommon situation in a mixed methods study, it may not have been feasible to split the data in this way. This situation would not have caused a problem because Dedoose is flexible enough that we could have used codes to represent each year of delivery rather than descriptor-values. In this case, one aspect of Task (c)'s context would have been different (i.e., what has been accomplished so far), and Task (c) could then have been fulfilled using the code co-occurrence chart rather than the descriptor × code count table, producing the same results as shown in Figure C2.4-8.

## 2.4.5 Case Study Conclusion

In this case study, we have provided an introduction to the *Five-Level QDA* method and its principles, and we have provided some examples of their application in Dedoose to indicate what is involved in most efficiently developing the expertise to harness Dedoose powerfully. The specific skills of each step of translation and the many illustrations in our textbooks facilitate gaining this expertise. But we are often asked about the more general nature of this expertise—what does it feel like? In the early years of our teaching, we concluded that the expertise lies in neither being a "splitter" nor a "clumper" when conducting qualitative analysis, but rather moving easily between "splitting"—working effectively at the detailed level of the "trees"—and "clumping"—pulling back and working equally effectively at the broader level of the "forest."

After we developed the *Five-Level QDA* method, we refined our views on the nature of this expertise and recognized that the contradiction between the nature of analytic strategies and software tactics calls for invoking three mind-sets (see Figure C2.4-7). When working at the strategy levels, we are thinking in an emergent mind-set, or a mode of thinking in which the next step of analysis is not predetermined or even presupposed by the former step but rather emerges from it. When working at the tactics levels, we are thinking in a step-by-step or algorithmic mode of thinking, in which each action taken in the software (selecting a menu item, pressing a button, etc.) has a predetermined effect. Working effectively at the middle level of translation between strategies and tactics invokes a third mind-set that is neither emergent nor algorithmic, but heuristic, in which prior experience in translating analytic tasks to software operations serves as a useful guide but not a rule book for how to proceed (for further information, see Translation as a Heuristic Process in Woolf & Silver, 2018, Chapter 6). Our conclusion is that a general description of the expertise of harnessing CAQDAS packages powerfully is to first recognize the relevance of these three mind-sets, and then to develop the skill of moving fluidly back and forth among them as the process of harnessing the software in the service of the analysis proceeds.

Figure C2.4-7 Facility in Three Mind-Sets

... emergent mindset...
... heuristic mindset...
... algorithmic mindset...
Level 1 : Objectives (research question & methodology)
Level 2 : Analytic plan (conceptual framework leads to analytic tasks)
Level 3: Translation
Representing the units of analytic tasks by actions taken on the most appropriate components of the software that fulfill the purpose of the analytic task in the context of what may come next
Level 4: Selected tools (straightforward choice of software operations)
and/or...
Level 5: Constructed tools (sophisticated use of custom or combined software operations)
...and on to formulating the next analytic task...


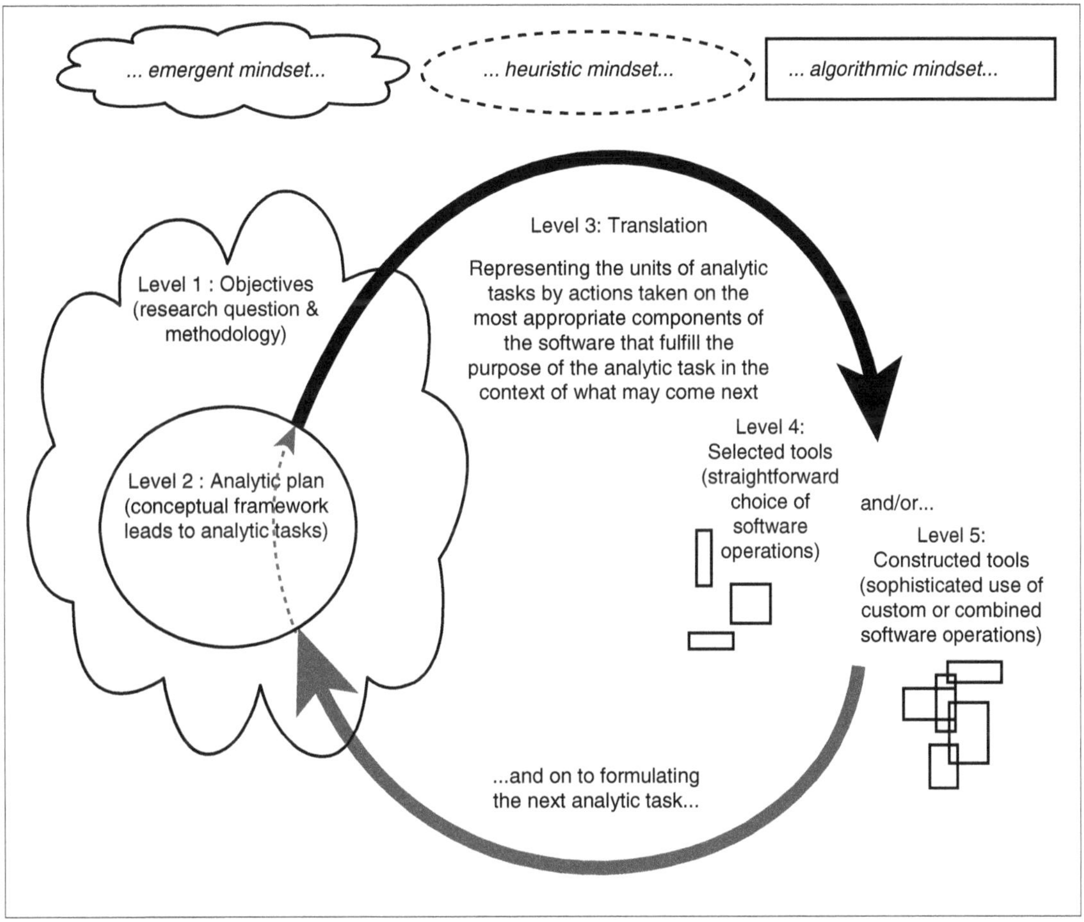

## 2.4.6 Case Study Appendix

Here, we describe the derivation of the three analytic tasks illustrated above in Section 2.4.3 "Translation in Action." This means describing in more detail the first two levels of *Five-Level QDA*, the two levels of strategy that lead to specific analytic tasks to be translated into software operations.

In the *Five-Level QDA* method, we move through a project in a series of *analysis phases*, each consisting of a cluster of analytic tasks. Each analysis phase is considered in its context, meaning what has been accomplished in the prior phases and what is anticipated to be accomplished in the coming analysis phase, depending on the outcome of the analysis in the current phase. The process of translation in a phase is documented in an Analytic Planning Worksheet, which comprehensively records the status of all five levels, both as an aid to thinking out the progress of the current phase and also to document the phase for later review or audit.

In this case study, we demonstrated one analysis phase containing three analytic tasks from a Critical Discourse Analysis of the speeches of former U.K. prime minister Tony Blair. This project was prompted by reading *New Labour, New Language* (Fairclough, 2000), which presents a theory of the political language of Tony Blair and the New Labour movement. An objective of the project was to explore whether Blair's rhetoric was specific to promulgating the New Labour movement or was more deeply entrenched. Fairclough identifies three analytically separable aspects of Blair's political language: (1) his rhetorical style, (2) the political discourse of the "third way," and (3) the genre of governance. The initial research questions therefore concerned whether any of the aspects identified by Fairclough related solely to Blair's position as leader of the New Labour movement or whether there were some that continued to be evident even after Blair left the office of U.K. prime minister. For the purposes of this case study, we focus on just one dimension of Fairclough's conceptualization of Blair's rhetorical style—his use of 15 keywords. These "New Labour Keywords" were identified by Fairclough as words that occur relatively most frequently in New Labour texts. To investigate Blair's use of New Labour Keywords after leaving office, the transcripts of the speeches he made in the 5 years after he left office (from June 2007 to September 2011) were accessed from his website. For the purposes of this illustration, we focus on a subsample of 15 transcripts (3 per year).

The phase of analysis discussed here is *Interrogate the distribution of New Labour Keywords by year.* Figure C2.4-8 shows the top half of the Analytic Planning Worksheet for this phase, documenting the Objectives and Methodology and Overall Analytic Plan (Levels 1 and 2a of the *Five-Level QDA* method). The worksheet also includes reminders of what had been accomplished up to this point in the project (Prior Completed) and what had been anticipated as happening next before the current phase began (Next Anticipated). These are important to include as they are part of the context of the analytic tasks in this phase and are used in Step 4 of translation to inform the choice of appropriate components in fulfilling each task.

The bottom part of the Worksheet is displayed in Figure C2.4-9. The left column lists the three analytic tasks that were undertaken in this phase and illustrated above. The middle column (Level 3: Translation) documents the thinking process for translating each task, and the right column (Level 4/Level 5) documents the software operations undertaken in Dedoose to accomplish each task. The final section of the Worksheet (Reflections) captures the analyst's thoughts about this phase of analysis.

# Figure C2.4-8 Objectives and Overall Analytic Plan Shown at Top of an Analytic Planning Worksheet

**PROJECT: Critical Discourse Analysis of Tony Blair's speeches post office. Phase 4: Interrogate the distribution of New Labour Keywords by year of speech delivery**

**Level 1:
OBJECTIVES &
METHODOLOGY**

### OBJECTIVES

To what extent are elements of Blair's rhetorical style, as identified by Fairclough in *New Labour, New Language*, identifiable in speeches he made during the four years after leaving office?

### GUIDING METHODOLOGY

"Theory-testing Critical Discourse Analysis'" of Fairclough's interpretation of Blair's rhetorical styles as a distinctive repertoire. Informed by Rosalind Gill's Discourse, Analysis process (in Bauer & Gaskell, 2000) but adapted to specifically test the applicability of Fairclough's (2000) theory of New Labour, New Language.

**Level 2a:
OVERALL
ANALYTIC
PLAN**

### CURRENT CONCEPTUAL FRAMEWORK
Visualization of Fairclough's theory

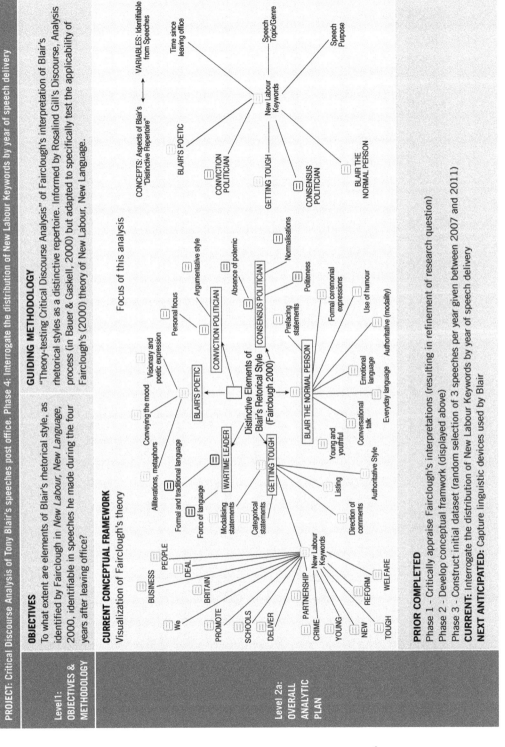

Focus of this analysis

### PRIOR COMPLETED
Phase 1 - Critically appraise Fairclough's interpretations (resulting in refinement of research question)
Phase 2 - Develop conceptual framework (displayed above)
Phase 3 - Construct initial dataset (random selection of 3 speeches per year given between 2007 and 2011)
**CURRENT:** Interrogate the distribution of New Labour Keywords by year of speech delivery
**NEXT ANTICIPATED:** Capture linguistic devices used by Blair

# Figure C2.4-9 Translating Analytic Tasks Using the Bottom Part of the Analytic Planning Worksheet

**PROJECT: Critical Discourse Analysis of Tony Blair's speeches post office. Phase 4: Interrogate the distribution of New Labour Keywords by year**

| Level 2: ANALYTIC TASKS | Level 3: TRANSLATION | Level 4: SELECTED TOOL or Level 5: CONSTRUCTED TOOL |
|---|---|---|
| a) Categorize speeches according to year of delivery | UNITS: Speeches, Year of delivery<br>PURPOSE: To group the 15 speeches according to the year in which Tony Blair delivered them, in order to later be able to interrogate all the speeches given in each year, and to compare speeches according to year of delivery.<br>POSSIBLE COMPONENTS: *Speeches*: MEDIA, MEMO, EXCERPT<br>*Year of delivery*: DESCRIPTOR-VALUE, CODE, MEMO<br>CHOSEN COMPONENTS: *Speeches*: MEDIA   *Year*: DESCRIPTOR-VALUE<br>EXPLANATION: Each speech has already been imported into the Dedoose-PROJECT as a separate MEDIA. DESCRIPTOR-VALUE representing each year of delivery (2007, 2008, etc.) can be linked to each MEDIA as relevant. | Selected tool<br>In the Descriptor Tab create a set Field for Year of Delivery with values for each Year within a set. Link each DESCRIPTOR-VALUE to the relevant media |
| b) Capture the occurrence of New Labour Keywords across all speeches | UNITS: New Labour Keywords<br>PURPOSE: To count the number of times Tony Blair used each New Labour Keyword in every speech.<br>POSSIBLE COMPONENTS: New Labour Keywords: EXCERPT, CODE, CODE-EXCERPT, MEMO, DESCRIPTOR-VALUE<br>CHOSEN COMPONENTS: New Labour Keywords: CODE (resulting in linked CODE-EXCERPTS)<br>Additional components from writing/visualizing purpose of task: CHART<br>EXPLANATION: Creating a CODE to represent each New Labour Keyword and linking it to each instance of each word will produce CODED-EXCERPTS and a count across all speeches | CONSTRUCTED TOOL<br>• Create one code to represent each New Labour Keyword<br>• Open the first media<br>• Use the search tool to find the first New Labour Keyword<br>• Navigate to each hit and link just the whole word to the relevant code<br>• Repeat for all New Labour Keywords in this media<br>• Repeat for all other media<br>• In the Analyze Tab choose the code Application chart (under Code Charts). |

| c) Compare the frequency of New Labour Keywords by year of delivery | UNITS: New Labour Keywords, Year of delivery<br>PURPOSE: To identify whether Tony Blair uses New Labour Keywords (in terms of frequency) over time.<br>POSSIBLE COMPONENTS: New Labour Keywords: EXCERPT, CODE, CODE-EXCERPT, MEMO, DESCRIPTOR-VALUE<br>Year of delivery: DESCRIPTOR-VALUE, CODE, MEMO<br>CHOSEN COMPONENTS: New Labour Keywords: CODE (and linked CODE-EXCERPTS)<br>Year: DESCRIPTOR-VALUE<br>Additional components from writing/visualizing purpose of task: CHART<br>EXPLANATION: During the previous tasks New Labour Keywords were represented using CODE (and linked CODE-EXCERPTS) and the different Years were represented using DESCRIPTOR-VALUES. It therefore makes sense to use these to accomplish this task. | SELECTED TOOL:<br>• In the Analyze Tab choose the Descriptor x Code Count Table |

**REFLECTIONS:** Coding the New Labour Keywords (NLKs) one-by-one allowed me to see context within which each word is used—it's clear that Blair is referring to e.g. 'people' in all kinds of different ways; therefore I will need to re-code for the difference. Initial thoughts relate to types of people he refers to (e.g. people in general, young people, people of faith) and also the tone of his reference to these people (i.e. positive or negative). In order to do this, I will need to create another set of NLK codes where the broader context (not sure yet whether just the sentence or a larger unit of meaning) is captured, then differentiate between different types of people. This needs to be done for each NLK. However, I think I need to read each speech in its entirety first to get a sense of the overall tone of the speech; I need to do this before coding for the various linguistic devices that Fairclough identifies. So I'm going to do that first, and write my thoughts about each speech in its entirety in a linked memo. I'll create a template for those memos to make comparative reflections. Then that can inform my coding of the linguistic devices.

It's also striking that some NLKs are very infrequently used (e.g. "crime", "deliver", "partnership" "promote", "reform", "schools", "tough", "welfare", "Young"). Need to go back to Fairclough to see what he says about how these were used by the New Labour Movement—were they tied into particular policies, etc. There's an important interpretation I need to do to explain why Blair is dropping his use of these words. Need to critically appraise the speeches and systematically look at the context in which each word is used in comparison to Fairclough's interpretation in order to do this.

## 2.4.7 Information About the Case Study Authors

**Christina Silver**, PhD, is a qualitative researcher and teacher of all the major CAQDAS packages, including ATLAS.ti, Dedoose, Discovertext, f4analyse, MAX-QDA, QDA Miner, Qualrus, NVivo, and Transana. She manages the CAQDAS Networking Project, based at the University of Surrey, UK. The project provides information, advice, training, and ongoing support in different software programs designed to facilitate qualitative and mixed methods analysis. Christina also undertakes research, training, and consultancy via Qualitative Data Analysis Services Ltd. and is the coauthor, with Ann Lewins, of *Using Software in Qualitative Research: A Step-by-Step Guide* (SAGE, 2014). Christina has trained thousands of researchers and students to use qualitative software since 1998. Her textbooks coauthored with Nicholas H. Woolf, *Qualitative Analysis Using ATLAS.ti, NVivo and MAXQDA: The Five-Level QDA® Method*, were published by Routledge in 2018.

**Nicholas H. Woolf**, PhD, is a qualitative research consultant and teacher of ATLAS.ti. He has taught graduate classes in qualitative methods, including at the University of Iowa, and since 1999 has taught approximately 300 ATLAS.ti workshops throughout North America for several thousand students. He has conducted and consulted on dozens of research projects in widely diverse fields, ranging from PhD dissertations to large-scale multinational studies. He gave the keynote address, "Analytic Strategies and Analytic Tactics," at the first ATLAS.ti User's Conference in Berlin, Germany, in 2013. His textbooks coauthored with Christina Silver, *Qualitative Analysis using ATLAS.ti, NVivo, and MAXQDA: The Five-Level QDA® Method*, were published by Routledge in 2018.

# Bringing Data Into Dedoose

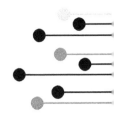

## 3.1 Gathering Mixed Data

This chapter discusses the types of data to gather for your Dedoose project and how to prepare these data for import.

Data gathering is different from browsing through convenient sources of information. As researchers, we do much more than browse and accumulate data; we purposefully gather data that meet the specific needs of the study design (Gibson & Brown, 2009). Observations, photographs, and in-depth interviews are commonly considered on the qualitative side, with counts, ratings, instrument scale scores, and population demographics on the quantitative side. Furthermore, the gathering of information continues to grow with ever-increasing access to an expanding variety of social media and digital resources.

The need for using the right tool for gathering and managing data has never been more important. Dedoose is specifically designed to manage mixed methods data gathering and to guide you through the analysis and interpretation process.

### 3.1.1 Data as Evidence

Data are the building blocks to produce evidence. In essence, data become evidence. Transforming data into evidence and capitalizing on the value of the data during analysis involves weaving credible information into a compelling argument (Bazeley, 2017; Gibson & Brown, 2009; Marshall & Rossman, 2015; Maxwell, 2013; Patton, 2015). Thus, how we as researchers use data shapes the quality of our findings and recommendations.

Mixed methods research requires the management of both qualitative and quantitative data. The complexity of mixing different types of data involves an interplay of field methods from two distinct paradigms with underlying methodological differences. Qualitatively, we primarily use data to better understand, explore, discover, or investigate a social phenomenon in its rich natural context. Quantitatively, we primarily use data to describe variation in a population or produce statistical findings that support or refute an interpretation of social phenomena (Creswell, 2017). Dedoose is designed to bridge these methodological differences by assisting researchers in building connections and relationships in both qualitative and quantitative data. Noteworthy questions usually arise during this process:

- What types of data promote quality in a credible mixed methods design?
- When is there too much data and when is there not enough data?
- How do we clean up and process data for Dedoose?

These are important design issues that this chapter considers.

## 3.1.2 Qualitative Data

A researcher can work with a wide range of qualitative data in Dedoose. Some examples of these qualitative data include field notes, observations, interview transcripts, focus group transcripts, public documents, historical records, images, audio recordings, video segments, social media, diaries, and personal journals. All these data types can be entered into a single Dedoose project.

**BRUCE'S TIP #8**

Media in Dedoose

All qualitative data sources in Dedoose are referred to as media. Any imported qualitative data can be found in the Media tab in Dedoose. If the imported data are quantitative, they can be found in the Descriptors tab in Dedoose.

A qualitative study is strengthened by incorporating all four types of data represented in Figure 3.1. Applying qualitative data triangulation to a mixed methods study offers a valuable means to assist researchers in carefully considering the inclusion of a diverse array of sources and promoting high-quality inquiry (McKenney & Reeves, 2012; Patton, 2015; Tashakkori & Teddlie, 2003).

As discussed by Kaczynski, Salmona, and Smith (2014), qualitative data triangulation comprises interview data (formal semistructured, informal conversational, focus groups), site documents/artifacts (official records, minutes of meeting, social media, correspondence), observation/field notes (social interactions, nonverbal actions, cultural context), and memos. These labels represent all-purpose placeholders; for example, in some studies, site documents may be referred to as artifacts. Grouping data into these classifications may stimulate consideration of gathering additional data from other areas of the triangle. In addition, an important benefit from this attention to detail is greater depth and deeper insights into multiple interconnected paths of evidence.

Figure 3.1  Building Credible Evidence From Multiple Data Sources

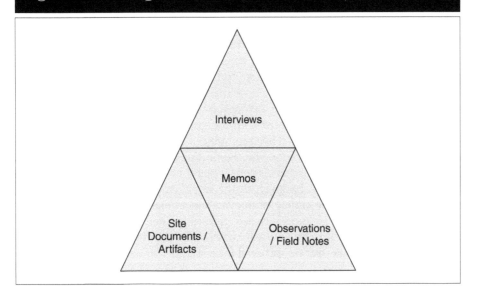

### 3.1.3 Quantitative Data

Quantitative data strengthen a mixed methods study with mathematical evidence, such as statistical models, and data gathered using standardized instruments. This generates numerical-based findings that enhance our broader understanding of the phenomenon under study. Dedoose supports the use of these numerical data as continuous number descriptor fields, as code weighting systems, and in examining change over time in longitudinal studies. By using these data to examine distribution plots, group comparisons, and chronological change and integrating them with qualitative data, we can generate findings to help address our research and evaluation questions (Bernard, 2013; Johnson & Christensen, 2017).

The flexible integration of quantitative functions in Dedoose allows quantitative interpretations to be appropriately broad so that a clear picture can be communicated to the intended audience. A few examples of numeric quantities and measurements of data include Likert-type scaled and closed response surveys, census records, and population demographic forecasting. Statistical outcomes are then used by the researcher to support claims leading to recommendations and conclusions.

### 3.1.4 Mixed Methods Data

Mixing these two distinct paradigms, qualitative and quantitative, allows for a blending of richer insights into the social problem of interest beyond what each paradigm may independently provide. Greater insights are thus achieved from flexible shifts in thinking and recognition of significant interconnections of data. This mixing process thus promotes compelling research by channeling the strengths of both qualitative and quantitative inquiry. The resulting complementary interplay of two distinct paradigms generates a synergy to support a wider range of research questions, greater insights, and stronger and more robust conclusions beyond what each paradigm may achieve on its own (Day, Sammons, & Gu, 2008; Tashakkori & Teddlie, 2013; Venkatesh, Brown, & Bala, 2013).

The application of mixed methods requires an appreciation and respect for both qualitative and quantitative inquiry. To be successful, you need to consider carefully your design thinking about how the data serve the research questions that frame the inquiry. Furthermore, before mixing data, you need to ensure that sufficient data have been gathered for both the qualitative and quantitative study in your mixed methods research. The credibility of a mixed methods study relies on an alignment of appropriate data with the findings and conclusions.

As the social science researcher designs a plan of action for a mixed methods study, careful attention must be given to the finer details of the data gathering process. Remember that the variety of information available to the social science researcher is only limited by the study design thinking being applied. Visualizing your study by creatively thinking outside the box can significantly strengthen the quality and range of data that are gathered for a study.

---

### EXERCISE
#### How Many Data Sources Can You Identify?

This exercise will help you during the early stages of designing your research study. Begin by thinking about data as the source of information to answer your research questions. Since researchers may allow the data sources to define and restrict the scope of a study, it is important to push your design thinking outside of the box. Really challenge yourself to think about what data you can draw on to best answer your questions. What is initially perceived as the limits of available information is often much smaller than what a study design can actually tap into.

1. Make a list of each type of data for your study.

2. Refer to Figure 3.1 and consider if you have overlooked any areas of the triangle.

3. Now let's get creative: Consider an interview for your study and write down as many types of data as you can think of that you can collect from that one interview. You will be using Dedoose, and not a filing cabinet, so you can be imaginative when thinking about these data.

4. Once you have really challenged yourself to think about this, refer to the appendix at the end of this chapter for a list of suggestions.

5. This exercise can be expanded by constructing a graphic that visually connects your data back to your research questions. To begin try browsing Google Images for sample graphics and flow charts related to your topic.

Visual representations of the data are useful for helping the researcher examine clear chains of evidence between the data and the research questions of a study. Refining these connections enhances the quality of data analysis and further assists with reporting credible findings.

A related point to this discussion is that working with mixed methods data allows the researcher to explore increasingly complex paths of inquiry. Here, the researcher has greater opportunities to explore unique combinations of data. Alas, your curiosity about the research topic may draw you to gather data outside the scope of the study. Curiosity-driven research can be compelling; just be aware that you may disappear down an irrelevant line of inquiry. It is important to balance these creative paths of inquiry by keeping all data connected and relevant to the focus and key research questions of your study.

Careful attention, thus, is warranted regarding what data are gathered. A strong mixed methods design incorporates the use of multiple data sources to promote deeper insights, better understandings, and more comprehensive interpretations. This attention to diverse points of view and perspectives enriches a study and promotes credibility and trustworthiness of findings.

## 3.2  Numbers as Data

From a mixed methods perspective, the application of numbers using Dedoose is neither qualitative nor quantitative. Rather, how you turn numerical data into meaning determines the application of the appropriate paradigm. In essence, the researcher determines how numbers are methodologically used. For example, a scale that weights 10 as high and 1 as low is a mathematical representation. The interpretation drawn from this, however, may be numerically measured quantitatively or descriptively interpreted qualitatively as a means to explore deeper paths of understanding. Of importance to this discussion is your approach to how you refer to numerical data in your justification of adopting a mixed methods study design.

### 3.2.1 Using Numbers Qualitatively in Dedoose

Numbers can be integrated into qualitative work in many ways and in doing so does not necessarily transform qualitative research into mixed methods (Bernard, Wutich, & Ryan, 2017; Maxwell, 2010; Ryan & Bernard, 2003). For example, numbers may be used to provide richer descriptive insights into the units of analysis under investigation or as mechanisms to facilitate enhanced pattern recognition as in cultural consensus models.

In another way, the researcher can use numbers, such as code weighting or descriptors in Dedoose, to overlay investigator-imposed dimensions that can be used to assist in unraveling multiple interpretations of qualitative content. It is recommended that this interpretation of numbers during qualitative analysis avoid the controversial use of quasi-quantitative claims that imply measurement (Erickson, 2007; Maxwell, 2010). Rather, such interpretations can be used as a means to identify paths of inquiry that would benefit from more detailed mixed methods analysis.

## 3.2.2 Using Numbers Quantitatively in Dedoose

This section discusses how Dedoose supports the direct use of numbers. Refer to Chapter 8: Working With Numbers in Dedoose, for a more detailed discussion of statistics in Dedoose. In SPSS, and other statistical analysis programs such as SAS/STAT, R, Stata, or Minitab, it is usually desirable to have demographic variables and other closed-ended responses, be they ordinal or nominal, in numeric form along with other continuous number data. For example, for Gender: 1 = male, 2 = female; Age-group: 1 = under 19 years, 2 = 19 to 25 years, . . . where "male," "female," "under 19 years," "19 to 25 years" are labels for the numeric proxies. In Dedoose, it is desirable to have as much transparency in the data points as possible. This simplifies interaction with the data since you do not have to reference a code book to remember whether "1" is male or female, or "5" is Asian, Hispanic, or White. Note that data exported from data collection services such as SurveyGizmo, Qualtrics, and SurveyMonkey typically are exported in the more transparent textual form.

Preparing a data set to maximize flexibility in analysis in both SPSS and Dedoose may require some variation. These preparation steps would be similar for other quantitative statistical analysis software programs. An example of variation for data points such as "Strongly Disagree," "Disagree," "Neutral," "Agree," and "Strongly Agree" shows the need to be prepared for quantitative analysis by conversion to numeric form. For convenience, all such conversion may be managed in Excel and then imported into Dedoose.

Preparing for analysis in SPSS:

1. Create copy of spreadsheet.

2. "Unpack" combined responses, for example, take responses to "favorite hobbies," turn responses to "select all that apply" into a set of variable such as "cooking: yes/no," "cycling: yes/no," and so on.

3. To facilitate quantitative analysis, convert all textual responses to numeric form.

4. Open spreadsheet in SPSS and where necessary add variable and value labels.

5. Calculate subscales.

Preparing for analysis in Dedoose:

1. The spreadsheet from above (after relabeling and unpacking) will serve as the primary data source.

2. The creation of subscales in SPSS is recommended before data can be fully prepared for Dedoose.

   a. While continuous variables in Dedoose are automatically converted into groupings when analyzing data in Dedoose charts, this conversion is based on an arbitrary algorithm that seeks to create equal groupings after an examination of range and nature of distribution along the numeric dimension.

   b. The key issue here is to consider in how many ways and in which ways one wishes to "slice" the population across these variables when looking for and within patterns in the qualitative data and how these data have been manipulated in any coding activity.

   c. In most cases, it is to your benefit when conducting your analysis that continuous variables be converted to categorical prior to import so that the decisions about how the population will be divided are controlled by you and your team and based on decisions that will best serve the research question.

## 3.3 Memos as Data

Both quantitative and qualitative inquiry are increasingly adopting the use of memos as data. The use of memos is an important part of many methodological traditions and teamwork practices. As shown in Figure 3.1, memos are strategically positioned at the heart of data triangulation. This position visually reinforces the point that every type of data that are gathered can be linked through memos. The growing use of memos underpins many theoretical orientations and is key to best practices in the tracking of design and analytical thinking during a project (Charmaz, 2014; Corbin & Strauss, 2015; Patton, 2015; Saldana, 2013). Also consider that quantitative and mixed methods practices are increasingly adopting the use of memos to support a robust code system development process in collaborative inquiry (Hesse-Biber, 2010a).

**BRUCE'S TIP #9**

Writing Memos in Dedoose

Memos are a great way to create an audit trail and track your work in Dedoose. You can also use memos to leave messages for other group members or research supervisors.

Memo writing is a research skill that must be applied early and often throughout a study to help manage data gathering and analysis. As memos are written and saved, they provide a documented audit trail of developing researcher insights and decisions. This is particularly critical as the growing complexity of a study progresses. Furthermore, memos promote transparency and improve communication with other stakeholders or research team members over the course of a research project.

Memos provide a unique function when conducting mixed methods research. Qualitative inquiry is primarily an inductive process of reasoning intended to promote openness to the voice of others, deeper insights, and better understandings into complex human issues. Quantitative inquiry is primarily a deductive process intended to support or refute assumptions and claims making up the interpretations that seek to describe and explain the why behind social problems. Mixed methods researchers engage in both processes by blending and shifting between inductive and deductive approaches throughout a study. This ebb and flow of shifting assumptions and insights can only be monitored by the researcher. Here is where memos can provide an invaluable role in documenting these shifts. These nuanced distinctions can lead to a greater understanding of what is going on in the study and help illuminate new insights.

When conducting a mixed methods study, memo writing must become ubiquitous. Data gathering of memos may be managed by creating four folders in Dedoose that are grouped into four distinct types.

- Methods memos

- Reflective memos

- Analytic memos

- Inductive–deductive shifts memos

*Methods memos* may be written any time a design issue is encountered or a modification in data gathering is considered. *Reflective memos* are similar to personal journals or diaries in which the researcher draws on distinct views and experiences. *Analytic memos* provide a means to capture and document preliminary interpretations and meanings. An *inductive–deductive shifts memo* is written each time the researcher intentionally applies inductive or deductive reasoning or unintentionally experiences a shift in reasoning. Together, these four types of memos document and support rich insights into the paradigm mixing process of the study and how analysis is evolving through interaction with the data.

Adopting a systematic approach to organizing memos is an important data management practice. The suggested four types of memos are useful to researchers as a means to stimulate writing and encourage frequent documentation. These four types, however, are not intended to represent rigid classifications. Find a system to capture memos that works for you. Researchers will frequently encounter an issue that may be grouped into more than one type. It is more important to write the memo than to hesitate and delay due to uncertainty regarding how to classify the subject.

The length of a memo is commonly one to three paragraphs. You may find that short notes such as annotations, notes-to-self, or observer comments may justify follow-up discussion that may be expanded on in greater detail through a memo. Short notes are useful bookmarks but are not a substitute for writing a memo. Conversely, when the length of a memo begins to grow, you are likely discussing more than one important topic. In such a situation, break the memo apart into multiple memos covering different topics.

As discussed earlier, memos provide an audit trail into the complexity of mixed methods analysis and interpretation. As you come to write up your research, you will likely find that you have not written enough memos as you re-create design decisions and interpretations over the length of a study. A helpful rule to follow about memos is to *write early* and *write often*. As well as using your memos as data, you can also use your memos to re-create your thinking when you come to write up your research as a linear artifact. However many memos you write, you will always think later that you could have written more.

In summary, memos are data, and as such are recognized as valuable evidence and analyzed alongside other data in a project. The researcher must apply the same analysis practices used to draw meanings from interviews, site documents, observations, and numerical interpretations to their memos. Reporting of memo analysis must ultimately be fully integrated into all other forms of mixed methods data analysis that are applied in a study.

Three important points to consider are as follows:

1. Draw on multiple mixed data sources.

2. Ensure each data source is relevant and aligned to the focus of the study.

3. Confirm that memos are included as data.

Memos in Dedoose are organized in a custom, user-defined, group structure depending on a project's specific needs. Memos can be free floating, not linked to any items in a project database, or linked to any number of items. Being group-based provides the freedom to organize memos in any number of ways. Finally, Dedoose memos can be easily exported to Word or Excel format files for local use in manuscript preparation, team discussion, data sharing, and report generation.

1. Create a new memo in Memos Workspace:

    a. Click the Memos tab.

    b. Click Create New on the top right.

c.   Title your memo.

d.   Add some content.

e.   Click Save.

2.   Create memo groups (only when creating a new memo or editing a memo):

a.   Click the Memos tab.

b.   Create a memo or click on one to edit it.

c.   Type into the Memo Groups field.

d.   Click Create Group.

3.   Linking memos to Projects items (create a memo for an excerpt):

a.   From Memos Workspace—Create new memo and "save" to prep for linking, or open an existing memo—then click the Memo Links button on the bottom of the pop-up.

b.   From an Object—open the Memos button or icon associated with the object you want to link.

4.   Exporting (XML and other formats) memos from Memos Workspace:

a.   Click Export, and select the desired format.

b.   NOTE: XML exports allow you to transfer memos between projects.

c.   If desired, provide a description.

d.   Select any linked items you wish to include in your export—

i.    Excerpts
ii.   Codes
iii.  Media
iv.   Descriptors
v.    Note that while excerpt text, codes, and descriptor content will be included, only media titles will be present in export

e.   Click Submit.

5.   Importing memos from Memos Workspace (allows users to share memos and associated content from one Dedoose project to another):

a.   Click the Import button on the upper right portion of the Memos tab.

6. Saving a Memo as a Project Document for Excerpting and Tagging:

    a. Click the Memos tab.

    b. Select the memos you wish to save as media files.

    c. Click the Create Document Copy.

    d. Documents versions of your selected memos will be created and will be viewable in the Memos tab.

**BRUCE'S TIP #10**

Write Memos Frequently

Memos help you capture your thinking about your research as it develops. Memos are data. Write memos early and often.

## 3.4 Case Study: Incorporating Mixed Analysis Into Your Study

This case study incorporates a qualitative approach using interviews that led to quantitative coded data identifying novel aspects of the attention-deficit/hyperactivity disorder–substance use relationship. Conceptually, this case is a mixed method analysis, not a pure qualitative analysis. It shows how Dedoose can be used to demonstrate mixed method features and how it can interact with other programs (Excel, SPSS) for subsequent analyses such as adding a quantitative scoring method and counting frequencies.

**THINK ABOUT, AND ANSWER, THESE QUESTIONS AS YOU READ THE CASE STUDY**

1. List all your qualitative data sources. Do your data relate back to your purpose and focus—can you connect them?

2. List all your quantitative data sources. Do your data relate back to your purpose and focus—can you connect them?

3. How are you mixing your data—through research design, through analysis, or through reporting? Does your design justify mixing?

# Incorporating Qualitative Analysis Into Psychiatric Research: A Case Study Using Dedoose to Examine Young Adults With Childhood ADHD

John T. Mitchell, Lily Hechtman, Desiree W. Murray,
Arunima Roy, & James M. Swanson[1]

## 3.4.1 Setting Up the Project

The Multimodal Treatment Study of Children with attention-deficit/hyperactivity disorder (ADHD), known as the MTA, was initiated as a 14-month, multisite randomized clinical trial that evaluated the effects of well-established treatments for ADHD (see Swanson, Arnold, et al., 2018, for an overview of the MTA). Ten months after the end of the trial (i.e., 2 years following treatment randomization), the MTA transitioned into an observational long-term follow-up study of the developmental course of ADHD. At that time, a local normative comparison group (LNCG) was added. In an extension of the MTA, a subsample of those with childhood ADHD ($n = 125$) and the LNCG ($n = 58$) in their early to mid-20s were examined in a qualitative study. This study, called the Qualitative Interview Study (QIS), explored various aspects of growing up with ADHD, including substance use (SU).

The relationship between ADHD and SU has been reported from a quantitative perspective in the MTA at different stages of development, including childhood (Molina et al., 2007), adolescence (Molina et al., 2013), and adulthood (Hechtman et al., 2016; Mitchell et al., in press; Molina et al., 2018). While these types of studies have yielded important information, qualitative methods can be used to complement this approach by providing additional information regarding beliefs about reasons for and the context of SU in the individuals' own words, revealing their own narrative account, and relying on their own experiences to yield novel insights (Weisner, 2002; Weisner et al., 2018).

The QIS involved the administration of the Ecocultural Family Interview adapted for the MTA—the M-EFI (Weisner, 2014; Weisner & Duncan, 2014). Cases were strategically oversampled for study participants with histories of persistent SU across four of the seven original MTA sites.[1] This yielded a total of 183 QIS participants when they were in their early to mid-20s, including 58 persistent substance users (39 ADHD, 19 LNCG) and 125 nonpersistent substance users (86 ADHD, 39 LNCG).

The primary findings from the QIS were published in a series of articles in the peer-reviewed *Journal of Attention Disorders* (Jensen et al., 2018; Mitchell et al., 2018; Swanson, Weisner et al., 2018; Wigal et al., 2018). Initial qualitative analyses in all these articles were conducted in Dedoose. In this case study, we discuss the initial approach adopted in the QIS and provide a case study of our analytic approach using Dedoose that yielded novel insights into facets of ADHD over the course of development into young adulthood from one of these studies: the QIS Emotion Substudy (Mitchell et al., 2018). This case study highlights the challenges and successes using Dedoose, including those associated with the coordination of a large number of interviews and subsequent transcription, scoring, analysis, and interpretation of the meanings discovered.

## 3.4.2 Data Sources

The purpose of the article by Mitchell and colleagues (2018), which we refer to as the QIS Emotion Substudy hereafter, was to explore the role of emotional functioning in the context of childhood ADHD and persistent SU. We considered two types of substance users: SU persisters and SU desisters. SU persistence and desistence was based on both the quantitative classification adopted for the entire QIS and the supplemental qualitative classification of SU persistence detailed in Jensen and colleagues (2018). This yielded a final study sample of 92 out of the 183 young adults in the QIS, which included 67 SU persisters (50 ADHD, 17 LNCG) and 25 SU desisters (20 ADHD, 5 LNCG). The remaining 91 QIS participants not included in the QIS Emotion Substudy were classified as SU abstainers ($n$ = 32), desisters with at least two previous assessments endorsing elevated SU ($n$ = 33), late starters ($n$ = 16), and resumers ($n$ = 10; see Jensen et al., 2018).

The M-EFI design and format is described in Weisner and colleagues (2018). In brief, these qualitative interviews were guided conversations lasting approximately 1.5 to 2 hours with interviewer prompts to cover a standard set of topics if narrative around these topics did not emerge otherwise. These prompts were piloted and refined with 16 separate young adults, as well as their parents—the topics covered particular domains of interest of the QIS. For the QIS Emotion Substudy, interviewer prompts that were particularly relevant included the following:

*What are the current stressors affecting you these days?*

*What makes you similar or different emotionally from other young adults?*

*When you first tried (insert substance), how did you feel?*

*What substance do/did you like the best?*

*What are some of the negative aspects of (insert substance)?*

*Did your emotions affect your substance use?*

Participants were invited to tell their own stories in their own words in response to these types of open-ended questions in an unstructured format.

The interviews were audio-recorded, transcribed, and uploaded into Dedoose. Challenges that arose with audio recording included quality of the recordings themselves, such as extraneous background noise during the interviews (which was particularly challenging when interviews were conducted at the interviewees' homes). Therefore, interviewers were tasked with modifying the interview environments accordingly and, in some cases, repeating what an interviewee said to ensure that it was captured in the recording. Once the audio recordings were transcribed, the study team edited the documents to remove personal data that may have identified study participants. Upon transcript de-identification, another challenge involved multiple study team members at each site uploading different documents. To minimize inconsistencies in labeling documents and to make particular transcripts easier to find within Dedoose, we used one centralized person to upload transcripts.

A team of raters was trained by one of the co–principal investigators of the QIS on how to score interview excerpts (i.e., excerpts defined as participant comments about a study topic; these could be a sentence fragment up to multiple paragraphs in length) within the transcripts. Each site contained at least one rater. To increase consistency across raters, an initial training on how to score transcripts within Dedoose was conducted in-person. This was followed by weekly conference calls by the team of raters and members of the study team with expertise in Dedoose to discuss unanticipated issues during the scoring process. The transcripts were scored according to a list of topics that were created a priori. Some topics were indexed, which simply meant an excerpt was about a particular subject area and involved indicating with a binary rating options if it was applicable (i.e., "yes" or "no" that it applies to an interview excerpt). Some topics were also rated using the Dedoose code weight/rating feature (e.g., on a scale from 0 = *perceived to be unimportant* to 8 = *perceived to be very important*). For the QIS Emotion Substudy, three topics were rated according to the 0 to 8 scale and reported in the publication:

Topic 1: Emotional states precipitate SU.

Topic 2: SU positively affects emotional states.

Topic 3: SU negatively affects emotional states.

Rating booklets were created for both the QIS and the QIS Emotion Substudy to provide additional guidance to assign a 0 to 8 score for an identified excerpt. Table C3.4-1 provides an example with Topic 3. Dedoose provides excellent

| Table C3.4-1    Rating Booklet Guide Example |
| --- |
| *Topic:* Substance use negatively affects emotional states (i.e., experiences regarding perceived negative impact of substance use on mood) |
| *Scoring options:*<br>0 = No mention involving experiences regarding the actual negative impact of substance use on mood.<br>1–2 = Low. Young adult reports some mild negative impact of substance use on mood (e.g., not feeling well for a short period of time on one or two occasions).<br>3–5 = Moderate. Young adult reports experiences with substance use negatively impacting mood, which may include mention of short-term and long-term negative impact of substance on mood.<br>6–8 = Substantial. Young adult perceives substance use as frequently having a negative impact on mood, including both short-term and long-term negative impact of substance use on mood. |

management of qualitative text data, great flexibility in indexing and code development, and memo and other functions to assist in these tasks. Finally, we also structured our code tree in a hierarchical manner both for organization purposes and to allow for more nuanced subcoding.

## 3.4.3 Data Management

Raters conducted two rounds of indexing and coding of the transcribed interviews in Dedoose. The first round was for the entire QIS sample; the second round was for the QIS Emotion Substudy.[2] Both rounds involved raters reading through the entire transcripts to select excerpts corresponding to a particular topic that would be indexed or coded. Once an excerpt was identified, the rater would provide a score of 0 to 8 using the Dedoose code weight feature for any applicable code(s). Raters regularly consulted the rating booklet and one another to maintain consistency between raters. Consistency across raters was a particular concern from the start. In addition to the challenges involved with raters dispersed across four different study sites, this process was carried out in two different rounds. To ensure consistency across the two rounds, raters held regular phone calls to allow for group discussion about issues that arose during the scoring process and to manage any "drift" from the initial training on how to score a transcript within Dedoose.

Additional indexing and coding were conducted to assess reliability between raters. This reliability testing was conducted within Dedoose in the Dedoose Training Center. Reliability testing had already been conducted with the full team of QIS, and it is described in detail in Weisner et al. (2018). Kappa coefficients were >.70 between raters when determining whether a topic should be coded. For the purpose of this case study, we will focus on the QIS Emotion Substudy reliability testing.

Reliability testing for the QIS Emotion Substudy involved 20 excerpts that had at least one topic scored by an expert rater. Raters were then assigned to view these excerpts in Dedoose within the Training Center and apply a score of 0 to 8 for any of the identified codes. Raters were blind to the expert ratings. Figure C3.4-1 illustrates the end result for a particular excerpt. Dedoose provides a Pearson product coefficient, $r$, for each individual rater after taking the reliability test. This correlation coefficient provides a summary of the relationship between that individual rater and the expert rater. This analysis indicated excellent interrater reliability with expert ratings (the mean $r = .88$, ranging from .79 to .98). However, for the QIS Emotion Substudy, the research team selected to calculate the intraclass correlation coefficient (ICC). The ICC is an extension of Pearson correlation coefficient and is a typical statistic used in psychological research when there are two or more raters to take their overall agreement into account. Dedoose easily facilitated these additional reliability assessments, since coding data can readily be exported and reimported in Dedoose. To do so, individual rater responses for each of the 20 excerpts were exported to an Excel spreadsheet for formatting and then exported to SPSS (IBM, 2013) to calculate ICC. Intraclass correlations indicated excellent consistency (ICC = .90) between raters.

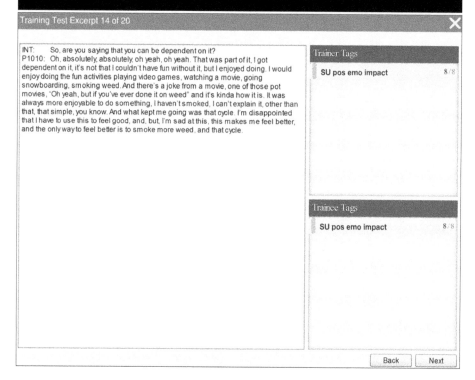

Figure C3.4-1  Example of an Interview Excerpt Used for Reliability Testing

INT:     So, are you saying that you can be dependent on it?
P1010:  Oh, absolutely, absolutely, oh yeah, oh yeah. That was part of it, I got dependent on it, it's not that I couldn't have fun without it, but I enjoyed doing. I would enjoy doing the fun activities playing video games, watching a movie, going snowboarding, smoking weed. And there's a joke from a movie, one of those pot movies, "Oh yeah, but if you've ever done it on weed" and it's kinda how it is. It was always more enjoyable to do something, I haven't smoked, I can't explain it, other than that, that simple, you know. And what kept me going was that cycle. I'm disappointed that I have to use this to feel good, and, but, I'm sad at this, this makes me feel better, and the only way to feel better is to smoke more weed, and that cycle.

Trainer Tags

SU pos emo impact                                           8/8

Trainee Tags

SU pos emo impact                                           8/8

Back        Next

## 3.4.4 Analysis Processes

*Analysis of Topics.* The first primary goal of this exploratory study was to examine group differences on the basis of ADHD status (i.e., ADHD vs. LNCG) and SU status (i.e., persistent vs. desistent) on the three emotion–SU topics (i.e., Topics 1–3 above). In addition to these three variables, an additional variable, a difference score of two topics, assessed the relative balance of positive and negative perceptions of SU—this variable was created by subtracting the average score on a scale of 0 to 8 for each young adult for Topic 2 from Topic 3. All inferential statistical tests were conducted outside of Dedoose. However, our initial analytic approach to visualize and assess trends in the data was conducted using Dedoose.

Initial analysis involved examining the data within Dedoose under the "Analyze" Workspace. This took many forms, including visually inspecting a three-dimensional code cloud or packed code cloud listed under "Qualitative Charts," group differences under "Mixed Method Charts," and the frequency of receiving a score for a particular topic by subject under "Media Charts." For example, Figure C3.4-2 displays a packed code cloud for the entire QIS. This is an interactive display in Dedoose and can select a certain topic to see a display of the

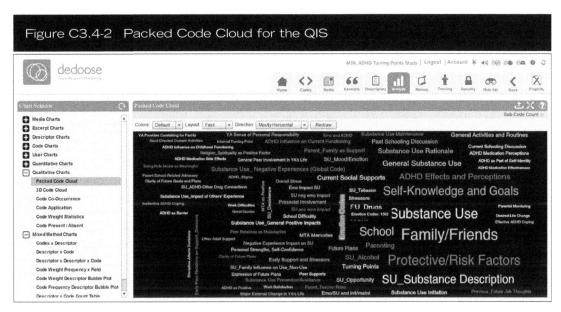

**Figure C3.4-2  Packed Code Cloud for the QIS**

*Note:* QIS = Qualitative Interview Study.

number of excerpts with this topic applied by a rater. By clicking on the actual topic in the cloud, all of the excerpts with this topic can be viewed and exported into a Word or Excel document.

For the QIS Emotion Substudy, we relied heavily on "Mixed Method Charts" to visually inspect any preliminary trends based on childhood ADHD group status and SU group status. Additionally, we used "Media Charts," then selected "Code Application" to inspect the frequency of a topic's selection. We further inspected qualitative trends by clicking on the frequency value in the table within "Code Application" to read participant comments. Another feature adopted within Dedoose involved the addition of a "Great Quotes" tag to index participant comments throughout the rating process that were exemplary and helped the study team convey meaning using the participants' own words. Use of the "Great Quotes" tag was important to balance out the need to closely read and score all of the transcripts while making it more manageable to navigate through all of the excerpts. In the QIS project, there were more than 13,000 excerpts. Having the "Great Quotes" tag provided an efficient way to go back into to Dedoose to identify particularly illustrative participant comments representing various topics.

The primary analysis involved a two-way between-groups analysis of variance (ANOVA) across all four topic variables to evaluate main effects for ADHD/LNCG group and SU persister/desister group, and their interaction. To do this, participant data were exported from Dedoose for reformatting within Excel. This involved exporting all Topic 1 to Topic 3 scores for each participant, as well as the participant's narrative comments in the excerpts each time a score was applied.

Most participants had multiple excerpts in which the same topic was scored. Within-participant means were calculated in Excel resulting in one score per participant for each of the three topics. Once these were calculated, the fourth outcome variable (i.e., the relative balance of positive and negative perceptions of SU) was calculated by subtracting the Topic 2 score from the Topic 3 score for each participant. The data were then imported to SPSS (IBM, 2013) and further examined using ANOVA. Effect sizes, Cohen's *d* (Cohen, 1988), were considered as well and were calculated within Excel.

*Analysis of Secondary Topics.* Because our analysis of the topics described above indicated a difference between SU persisters and desisters for Topic 2 (i.e., SU positively affects emotional states), we conducted an exploratory qualitative analysis of participant narratives for this topic at a substance-specific level. This analysis focused on cannabis, alcohol, and cigarettes since 82% of the excerpts involved at least one of these substances. A rater read through these excerpts to identify themes involving the role of emotion in SU. For each substance (i.e., cannabis, alcohol, and cigarettes), the rater identified excerpts that indicated if it was perceived to either enhance positive mood, reduce negative mood, or improve ADHD symptoms.

The prevalence of endorsing these themes for cannabis, alcohol, and cigarettes was recorded in Excel and exported to SPSS so that chi-square analyses could be conducted between three different groups: (1) ADHD SU persisters, (2) LNCG SU persisters, and (3) ADHD SU desisters.[3] This analysis allowed us to report on the frequency of each qualitative theme endorsement for each individual substance between groups, which yielded novel insights about ADHD and SU. For example, 50% of the ADHD SU persisters indicated that they perceived cannabis to improve their ADHD. This rate was significantly higher than the LNCG SU persisters (13%) and ADHD SU desisters (12%). Example statements from participants helped us better understand these sometimes complex perceptions. For example, even though some reported that cannabis improved their ADHD symptoms, they conflated the impact on ADHD symptoms with impact on mood.

### 3.4.5 Reporting the Project

In the QIS Emotion Substudy, Dedoose was used in collaboration with Excel and SPSS. Coding and indexing of transcripts was completed in Dedoose first for the entire QIS sample and then for the QIS Emotion Substudy that included a project-specific rating guide. Reliability testing was also conducted in Dedoose. For further discussions on the study design and analysis procedures, refer to Mitchell et al. (2018). The QIS Emotion study had the considerable benefit of access to all the narrative data from the entire sample of 183 cases—readily accessible across all the study sites, with demonstrated reliability, and ready for further analysis. As noted, however, all inferential statistical analyses were conducted in SPSS after some data preparation in Excel. The latter included using Excel to establish individual participant mean scores for each topic and calculating effect sizes. The preparatory steps and preliminary analysis in Dedoose prior to exporting must also be considered given Dedoose's data visualization features. For instance, visualizing the frequency of code application differences between subjects distinguished by SU group status and/or ADHD group status was valuable in the early phase of data analysis. These features in Dedoose for visualization and exploration of narrative data, both coded and full text, were very useful in providing guidance for subsequent analyses.

## 3.4.6 Looking Back

The QIS was conducted across four study sites. Dedoose provided a shared platform that all team members could access to carry out their work, in real time, and with the assurance of always up-to-date data. This eased logistical demands of raters in many different locations, regardless of their computer platform, to simultaneously review transcripts and helped coordinate raters across sites in taking the reliability tests. At the same time, having shared access by all team members allowed those responsible for analysis to immediately access ratings. The use of the Dedoose code rating feature was valuable to our findings inside Dedoose and our quantitative analyses carried out in SPSS. A final consideration for the QIS Emotion Substudy was that coding and indexing were conducted in two waves. Having an initial round of indexing and coding for the QIS study was helpful to formulate and refine research questions about the role of emotion in SU for those with ADHD in childhood. That is, the research team was able to observe participant narratives from the first round and consider those narratives in conjunction with knowledge about what we know—and don't know—about emotion as it pertains to SU in ADHD, which then led us to formulate stronger questions for the next round.

## 3.4.7 Case Study Conclusion

In conclusion, this case study incorporated a qualitative approach to understand and inform future research questions about emotion and SU among young adults with a history of ADHD. The qualitative interviews led to quantitative coded data that allowed us to identify novel aspects of the ADHD–SU relationship. How our team capitalized on what Dedoose offers demonstrates its mixed method features and how it can interact with other programs (Excel, SPSS) for subsequent analyses. At a more general level, this case study illustrates how Dedoose can be used in psychiatric research to uncover complex relationships by incorporating a qualitative perspective alongside quantitative findings.

*Acknowledgements.* We appreciate feedback from Thomas S. Weisner, PhD, on an earlier draft of this case study.

### 3.4.8 Information About the Case Study Authors

**Dr. John T. Mitchell** is with the Department of Psychiatry & Behavioral Sciences, Duke University Medical Center, Durham, North Carolina.

**Dr. Lily Hechtman** is with the Division of Child Psychiatry, McGill University, Montreal Children's Hospital, Montreal, Quebec, Canada.

**Dr. Desiree W. Murray** is with the Frank Porter Graham Child Development Institute, University of North Carolina, Chapel Hill.

**Dr. Arunima Roy** is with the Division of Molecular Psychiatry, University Hospital Würzburg, Germany.

**Dr. James M. Swanson** is with the School of Medicine, University of California, Irvine.

Contact Information: John T. Mitchell, PhD, Department of Psychiatry & Behavioral Sciences, Duke University Medical Center, 2608 Erwin Road, Pavilion East, Suite 300, Durham, NC 27705, USA; Phone 919-681-0012; Fax 919-681-0016; john.mitchell@duke.edu.

### 3.4.9 Notes

1. Duke University Medical Center, Montreal Children's Hospital, University of California at Berkeley, and University of California at Irvine.

2. Additional indexing and coding were conducted in the Jensen et al. (2018) and Swanson et al. (2018) studies as well. Please see each respective publication for additional details on those procedures.

3. Pairwise comparisons excluded the LNCG SU desister subgroup given its small sample size.

## 3.5 Conclusion
• • • • • • • • • • • • • • • • • • • • • • • • • • • • • • • • • • • • • • • • • • • • • • • • • • •

Chapter 3 brings an end to the first section of this book about Research Foundations. You have been introduced to Dedoose and spent some time thinking about your study design and how you will proceed with your data analysis. Part II is about Data Interaction and Analysis. It introduces some of the challenges of working in teams in Chapter 4 and then discusses the qualitative component of a mixed methods study in Chapter 5.

Chapter 6 then introduces mixed methods analysis with Chapter 7 describing some more complex issues, including filtering your data and working with visualizations. These upcoming chapters really give you a chance to develop your thinking around your study design and analysis and how to successfully work with Dedoose.

# APPENDIX: TYPES OF INTERVIEW DATA

This list of different types of data that you can collect from a single interview was compiled by us during many workshops where we had participants take part in this activity. It is not a comprehensive list and only serves to illustrate different types of data that you can collect associated with interviews.

1. Memos: four types

2. Transcripts

3. Demographic data about participants

4. Translation

5. Observer comments/notes to self/annotations

6. Field observations—during interview

7. Field notes—interview site (setting)

8. MP3/MP4—audio/video recordings

9. Site documents, for example, organizational website/mission statements/policy documents

10. Interview artifacts, for example, drawing how they see the organization

11. Photographs

12. Diagrams of interview site

13. Incentives (if any)

14. Vignettes

15. Predata, Postdata

16. Sample summary data

17. Consent forms/institutional review board/ethics/interview protocol

18. Tracking data

19. Geographic information systems (GIS) and spatial data for geospatial analysis and cartographic mapping

20. Sociograms

21. Social media

22. Email chains—correspondence before/during/after

23. Power dynamics

24. Participant journals/memos/diaries/reflections

25. Member checks

# Data Interaction and Analysis

Strong research anticipates the emergence of important themes and articulates how the analysis process relates to the focus or the central research question of a study. When it comes to the particular themes that will be used to frame a study, tracking their identification, definition, and rules for application to qualitative content is a fundamental part of mixed methods and qualitative analysis (Ryan & Bernard, 2003). Throughout a study, it is essential to identify which themes and findings are relevant and help address research questions as opposed to those that are more fractured or idiosyncratic. Regular reflection on the central research question will help ensure that those most relevant themes are recognized and incorporated into later analysis. Finally, with a mixed methods approach, it is critical to be thoughtful and intentional in deciding what different kinds of data will be drawn on and how these data will be intertwined toward maximizing the value of how the analysis will support research question arguments.

We begin Part II of the book by considering how best to work in research teams with a particular focus on code system development, coding, and team-related issues. Research collaboration is increasing as cloud-based technologies allow teams to work together in real time. This part of the book focuses on data interaction and analysis, looking first from a qualitative point of view and then moving to mixed methods. Here, issues about data complexity are considered, including challenges of mixing your methodologies and mixing your data.

# CHAPTER 4

# Teamwork Analysis Techniques

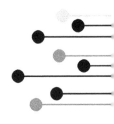

Working in teams is both rewarding and challenging. In this chapter, we consider team dynamics and collaborative techniques to improve mixed methods research team practices. We recognize that mixed methods research requires both quantitative and qualitative methodological skills. However, a single researcher having research expertise in both paradigms is often out of the ordinary. Furthermore, a single researcher can find it inefficient to concurrently manage distinctly different data management and analysis practices (Caruth, 2013). This chapter offers insights into teamwork, which is often an overlooked and taken-for-granted part of mixed methods research.

Mixed methods research teams may comprise individual members with expertise in a wide range of methodological skills. Additionally, team members may be chosen to represent diverse social science disciplines and distinctively different methodologies. Given this diversity, it is important that methodological respect between team members is maintained and valued (O'Cathain, Murphy, & Nicholl, 2008b).

Supporting collaborative qualitative and mixed methods work is fundamental to Dedoose's design and, as such, is a unique strength of the Dedoose platform (introduced in Chapters 2 and 3). In this chapter, we first talk about how to work successfully in teams and then expand on the Dedoose features and functionality related to teamwork showing how they can be capitalized on throughout the course of a project.

## 4.1 Team Management

The emergence of cloud technologies in general has stimulated team collaboration and presents new challenges beyond those that researchers have experienced using traditional machine-based software. In this chapter, Dedoose is presented as a platform that, when used to its full capability, can greatly increase the efficiency and effectiveness of how teams can work together in collaborative research and evaluation projects.

In our recent survey (described in Section 3.4) conducted with a sample of individuals of varying level of experience with qualitative and mixed methods research and the tools developed to support this work, the clear majority of participants agreed with the notion that collaboration in their area of work is important and valuable. Accordingly, it is noteworthy that one of Dedoose's strengths is how multiple team members can work simultaneously, in real time, from any Internet-connected computer or tablet device. Dedoose allows individual members to work synchronously on a single project regardless of geographic location, number of team members, or different time zones.

## 4.1.1 Team Dynamics

Researchers and evaluators working in teams often neglect to seriously consider how to create an environment and communication systems that will bring out the best in each team member and help the team work effectively and productively. Rather, they commonly charge ahead into the project without thinking about how this might negatively affect the quality of the overall design and the smoothness of how each stage of the project will unfold. To further complicate the matter, each individual—who might range from new students with no research experience, to senior faculty with long histories of published work, to experienced principal investigators, to community members—comes to the project with different strengths, weaknesses, and experiences related to the specific content area of the work, methods in general, and the use of technology. Ideally, the collective set of strengths will be complementary in nature, and if the team comes to work in a coordinated way, it will function effectively and productively.

Team collaboration and group dynamics provide a useful framework for better understanding the developmental process that a research and evaluation team may experience. The Five-Stage Team Development Model was first introduced by Bruce Tuckman (1965) and expanded with additional stages of team processing 13 years later (Tuckman & Jensen, 1977). This model was developed in the context of a review of the formation of "team" in group therapy, natural settings, and the laboratory. Application of this conceptual understanding has proven to promote team effectiveness and has been adopted and modified for use in a wide range of disciplines, including organizational development, educational leadership, group dynamics training, and project management.

Building on this earlier work, a conceptual framework for mixed methods research teams is presented to align with social science research and evaluation team collaboration practices. This mixed methods research team model comprises seven phases through which most teams will pass: (1) forming, (2) storming, (3) norming, (4) performing/analysis, (5) adjourning/reporting results, (6) reforming/follow-up, and (7) progressive performing (see Figure 4.1). By anticipating these phases, teams may avoid situations that can cause the team and the project to fail.

This mixed methods research team model demonstrates a relationship between the productivity of team members and the time on task required to complete a project. Considering this fluctuating path, it is noteworthy that changes in team membership may require a team to reform and revisit the subsequent stages of the process.

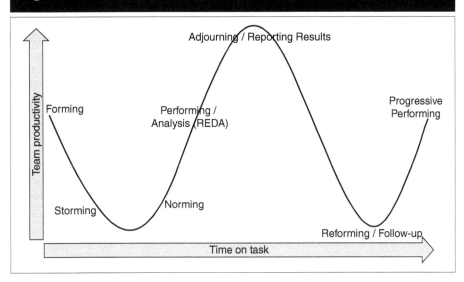

Figure 4.1   Teamwork Model

*Source:* Adapted from Tuckman and Jensen (1977).

The teamwork model is presented in Figure 4.1 as a representation of the life cycle of a team working on a research or evaluation project that involves the use of technology. Here are some ideas to work with when you next work in a mixed methods research team.

### 4.1.1.1 Forming

As noted above, it is important to keep in mind that even if the members of the group have worked together in the past, each project is unique and justifies consideration of the "forming" stage of the team-building process. Part of what you are doing in this stage is identifying who is on the team and what strengths, experiences, and technological skills each member brings. What are the specific tasks to be carried out? Is there a managerial hierarchy among the members and are there clearly identified leaders? It is important that each team member carefully considers their roles and responsibilities in the design and delivery of the project and their preparedness to do so. Key questions to be discussed at this stage include the following: What benefits do you bring to the team in terms of specific software, research methods, management, and presentation skills and experiences? What do you expect from other team members? And, can all members come to a consensus about the distribution of roles and responsibilities? With this information on the table, tasks focused on data gathering, data management, and analysis in Dedoose and overall team management can be determined and assigned.

### 4.1.1.2 Storming

This is a largely inevitable and often highly challenging phase for any team. Team members arrive with both good and bad historical experiences related to working with others, and this phase is a bit of a shaking out. Any team must take clear steps to ensure that all individuals remain engaged, prevent any sense of team member isolation, and avoid a groupthink mentality that might discourage creativity and responsibility. At this point in the process, it is critical to remember that effective communication will be fundamental to all members of the team, regardless of status or role, in working through this necessary process. It can also help to keep in mind that the use of technology in this communication process can create its own problems. For example, messaging through Twitter or text can be misinterpreted, and other technology-based communication (e.g., email, Skype, Google Hangouts, WebEx, or other platform) is different from what takes place in a face-to-face meeting. Team leaders will benefit from keeping in mind that these challenges can arouse emotions and other internal insecurities that may affect team members' ability to communicate clearly. Respectful and forthcoming communication will encourage the establishment of a trusting atmosphere that will, in turn, help the team advance to the next stage of the process. Regrettably, some organizational teams find themselves unable to move beyond a storming experience because of insufficient effort, member unwillingness, or significant incompatibility of the team structure, which leaves them locked in a destructive group dynamic cycle.

### 4.1.1.3 Norming

At this stage, team members have advanced together as a group, and each has progressed toward feeling valued, capable, and prepared to contribute to the overall team effort. By now, roles are clearly identified and responsibilities distributed, team interactions are positive and productive, and team protocols are established. Together, this sets the stage for the team to move into a highly productive period. Team members are ready to work in a strong, collaborative, and open environment, each armed with the appropriate technologies for their tasks, and where creativity and certain levels of risk are valued.

### 4.1.1.4 Performing/Analysis

This is a highly productive time for the team. The team demonstrates clear, shared understandings about the research or evaluation project and is actively engaged in project tasks. Technologies are in place to support each member with the tasks for which they are responsible, including communication, data gathering, management, analysis, and the preparation of project deliverables. These technologies can include phones; recording equipment; email addresses; computers; tablets; Internet access; MS Word, Excel, and PowerPoint; SPSS or SAS; and Dedoose. This is the period where all members of the team have a clear awareness about and connectedness with the team and their shared goals. Finally, during this stage, critical interactions among team members are encouraged; all views are sought, communicated, discussed, and shared; and the team is acting productively toward meeting the project goals.

### 4.1.1.5  Adjourning/Reporting Results

During this later phase, team members are effectively using their technologies to produce final reports, recommendations, and/or other deliverables, and there is thorough and clear communication with all project stakeholders. The project is then brought to a close, and the reporting of findings and recommendations is achieved through the visualizations, reports, publications, and presentations generated in the previous phase. Finally, the team can consider future directions related to the completed project as individuals or the team as a whole.

### 4.1.1.6  Reforming/Follow-Up

Reforming requires a return to the beginning of the life cycle and can occur on receiving any stakeholder feedback that requires requiring further action from the team. For example, receiving feedback from a journal reviewer or a new senior researcher who joins the team may stimulate new thinking about how the work is being conducted. Stakeholder buy-in and the utilization of deliverables are particularly important in this stage. If there has been any change in team membership, technology, or the project overall, the team is reformed and will return to a storming phase to sort through any significant changes toward returning the team to a norming state. Under some circumstances, taking the team apart and reforming/reconstituting the group may be helpful in progressively reaching even stronger performance capabilities and promoting a collaborative culture of excellence to better meet project and stakeholder needs.

### 4.1.1.7  Progressive Performing or Adjourning

This is the time to stop and, assuming the team was indeed productive, to celebrate success. Acknowledging the team accomplishment in the research or evaluation project is an important step to take before taking on new challenges. Here, we note that in any group there may have been constructive conflict and that even high-performing groups have limitations. It can be valuable for the team to reflect on the entire process so that each member can learn and grow through their experiences and the reflections of others. While we believe that working with teams is important, one must keep in mind that each time a research and evaluation team begins a new project, the team process begins anew. Regardless of whether the members have worked together before, taking on a new project and/or new team members makes the team new and different and requires revisiting the team-building process.

## 4.2  Collaborative Interpretations

Before talking about how teams work together to build and apply code systems from a process perspective, and then within the Dedoose environment, we turn to a discussion of multiple meanings and moving toward a shared understanding when coding in teams, analyzing data, and presenting findings.

The development and application of codes systems is one of the most fundamental activities in qualitative research. Code systems evolve into the framework of themes or concepts that are then used to organize the information contained in qualitative data that address the research questions and then used to communicate research findings to a consumer audience. Key questions here include the following:

1.  Where do good codes come from?

2.  How do we determine if they are valuable and useful?

3.  How does one know if the codes in a complete code system are sufficient to address the research questions?

Let's begin by thinking about where codes come from. Part of answering this question is determined by the nature of your data within a particular project and the philosophical perspective from which you are working. If, for example, the data come from a survey where participants responded to brief open-ended questions, the questions themselves may be a useful starting point. Similarly, consider if your data were gathered through interviews or focus groups with some clear structure to the interview or group guide protocol. Under these circumstances, it is likely that participants will be responding to the questions themselves, and so, again, they may serve as a start to building the code system. Things become more challenging when dealing with data in flowing interviews/ conversations with relatively little structure to the inquiry. Turning to these more open-ended transcripts, field notes, and observational notes, you might also begin with some structured format (Mulhall, 2003; Wald, Davis, Reis, Monroe, & Borkan, 2009). When this is the case, the nature of the overall content structure may suggest some useful initial code categories. In contrast to this more structured approach to code identification, we believe a more interpretive and constructionist perspective can be taken toward the discovery of emergent and informative codes as the data are examined. In practice, we typically recommend starting with broader codes that are relatively easy to apply and then work within these larger categories toward more nuanced and idiosyncratic subcodes. That said, maintaining an open approach to coding will help ensure that valuable content will not be overlooked.

Overall, Dedoose is suited to support work that falls anywhere along the philosophical spectrum of where and how codes are identified. From a technical perspective, codes can be added to the system and applied to the content at any time, prior to data interaction or as needed with more emergent codes, and the structure of the tree itself can be easily modified as the overall system evolves over the course of exploration and discovery.

Regarding how you determine what makes a useful code, we advise you to reflect on your research questions often as they will provide important guidance. What specific questions do you intend to address? What evidence will you need to support the anticipated findings of the research project? With those questions as a starting point, are the data rich and broad enough to make successful arguments? Were the data gathered from the right sample of people or places? Reflecting on questions like these throughout the course of a project will enhance the ultimate credibility of a study. Again, the code system is intended to provide a structure for what you will learn from the qualitative data and then communicate findings. So these questions will guide your work to develop a structure that will be effective and will help ensure your arguments are clear and strong.

Beyond the possible codes that may come from structured data gathering protocols (i.e., using the questions themselves as initial codes), how else may valuable themes be discovered? Ryan and Bernard (2003) offer a variety of approaches to consider. Keep in mind that while qualitative data are often rich with interesting information, the coding process is a data reduction strategy that helps us narrow our scope of inquiry with the hopes of discovering other important information that may not be readily apparent in the raw data. Miles and Huberman (1994) say that data reduction

> refers to the process of selecting, focusing, simplifying, abstracting, and transforming the data. (p.10)

In addition, data reduction, in their view, occurs continuously throughout the life of any qualitative project (Miles and Huberman, 1984; 1994).

So what does all these have to do with collaborative interpretations? One of the most common criticisms of qualitative research is focused on the subjectivity that may be injected in the process. In response, many argue that proper and regular reflection, iterative data processing, within- and across-case comparison, extensive use of memos, and thorough documentation can largely address these concerns (Ayres, Kavanaugh, & Knafl, 2003; Finlay, 2002; Mauthner & Doucet, 2003; Underwood, Satterthwait, & Bartlett, 2010). We further believe that this process can be even more effective when done collaboratively by making an investment in team communication as fundamental to the process (Anderson, Guerreiro, & Smith, 2016; Belgrave & Smith, 1995; Broer et al., 2016). Given that a major driver behind the Dedoose design is to support collaboration, the Dedoose environment is ideal for this critical aspect of reflective, iterative, and collaborative code system development, excerpting and tagging qualitative content, and the interpretation of findings. That is, the results of a collaborative team effort in finding, exploring, and articulating meaning in qualitative data can be helpful in producing convincing, arguably more objective, and valuable findings.

## 4.3   Coding in Teams

Following on from our line of argument in the previous section, coding in teams can bring greater insights to the analysis. In this section, we discuss strategies for coding in teams, first without software, and then in Section 4.4 using Dedoose.

The initial discussion highlights strategies we used to meet the challenges of a large multimember, multisite research project. We knew we needed coordinated teams to meet all project goals. Importantly, we knew that if we were going to do the work well and build a strong body of evidence, we needed to think ahead as much as possible. How would our teams need to be set up to ensure that everyone was well trained and prepared to meet their responsibilities? If we could build well-coordinated, properly staffed, well-trained teams, we would be ensuring that all aspects of the work would be as efficient and high quality as possible. In the end, many Dedoose features were invaluable in the team coordination, building of consistency across team members, and centralizing the work to allow for effective data management, integration, and analysis.

The broader investigation was to understand the impacts of an experimental literacy curriculum put into Head Start programs in Los Angeles and Florida. Our role was to learn more about the literacy environments in the homes where these children lived (Lieber, 2016). Essentially, we were asking, "What is taking place in these homes that will support the children's development of skills they would later need to learn to read?"

### 4.3.1 The Head Start Literacy Study and Teamwork

The more specific goals of the study were to (a) identify a key set of themes that could be used to describe the activities and routines in family homes that can influence the children's development of skills understood as necessary for later learning to read, (b) define and develop criteria to distribute families across a range of quality for each of the key themes that would allow for distinguishing subsets of families showing different levels of quality, and (c) explore variation across these theme quality–dimensions (Lieber, 2016). Overall, the research plan would lead to evidence that would help our understanding of how subsets of families can be distinguished from one another and how such variation can expose strengths and weaknesses in the ways families seek to manage the challenges of their circumstances as they raise their children. This was a multiyear, team-based project that included several cohorts of assistants at the data gathering and management stages and, so, required a number of visits to the team-building and maintenance process to ensure the generation of high-quality results over the course of the project.

This project presented many challenges related to team coordination, communication, management, and quality control with respect to the code system. Furthermore, in addition to traditional content coding across a set of themes, the project also included the use of code ratings to index the relative quality of parenting practices across these themes. Code ratings/weights, to be discussed in depth in Section 5.2.4, is the simple idea of overlaying qualitative content across a numerical dimension to index variation on observed quality, strength, depth, perceived importance, sentiment, or any characteristic where commonly coded content can be overlaid across such a dimension. This is one of many ways to transform or quantify qualitative content and allows the researcher to introduce another dimension to the overall project database.

**BRUCE'S TIP #11**

Code Ratings and Code Weights

In some contexts, code ratings are used differently than code weights. However, in the Dedoose environment, they are mechanically identical.

## 4.3.2 Coding With the Literacy Project Team

Strong and robust coding ensures the development of a database that allows for analysis to produce findings that matter. Working in teams can make the process of developing a code system more challenging, but in turn, it demands a level of communication, articulation, and documentation that will ultimately be clearer and more valuable to consumers of the work. Good teamwork also welcomes, and benefits from, diverse perspectives and provides supports for less experienced members. Central to the establishment of a sound and valid database on which analysis could take place with confidence is the need to ensure consistency in code application and code weighting decisions across all contributing team members.

The basis of this process was founded on preliminary work carried out by the project principal investigators and key staff who had first come together as a team through the forming, storming, and norming processes. Interview protocols were designed and tested with field staff, and early data were explored in depth to identify the key themes being communicated by research participants about their home literacy environments. The team coded data from a range of participant families and continued to revisit the emerging code system until there was a shared sense that all important content being communicated was being represented by the code system, and there was a shared understanding of where codes should and should not be applied. Finally, a series of "tests" to assess interrater reliability were undertaken to demonstrate and document a commonly understood set of code application criteria across team members.

This work resulted in the development of a comprehensive and well-documented code book. It is important to remind the reader that, as this project took place over many years, there was some rotation in assistants who were responsible for the coding of and application of code weights to the qualitative data. In the literacy study, their training began with an iterative process of code book study, team meetings, code application testing, and code weight decision practice and testing. With this partly revolving team, we were able to establish and maintain satisfactory standards that eventually allowed each member to contribute to the building of the database as effectively as possible. The code and weight application criteria were discussed extensively with all new project staff, and anyone responsible for working with qualitative data was required to meet acceptable standards, as assessed by Dedoose Training Center tests, before being allowed to work independently.

It was through these processes and procedures, akin to our adapted team development model, that high standards were established, periodically monitored, and maintained. In this exemplar case, and particularly for longer term projects, an iterative application of the team development model can be most effective. Testing for interrater reliability can be as important as testing for how individuals apply codes and code weights over time. Checking both across- and within-team members on a periodic basis can help ensure the consistent interaction with, coding of, and transforming of qualitative data over time. Thus, a revisiting to the key conversations and processes that take place in the context of our adapted model is fundamental to the production of high-quality results and findings that will be of value to stakeholder groups.

## 4.4 Bringing Procedures Into the Dedoose Environment

From its beginning, one of the key drivers behind the design and development of Dedoose was to support both collaboration and dealing with the various types of data being used in mixed methods work. Accordingly, a range of Dedoose features and functionality are focused specifically on meeting these collaboration and data interaction, transformation, integration, and analysis needs. As a starting point, being web-based, Dedoose is a natively collaborative environment where any number of individuals can be working together in real time from any Internet-connected computer or tablet.

As discussed in Section 2.3.4, access to a project is controlled by project creators and various levels of access to any Dedoose project can be managed at a very granular level to limit individuals' access privileges. Access groups can be added to a project within the project Security Center with varying levels of privilege depending on the responsibilities of each team member. For example, a typical user group in many projects is what we call a "Standard

Assistant." These are team members whose responsibilities include the uploading of qualitative media, linking these media to the descriptor information that distinguish one research participant or setting from another, and creating and tagging excerpts with codes and code weights. What "Standard Assistants" cannot do in a project is modify the code system in any way, change descriptor information, modify or delete data that they did not create themselves, or enter the Security Center. With groups such as these, each team member can carry out their assigned responsibilities while maximizing the protection of the overall database.

Overall, the Dedoose project Security Center is designed to allow project creators to control the limits of privileges for those they have invited to join the project and maximize database protection. Finally, it is worth mentioning that information on the specific individual responsible for creating data in a project is recorded and retained, and often visible, within the database. This information, as discussed in the next section, can be valuable for filtering and sorting.

## 4.4.1 Team Coding and Establishing Consistency in Dedoose

Now that you understand how access privileges are assigned in a Dedoose project, the remainder of this section will cover excerpting and coding as a group and what Dedoose offers to help you do this with high-quality methodological rigor. With the growing importance in the value of research collaboration, there are several Dedoose features and functions to serve this goal.

With a fundamental belief that productive teamwork requires communication and practice within any project, and apart from the fact that all team members can work simultaneously in real time within a project, Dedoose offers three basic approaches to the establishment of consistency and transparency in how a team carries out its collective work (as shown in Figure 4.2): coding blind, coding in parallel, and a Training Center to test for interrater reliability (Dedoose, 2017).

It is also important to remember how the Dedoose memo system can be used to support this "coming together" as a team narrows in on a commonly understood coding system, code application criteria, excerpting style, and use of the weighting system. The memo system (review Section 3.2 for more detail about memos) is flexible and an ideal feature to employ as you document your thought process at any meaningful point during your asynchronous work. Documenting thoughts about challenges to any decisions and "notes to self" about possible later analytic direction is extremely valuable to the codebook, database, analysis direction, and overall project maturation.

When you start to code, it is important to keep in mind that creating and tagging excerpts involve two distinct decisions. The first is to determine where an excerpt starts and ends. In a flowing interview transcript, this determination can be challenging as it is often not clear where a complete thought has been reported with sufficient context to define a useful excerpt. Not surprisingly, when dealing

Figure 4.2  Consistency in Team Coding

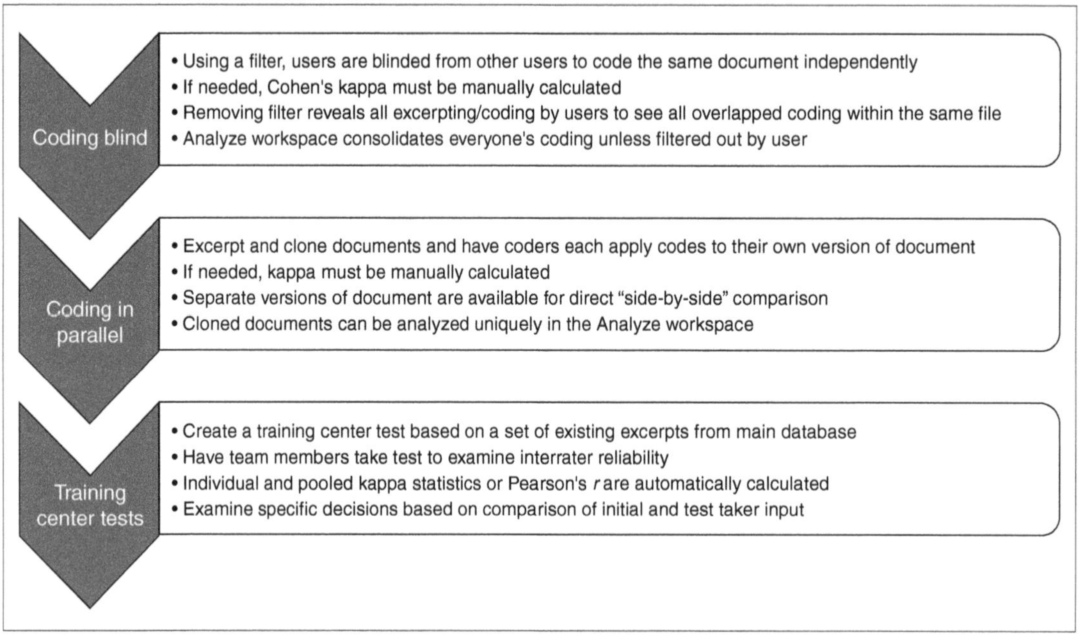

**Coding blind**
- Using a filter, users are blinded from other users to code the same document independently
- If needed, Cohen's kappa must be manually calculated
- Removing filter reveals all excerpting/coding by users to see all overlapped coding within the same file
- Analyze workspace consolidates everyone's coding unless filtered out by user

**Coding in parallel**
- Excerpt and clone documents and have coders each apply codes to their own version of document
- If needed, kappa must be manually calculated
- Separate versions of document are available for direct "side-by-side" comparison
- Cloned documents can be analyzed uniquely in the Analyze workspace

**Training center tests**
- Create a training center test based on a set of existing excerpts from main database
- Have team members take test to examine interrater reliability
- Individual and pooled kappa statistics or Pearson's $r$ are automatically calculated
- Examine specific decisions based on comparison of initial and test taker input

with flowing open-ended data, different members of a team will often have different interpretations of where a complete thought is represented and, as such, where an excerpt is to be defined. The second decision is to select the appropriate codes for the given passage based on a recognition of the "meanings" identified and understood in the passage and the currently established codes or possible expansion of an evolving code system (Ryan & Bernard, 2003). This second decision can be challenging in its own respect depending on the levels of nuance represented by the overall code system, the level of clarity with which team members have defined code application decisions, and the degree to which the code application criteria have been communicated across team members via practice, discussion, and documentation (Dey, 1993; Jehn & Doucet, 1996, 1997). We argue that while the first decision, excerpt location, can be thought of as a matter of style, there are many implications of variation in style depending on the level of context surrounding the specific content that justifies the application of a code. On the other hand, the second decision, code selection, points more directly to how different members of the team are understanding the code application rules, how well the rules are articulated, and how consistently the team can be expected to perform as they code.

In some arenas, excerpt delineation is discussed in the context of a "splitting" versus a "chunking" style. Splitters tend to create multiple briefer excerpts, applying fewer codes to each. Chunkers, on the other hand, tend toward creating longer more contextualized excerpts, applying more codes to each. The interrater reliability and validity questions ask, "Did independent coders decide to apply the same codes based on the content they were viewing, regardless of whether they were dealing with more or fewer excerpts?" For example, if given a paragraph from a transcript, a "splitter" might create three excerpts with one code applied to each. A "chunker," on the other hand, might create one excerpt with the same three codes applied. If it can be demonstrated that the decision to apply each of the three codes was based on the same portion of the overall paragraph, regardless of whether the paragraph was split into three excerpts or left as a whole, the code application decision of both coders was identical—hence, in concept, there is perfect interrater reliability.

## 4.4.2 The Case for "Chunking"

Qualitative data allow us to learn about the rich, natural, complex, and contextualized ways in which our research participants experience their lives. Many have argued that context is foundational in our ability to understand the real meanings in the "how" and "why" of life (Michler, 1979; Weisner, 1996, 1997; Yoshikawa, Weisner, Kalili, & Way, 2013) beyond simply the "what" and "how many?" "We rely on context to understand the behavior and speech of others and to ensure that our own behavior is understood, implicitly grounding our interpretations of motives and intentions in context" (Michler, 1979, p. 2).

Recognizing that excerpting and coding qualitative content is a data reduction strategy, it is important to keep in mind what will be experienced in later analytic activities (Guest, MacQueen, & Namey, 2012). Accordingly, we argue that sufficient context is fundamental to a full understanding of the meaning contained within excerpts and erring on the side of too much context in an excerpt is far more desirable than too little. Again, "splitters" tend to create smaller excerpts that are tagged with small numbers of codes. For splitters, imagine doing a search and retrieve for commonly coded excerpts. Results will include many short excerpts that are always limited to the range of the excerpt itself and completely out of context. Remember, when you are creating excerpts, you are viewing or listening to the entire media file, so that the context is present and broader meanings may be clear when you are engaged in the process. Unfortunately, for splitters, when they later review excerpts out of context, they often find themselves needing to return to the context to be reminded of the broader meanings and reasons for having applied particular codes. That is, you have the fuller picture in mind when creating excerpts, but it is useful to imagine what information will be at hand when later reviewing the excerpts in retrieved lists out of context.

Taken all together, and given our experience with research and in our consultation with others in academia, we encourage a more chunking style when creating excerpts. When doing so, you are more likely to ensure you've good context and you'll have set up the project to take full advantage of the Dedoose analytic features. In short, "chunkers" gain two major benefits:

1. Excerpts contain sufficient context to later understand why particular codes were applied—essentially the major intention of the data reduction strategy.

2. Many of the analytic features in Dedoose, such as the code co-occurrence matrix, are far more valuable in the subsequent analytic phase of a study.

### 4.4.3 Coding Blind

As a team prepares to begin the excerpting and coding process, we believe that it is valuable to have some understanding of how anyone involved will naturally make these two distinct decisions: (1) deciding where to create excerpts and (2) deciding which codes to apply. Coding blind in Dedoose is a valuable strategy for discovering the different ways in which individuals in a team independently make these decisions. Using Dedoose filtering capabilities, users can view a document or other media file without viewing the work contributed by others. The primary goals here are twofold. First is to get a clearer understanding of where team members are independently making decisions about excerpt location, which content contains meaning worthy of excerpting, and where meaningful excerpts start and end. Second is to begin understanding decisions about when to use existing codes to capture all important content in the data and where new codes may be needed to ensure a sufficiently comprehensive system that will allow the team to address all the research questions. Coding blind is typically an early-stage team behavior discovery exercise, as it is important to the overall project quality that the team intentionally and thoughtfully adopts common excerpting and code application decisions.

### 4.4.3.1 Coding Blind as a Team Member

Coding blind is accomplished by taking advantage of Dedoose filtering capabilities through which a user can view a document or other media files and create and code excerpts without the ability to view any work contributed by others.
Here's how you do it:

1. Each user logs into Dedoose and, before accessing a media file, filters out the work of others via the Data Set Workspace functions:
   a. Enter the Data Set Workspace.
   b. Select Users tab.
   c. Click De-Activate All.
   d. Click once on your username in the list.

e. Click Dataset tab.

f. Check to ensure that User item in Current Data Set panel is one out of the total users on project.

g. Close Data Selector panel.

2. Once the user activates this filter in Step 1, they can only see the work that they have contributed to the media file. At this point, the user can carry on with their own excerpting and tagging activity without any distraction/contamination from viewing the work of others.

3. Each user does their work in this manner on the same media files.

4. The full team can later view the media files with all work showing and can clearly identify any variation in excerpting and coding decisions.

**BRUCE'S TIP #12**

Active Filter Indicator

Note that when a filter is active in Dedoose, there are two visual indicators. The Data Set Workspace icon is shaded red and a "funnel" icon will appear in the panel header for media files and other analytics—which serves as a toggle to view the filtered data or all data.

### 4.4.3.2 Coding Blind as an Administrator

As the project administrator, you can set up coding blind exercises by granting team members different levels of access (security groups) via the Security Workspace:

1. Click the Security Workspace tab.

2. Click Add Group.

3. Provide a Title.

4. Select the Project-Wide Assistant with Isolated Excerpt Access group.

5. Click Submit.

6. Drag and drop users into the group.

For more information on the Security Workspace, and adding users to projects, see Section 2.3.4.

**BRUCE'S TIP #13**

Security Group Access to Filters

If you create the filter yourself, you will have total control over what you see. If you are placed in a security group by the project administrator, you only have the access level granted to that group.

### 4.4.3.3 Reviewing the Coded Blind Work

With the information gained from the coding blind exercise, the team can then discuss excerpt location decisions, code system adequacy, coding decision criteria, and, most important, attaining consensus on the excerpting style that all team members will adopt moving forward. It is important to keep in mind that the "style" with which excerpting is carried out is not as critical to interrater reliability and validity in coding decisions. That said, implementation of a relatively consistent style across team members can help support any conclusions that may be drawn based on the quantification of any excerpting/coding activity. Finally, when evaluating findings from these exercises, it is also valuable to keep in mind how tasks will be distributed among team members and how quality control will be monitored. There are many ways to "divide and conquer," and the team will benefit from having made clear strategic decisions on how this is put into practice.

## 4.4.4 Using Document Cloning for "Apples-to-Apples" Coding Comparison

Following the establishment of a consistent excerpting style and initial pass at using the emerging code system, taking advantage of the Dedoose document cloning feature is a logical next step. The primary goal of the document cloning functionality is to more closely assess code application decisions without concern for the excerpting decision—in a sense, more of an apples-to-apples comparison of coding. The document cloning feature essentially creates an identical copy of media files with all excerpts in place to facilitate coding in parallel. To use this approach, the following is done:

1. One or more "trusted" team member(s) is assigned responsibility for creating excerpts in a text file, but not applying any codes. Key here is to apply what was learned from the coding blind process regarding excerpting style and, at the same time, making sure that all important content in a media file that will be valuable to addressing the research questions is included in the set of excerpts within each file.

2. The text files are then cloned with a copy for each team member. The clones are basically identical copies of the documents with all excerpts in place. Once excerpted, do the following:

    a. Open the document.

    b. Click Edit Document.

    c. Click Clone Document.

    d. Once the cloning is completed, the cloned copy will be loaded with the same name as the original file. At this point, we strongly recommend editing the document title using a clear naming convention identifying the document for each team member, for example, "doc 1_person 1," "doc 1_person 2," and so on.

3. Each team member then accesses their copy of any cloned files assigned to them and applies codes to the existing excerpts.

4. From these fully coded copies, there are a variety of ways to compare and contrast the coding decisions made by each team member. With this knowledge, the team is now prepared to continue, in more depth, the conversation about the adequacy of the code system and refining code application criteria toward a comfortable and shared understanding.

**BRUCE'S TIP #14**

Edit Document Title Function

When you clone any document, it is best practice to edit the document name. Editing the document title can also be done via the Edit Document function:

1. Click Edit Document.

2. Click the Title bar.

3. Edit the Document Title.

4. Click Submit.

Coding blind and independent coding using the cloning feature can continue in an iterative manner until such time when the team feels confident in the overall structure of the coding system and its ability to independently apply codes in a consistent manner. Once achieved, the team may wish to more formally assess interrater reliability using the Dedoose Training Center.

## 4.4.5 The Dedoose Training Center

The Dedoose Training Center was designed to create and provide access to tests that will formally assess the consistency of coding decisions by any pair of coders or within coders over time (Figure 4.3). Any user with sufficient permission in the project can take a Training Center test by selecting it and clicking "Take this Test."

To make use of the Training Center tests for code application decisions, follow these steps:

1. One or more team members create and code excerpts within project media files. It is usually best to ensure that the content coded for Training Center tests represent the full range of variation in the study data. This full representation then truly challenges the team to thoughtfully apply all important codes in the code system across the real variation in the content that will be seen over the course of the project.

2. Training Center tests are created by first selecting a set of codes on which a test will focus and then selecting representative text excerpts from the master project (as created in Step 1).

3. Other members of the team, including those involved in the initial test excerpt creation, then take the tests.

4. When taking a test, you are presented with the set of codes assigned to the test and then, in turn, the content for each test excerpt, but there is no indication of which codes were applied to the excerpts when created in the master project.

5. Results include Cohen's kappa coefficient for each code, a pooled kappa for the full set of codes in the test, and detailed information showing each excerpt's content, the codes applied in the master project, and the codes selected by the test taker.

Figure 4.3  Training Center Test

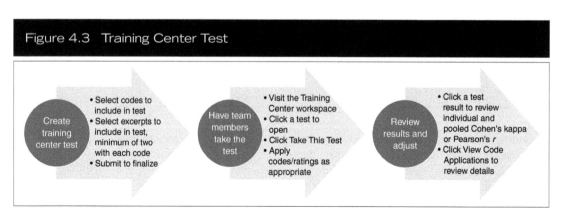

### 4.4.5.1 Training Tests and Code Weighting

As described in Sections 5.2.4 and Chapter 8, the use of the Dedoose code weight/rating feature allows investigators to overlay numeric dimensions on coded qualitative content. Creating Training Center tests for code weightings/ratings is similar to code application tests in the selection of particular codes and sets of excerpts to include. The key difference is that with these tests the excerpts are presented with the codes applied and the code weight/rating value is set to the default as per the code definition and scale specification.

1. In the case of a code weighting/rating test, you are presented with the codes applied and the default weight/rating value.

2. Test takers are tasked with selecting the appropriate codes for each excerpt in the test or setting the code weight/rating value.

3. The results will then include Pearson's correlation coefficient for each code and, like with code application tests, access to detailed information regarding the code weight decisions on a code-by-code basis.

When test results are less than acceptable, the team can examine and discuss, in detail, where inconsistencies were observed. This information is critical to review to understand the nature of the inconsistencies. Does the code system need further refinement, perhaps changing, adding, or deleting codes? Do particular team members struggle with particular codes? Do some members tend to agree more consistently than others? Engaging in and documenting the course of this process and discussion until acceptable results are achieved serves to build the shared understanding across team members. When this is done well, it enhances the internal confidence of the team in its methodological integrity and, when communicated to others, will instill confidence in the quality of the work. Where test results show acceptable levels of interrater reliability, Cohen's kappa and/or Pearson's correlation coefficients can be noted for inclusion in presentations or manuscripts. Again, these metrics are strong evidence of the relative rigor demonstrated by the research team and are valuable evidence to include as part of the methods section in any avenue of project dissemination.

## 4.5 Team Conduct Rules

We believe teamwork can be a valuable part of qualitative and mixed methods work and great teams produce strong research and evaluation findings. The team-building model presented here illustrates the process that most groups will experience when working with others on a consistent basis. An important element in team dynamics involves the formation of teamwork rules of conduct that are ideally established as the team forms. This step acknowledges the importance of each team member and that early attention improves team dynamics and performance.

The following is offered as a starting point for building a research or evaluation team's rules of conduct:

1. Establish formal rules of communication and ensure that appropriate and necessary technologies are provided. This may be best done early in the design and development of a project. Carefully discuss the procedures and meanings of each rule to promote clarity and consistent adoption. To ensure optimal communication, and depending on the nature of the topic, it can be helpful to decide and agree on how and when communication should take place and via what mechanism (e.g., email, texting, phone calls, face-to-face meeting, or some other manner).

2. Work to recognize and respect different styles of decision-making and how individuals respond to conflict toward creating open channels of communication among all team members. When done well, all will find increased comfort in expressing their feelings and ideas. Furthermore, when these communications are available to the team, everyone can consider and decide how things might be done differently and can hope to benefit from the team's increased cohesiveness and productivity.

3. Once the project is under way, reflection on design choices can help maintain focus and momentum. Establish procedures for the uniform adoption of flexible emergent design issues. Research and evaluations rarely progress as expected when they first begin, so anticipate the likely need for some flexible thinking. This challenge is magnified when working in teams, but the quality of the outcomes will be higher with regular evaluation, some creative thinking, and good communication.

4. As the codebook is a central part of all projects, we recommend that one person is assigned as the codebook master (Kaczynski, Miller, & Kelly, 2014). An oversight team can then assist the master by suggesting revisions after periodic review on the following:

   - How much context in excerpting is needed?
   - Can team members freely make new open codes?
   - Can team members establish and document clear code definitions?
   - How to change code meaning?
   - What are the procedures to merge/delete codes or change the hierarchical structure of the system?

5. Professional development and training in methods and data analysis technology are best accomplished when they are ongoing throughout a team study at appropriate times.

In practice, Dedoose has many features to facilitate taking the teamwork model approach perspective into this process. Working on shared data in real time, the use of analytic and other memos to track thought processes and communicate to team members, integrated chat features for real-time communication, and various features for developing and testing a well-documented code system can help ensure the overall quality of work. Collaboration in all stages of this process has many challenges and may arouse frustrations (Gerstl-Pepin & Gunzenhauser, 2002), but where carried out successfully and openly, the rigor of the methods employed will be transparent, and this rigor can be communicated to consumers of the work, and it is hoped that it will instill higher levels of confidence in the findings (Anderson et al., 2016).

The following case study highlights some of the issues that you may encounter when working with large teams across cultural boundaries. It describes a qualitative investigation of different domestic and international perspectives on some U.S.–Mexican and Russian policy issues and will give you some ideas about the strategies you might use when working in Dedoose with a large and diverse team.

## 4.6 Case Study: Large-Scale, Multilanguage, Cross-Cultural Analysis With Dedoose

........................................................................

---

**THINK ABOUT, AND ANSWER, THESE QUESTIONS AS YOU READ THE CASE STUDY**

1. Who is on your team; what are their roles and responsibilities?
2. What rules or guidelines would help your team be productive and successful? Use the case study to help you with ideas for this.

---

### Large-Scale, Multilanguage, Cross-Cultural Analysis With Dedoose

#### Ryan A. Brown & David P. Kennedy

In 2012, the Intelligence Advanced Research Projects Activity (IARPA) asked RAND to conduct a qualitative investigation of different domestic and international perspectives on three policy issues or "cases": (1) "Illegal Drugs"—drug trafficking across the U.S.–Mexico border, (2) "Caspian Sea"—territorial conflict between Russia and Iran regarding the Caspian Sea, and (3) "Russian Politics"—conflict between different Russian political parties. IARPA was particularly interested in examining "cross-cultural" similarities and differences—namely, Mexican vs. U.S. perspectives on drug trafficking, Iranian vs. Russian perspectives on the Caspian Sea, and perspectives from supporters of different Russian political parties (Left, Center, and Right); these various countries and political parties were labeled "protagonists" for each case, and they helped define our sampling strategy for qualitative interviews. For each case, IARPA also defined four or more topical dimensions to cover in our research; for example, the Illegal Drugs case included "Wealth and Poverty" and "Market for Drugs" as required topical domains (see Figure C4.6-1).

This topical breadth and expansive cross-cultural frame already extends beyond the typical constraints of qualitative research. In addition, IARPA wanted to know what respondents thought of their own country's (or political party's) position and policies for each issue, they wanted to gather data on perspectives of the other country (or political party), and they also wanted to know what respondents thought opposing countries (or parties) might think of their own home country or party. Finally, IARPA was very interested in the linguistic subtleties used to talk about these policy issues and required us to collect and analyze data in the native language of each country—Russian, Farsi, Spanish, and English.

In this case study, we focus on how Dedoose's capabilities allowed us to collect and analyze data from 150 qualitative interviews conducted in four different countries across the globe (see Figure C4.6-2). We illustrate how Dedoose's management features, data visualization capabilities, and collaborative analytic platform allowed us to manage an international team of interviewers working for four different subcontractors as well as a local team of more than 30 coders proficient in Russian, Farsi, Spanish, and English. Our research task also involved creating structured survey items for quantitative cultural consensus analysis (Weller, 2007), and we describe how Dedoose enabled us to work across four different languages to produce a common set of items across protagonists.

### Figure C4.6-1   Example Case: Illegal Drugs

| Cultural Perspectives | | | | | |
|---|---|---|---|---|---|
| | Mexican Beliefs | | | U.S. Beliefs | |
| Problem Aspects | Mexico's perceptions of... | Mexico's view of U.S. position on... | Problem Aspects | U.S. perceptions of... | U.S.'s view of Mexico's position on... |
| Illegal Drugs | | | Illegal Drugs | | |
| Mexican Government's Handling of Drugs | | | U.S. Government's Handling of Drugs | | |
| Market for Drugs | | | Market for Drugs | | |
| Wealth and Poverty | | | Wealth and Poverty | | |
| The Other | | | The Other | | |

**Figure C4.6-2  Sampling Strategy**

| Case | Protagonist 1 | Protagonist 2 | Protagonist 3 |
|---|---|---|---|
| Illegal Drugs | 30 United States (10 each from Washington, D.C.; Austin, Texas; and Los Angeles, Calif.) | 30 Mexico (10 each from Mexico City, Guadalajara, Monterrey) | n/a |
| Caspian Sea | 30 Iran (travelers to different regions from different parts of Iran) | 30 Russia (from Nizhny Novgorod and Moscow) | n/a |
| Russian Identity | 15 from Russia (Center) | 15 from Russia (Left) | 15 from Russia (Right) |

## 4.6.1 Setting Up the Project

Because we were dealing with four different languages and three topically distinct "cases," we set up individual Dedoose projects corresponding to each language within each case. Thus, we created one project for English-speaking (U.S.) interviews in the Illegal Drugs case and one for Spanish-speaking (Mexican) respondents. Likewise, we created a Russian and Farsi project for the Caspian Sea. The Russian Politics case required only a single Dedoose project, as all interviews were in Russian. We designated experienced qualitative researchers to lead each of the five Dedoose projects. These project leads each had some basic bilingual proficiency, but they primarily relied on their fully bilingual coders to conduct the coding in Russian, Farsi, and Spanish.

Dedoose allowed our team to efficiently scale up a number of our existing practices that enable rapid collection and rigorous analysis of qualitative interview data. Specifically, we use a grid-based interviewing method (Brown et al., 2012; Brown et al., 2013; Kennedy et al., 2012) that aligns major topical dimensions with one another to create a nonlinear reference guide for interviewers (see Figure C4.6-3). This allowed us to ensure similar topical coverage across interviews while allowing the conversation to flow naturally from one topic to another (rather than constraining conversational topics in a linear fashion). As Figure C4.6-3 illustrates, the grid format was particularly well-suited for the cross-cultural and broad topical demands of this research project.

After interviews were completed, interviewers completed a structured "debrief note" form that required them to summarize core topical areas that cut across dimensions and specific "cells" of information in the interview grid. This served two purposes. (1) It provided direct feedback to interviewers on how well they covered key topical domains and, therefore, allowed better interviewer management. (2) Debrief notes required interviewers to begin synthesizing and analyzing collected data and to start describing themes for analysis. These focused themes allowed us to more quickly develop codebooks than lengthier, less focused transcripts.

**Interview Grid: Illegal Drug Trafficking Between Mexico and the U.S.**
**"There is a lot of discussion about the illegal drug trade between Mexico and the U.S.**
**Please tell me what you think about this."**

| | Overview | What Do People in Mexico Think? | What Do People in the U.S. Think? |
|---|---|---|---|
| Mexican Government Policy | □ What is the Mexican government doing about the problem?<br>□ What is the history?<br>□ What will they do in the future?<br>□ How does this situation impact:<br>　□ Poverty?　□ Military/Police?<br>　□ Violence?　□ Economy?<br>　□ Treatment?　□ Education? | □ What are the different opinions of Mexican government policy in Mexico?<br>□ Who has these opinions?<br>□ What are they happy with? Why?<br>□ What don't they like? Why?<br>□ What do they want the government to do? Why? | □ What are the different opinions of Mexican government policy in the U.S.?<br>□ What does the U.S. government think?<br>□ What do the U.S. people think?<br>□ What are they happy with? Why?<br>□ What don't they like? Why?<br>□ What do they want the Mexican government to do in the future? Why? |
| U.S. Government Policy | □ What is the U.S. government doing about the problem?<br>□ What is the history?<br>□ What will they do in the future?<br>□ How does this situation impact:<br>　□ Poverty?　□ Military/Police?<br>　□ Violence?　□ Economy?<br>　□ Treatment?　□ Education? | □ What are the different opinions of U.S. government policy in Mexico?<br>□ What does the Mexican government think?<br>□ What do the Mexican people think?<br>□ What are they happy with? Why?<br>□ What don't they like? Why?<br>□ What do they want the U.S. government to do in the future? Why? | □ What are the different opinions of the U.S. government policy in the U.S.?<br>□ Who has these opinions?<br>□ What are they happy with? Why?<br>□ What don't they like? Why?<br>□ What do they want the government to do? Why? |
| Supply / Demand | □ Where do the drugs come from?<br>□ Who is producing them? How? Where?<br>□ In Mexico? □ In the U.S.?<br>　□ Other?<br>□ Who are the people purchasing the drugs? Where are they?<br>□ How are drugs moving from suppliers to those buying them? | □ What do people in Mexico think about drug supply and demand?<br>□ What do they think about demand and supply in Mexico?<br>□ What do they think about demand and supply in the U.S.? | □ What do people in the U.S. think about drug supply and demand?<br>□ What do they think about demand and supply in the U.S.?<br>□ What do they think about demand and supply in Mexico? |

| | | | |
|---|---|---|---|
| Wealth / Poverty | □ What role do wealth and poverty play in the illegal drug situation?<br>□ What is the effect of wealth and poverty in the U.S.?<br>□ What is the effect of wealth and poverty in Mexico? | □ What do people in Mexico think about the role of wealth and poverty?<br>□ What do they think about wealth and poverty in Mexico?<br>□ What do they think about wealth and poverty in the U.S.? | □ What do people in the U.S. think about the role of wealth and poverty?<br>□ What do they think about wealth and poverty in the U.S.?<br>□ What do they think about wealth and poverty in Mexico? |
| Compare / Contrast | □ How is the illegal drug situation similar to other conflicts between the U.S. and Mexico?<br>□ Immigration?   □ Tourism?<br>□ How are they different? | □ How are Mexican opinions similar regarding other conflicts between the U.S. and Mexico?<br>□ Immigration?<br>□ Tourism?<br>□ How are they different? | □ How are U.S. opinions similar regarding other conflicts between the U.S. and Mexico?<br>□ Immigration? □ Tourism?<br>□ How are they different? |

Interviewers who were bilingual sometimes wrote these notes in English, but most interviewers wrote debrief notes in their native language for later translation.

As part of our standard practice for qualitative research, we use the Livescribe Smartpen© to record interviews while taking written notes during the interview that paralleled the protocol matrix structure. Livescribe Smartpens allow the researcher to record audio while writing, and the recorded notes are accurately transcribed and can be shared through the cloud (**www.livescribe.com**). This allowed interviewers to easily revisit relevant portions of the audio recording while writing up debrief notes. Interviewers learned to use marks and written phrases to flag interview content covering specific topics in the interview grid and debrief notes. This allowed them to include relevant verbatim quotes in their debrief notes, further increasing the utility and richness of debrief notes as a data source.

Because of the short turnaround time required to complete data collection and analysis and limitations to available staff with language and methodological expertise, we needed to train and manage a large, globally dispersed group of interviewers and coders, including remote training through several project subcontractors. To assist with data collection quality control, we relied on structured feedback forms to provide consistent critiques of interviewing style and debrief note quality. First, we trained our RAND team of bilingual coders to become proficient in qualitative interviewing skills; these interviewers first conducted practice interviews in English, which were checked by the project managers. We then had our RAND team conduct interviews in Farsi, Russian, and Spanish and critique one another's interviewing style. Finally, RAND project managers and coders trained our international subcontractors, mentoring them through several practice interviews until quality improved sufficiently for our subcontractors to conduct unsupervised field interviews.

A crucial preparation step for our project was to train coders with little (or in some cases no) prior qualitative coding experience. For these coders, we conducted two half-day training sessions that started with an introduction to the project and qualitative coding in general and proceeded to a coding test in Dedoose consisting of a multiple-choice test matching codes to excerpts. In addition to training coders to identify text that matched code definitions, we also discovered that these coding tests revealed existing inconsistencies or lack of clarity in some of our coding definitions, prompting team discussions and sometimes revisions to code definitions. Rather than requiring that new coders achieve a certain kappa on their first test, we used test results to engage team members in code application "deconfliction" sessions so that team members educated and learned from one another. And rather than limiting this dynamic to training, we carried this practice through the rest of the project, holding regular meetings within and across coding teams and engaging regularly on an internal social collaboration platform (see Figure C4.6-4).

## 4.6.2 Data Sources

Our interviewing and debrief note process resulted in two primary forms of documents for analysis in Dedoose: (1) English debrief notes (often translated from another language) and (2) native language transcripts in Farsi, Russian, Spanish, or English. English debrief notes allowed us to develop our initial coding scheme and enabled us to easily talk across different projects (and languages) corresponding to the same case. We then employed the coding scheme developed with English debrief notes on native language transcripts. This led to some further adjustment and revision of our coding scheme when coders discovered content or subtlety in meaning that was not adequately captured in English debrief notes.

## 4.6.3 Data Management

Dedoose's extensive data management tools afforded us multiple capabilities for the complex, multilayered personnel and data oversight required to execute this cross-cultural project. As mentioned in Section 4.6.2, we produced two primary types of documents for each respondent—(1) English debrief notes and (2) native language transcripts. The "Data Set" feature in Dedoose allowed us to easily stage our analysis to first code debrief notes in order to develop our coding architecture and later move on to native language transcripts in order to refine and finalize our codes, referring back to debrief notes when an English example was needed. We used similar file naming conventions and the Document sorting feature in Dedoose to ensure that we could easily match English debrief notes with native language transcripts for the same participant.

Dedoose's "Descriptor" feature allowed us to code respondent age, gender, and other demographic characteristics for later subgroup analysis. This was particularly useful when pulling content and quotes to create structured survey items;

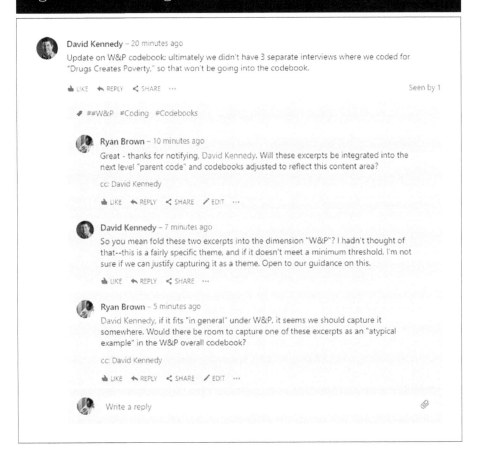

**David Kennedy** – 20 minutes ago

Update on W&P codebook: ultimately we didn't have 3 separate interviews where we coded for "Drugs Creates Poverty," so that won't be going into the codebook.

👍 LIKE   ↰ REPLY   ＜ SHARE   ⋯                                          Seen by 1

🔖 ##W&P  #Coding  #Codebooks

**Ryan Brown** – 10 minutes ago

Great - thanks for notifying, David Kennedy. Will these excerpts be integrated into the next level "parent code" and codebooks adjusted to reflect this content area?

cc: David Kennedy

👍 LIKE   ↰ REPLY   ＜ SHARE   ✏ EDIT   ⋯

**David Kennedy** – 7 minutes ago

So you mean fold these two excerpts into the dimension "W&P"? I hadn't thought of that--this is a fairly specific theme, and if it doesn't meet a minimum threshold, I'm not sure if we can justify capturing it as a theme. Open to our guidance on this.

👍 LIKE   ↰ REPLY   ＜ SHARE   ⋯

**Ryan Brown** – 5 minutes ago

David Kennedy, if it fits "in general" under W&P, it seems we should capture it somewhere. Would there be room to capture one of these excerpts as an "atypical example" in the W&P overall codebook?

cc: David Kennedy

👍 LIKE   ↰ REPLY   ＜ SHARE   ✏ EDIT   ⋯

Write a reply                                                              📎

specifically, this helped us ensure that we were drawing content that spanned diverse demographic categories within each project.

Dedoose's user permissions and staff tracking features were crucial for the management of our project. In particular, we restricted most coders so that they could not alter our coding scheme. This forced coding teams to hold open discussions on RAND's internal social collaboration software platform in full view of qualitative project leads before deciding to change the coding scheme to accommodate instances of new (or imperfectly fitting) data. These open team discussions helped clarify codes and the meaning of specific excerpts of text, as well as occasional adjustments to the coding scheme itself. Code Application visualizations tracking allowed project leads to examine coding progress by specific team members. This in turn prompted project managers to check in with coders separately or hold group discussions to reallocate documents to coders with more time, to discuss codes that seemed to be underused, and to discuss whether certain codes could be eliminated or combined (based in part on results from the Code Co-Occurrence Matrix).

Another Dedoose feature that allowed our teams to work rapidly across multiple languages in parallel is the ability to create and edit Memos as a collaborative team. As coders or project managers noticed an unresolved issue with a code definition, excerpt, or even an entire document, they created a Memo linked to the code, excerpt, or document and labeled it as "unresolved," changing this status to "resolved" once the team had worked through the issue in a meeting or via our social collaboration software platform. As we developed very detailed code definitions, we also included these as Memos attached to specific codes.

## 4.6.4 Analysis Processes

Analysis for this project presented several core challenges. The size and pace of the project required a team of more than 30 coders to work at half- to full-time for several weeks in a row in order to complete the coding process. Moreover, coders were working in English, Farsi, Russian, and Spanish simultaneously. The web-based, collaborative team environment provided by Dedoose was absolutely crucial for this project. Trying to conduct this sort of large-scale, multilanguage, fast-paced analysis on a single-user platform (and emailing files back and forth) would be a nonstarter; this project simply would not have been possible without Dedoose.

As described in the introduction to the case study, the IARPA project sponsor required us to cover a broad set of predefined topical areas or "dimensions" for each case. This meant that each coding team had to cover a large number of codes—more than 100 for the Russian Politics case and close to 100 for each country in the Illegal Drugs and Caspian Sea cases. In our experience and based on previous research (Miller, 1956), some individual coders may have difficulty keeping more than 10 codes in mind while reading and coding notes or transcripts. This meant that we needed to assign groups of coders to specific dimensions to keep coders from being too overwhelmed with coding options. With multiple groups of coders analyzing the same document, management of excerpt creation and editing was critical. We instructed coders to use the most comprehensive passage of text they could while coding rather than creating excerpts at the sentence of phrase level. Similarly, coders were required to use preexisting excerpts created by other users whenever possible rather than creating overlapping excerpts. Dedoose's ability to quickly visualize User charts, especially excerpt creation, helped greatly with this complex management task.

Within dimensions, content was sometimes significantly different for each country. For example, within the broad topic of "wealth and poverty" in the Illegal Drugs case, several Mexican respondents described how drugs themselves can drive individuals, families, and even countries into greater poverty. However, no U.S. respondents described a similar theme. These differences in emphasis meant that coding schemes for a case were identical at the top or "parent" level of codes, but they diverged at the "child" and "grandchild" levels. Dedoose's flexible, agile system of adding, deleting, and moving codes enabled our teams to maintain parent-level equivalence of coding structure while making country- (or political party-) specific adjustments at a more fine-grained level.

The cross-cultural comparative demands of this project, along with the specific topical interests of our client (IARPA) required close attention to the unique content and cultural context of each country while still allowing for cross-cultural (or cross-political party) comparison within cases. This meant that we needed to hold occasional meetings with project managers representing different countries (or parties) to examine our emerging coding schemes and see where content overlap was occurring. This allowed us to develop some parallel codes across countries (or parties) without content from one country (or party) unduly influencing the analytic process of another. Two Dedoose capabilities facilitated coordination during these "consilience" meetings: (1) Dedoose's code export processes allowed us to create and compare Excel databases of emerging coding structures and (2) Dedoose's web-based format allowed us to easily switch between countries and directly examine excerpts related to each code.

To meet the client's desire for a validation of the qualitative results, we conducted follow-up structured interviewing and quantitative analysis based on a questionnaire consisting of structured survey items that we developed from our coding output (paraphrased or verbatim quotes). The questionnaire was used to conduct Cultural Consensus Analysis (Weller, 2007). This required us to have large face-to-face team meetings in which pairs of countries (or in the Russian Politics case, the entire coding team) met together and created as many items as they could that represented similar constructs shared across both protagonists. This required extensive discussion and translation back and forth from English into Farsi/Russian/Spanish and back again. Dedoose's ability to export codes along with coded excerpts allowed these complex, demanding meetings to proceed as smoothly as possible. These meetings produced the final Cultural Consensus Analysis instrument that we used successfully to test validity with separate, larger quantitative samples for each case (see Figure C4.6-5).

Overall, we identified eight unique Dedoose features that were critical across the entire analytic process (i.e., after interviews were conducted): (1) team-based cloud features, (2) User Group and user permissions management, (3) Data Set capabilities, (4) Memos, (5) User Code Application charts, (6) Code Co-Occurrence charts, (7) Excerpt navigation and display, and (8) the Dedoose Training Center. Figure C4.6-6 illustrates how each of these eight Dedoose features were critical components of our analytic process, highlighting the analytic steps for which each of these features played a necessary role. As can be seen in Figure C4.6-6, every analytic step relied on Dedoose's team-based, cloud-enabled collaborative architecture.

## 4.6.5 Reporting the Project

Our IARPA sponsor viewed the coding scheme we developed for each case as the primary analytic output and was not interested in extensive methodological, topical, or theoretical discussion. To that end, IARPA wanted an efficient yet comprehensive "user's guide" to the codes we developed for each country (or political party) within each case. To satisfy our client's needs, we created separate reports for each case (Illegal Drugs, Caspian Sea, and Russian Politics). The main body of

## Figure C4.6-5  Caspian Sea: Items Driving Russian Cultural Consensus

| Item Dimension | Mean | Component 1 Score | Item Text |
|---|---|---|---|
| Value | 1.16 | −1.45 | Caspian gas and oil deposits are valuable to Russia. |
| Regional Roles | 1.25 | −1.34 | Russia is strong. |
| Religion | 1.25 | −1.34 | Iranians absorb Islam with their mothers' milk. |
| Regional Roles | 1.26 | −1.27 | Russia is more powerful than Iran. |
| The Other | 1.29 | −1.26 | The Iranian government is built on Islam. |
| The Other | 1.29 | −1.24 | Iran has deep historic and cultural roots. |
| The Other | 1.36 | −1.13 | Iranians are very religious. |
| Religion | 1.38 | −1.07 | Islam is strict. |
| Value | 1.44 | −1.02 | Russia needs access to the Caspian Sea to protect its southern borders. |
| Regional Roles | 2.46 | 1.04 | The Caspian issue is the only disagreement between Russia and Iran. |
| Regional Roles | 2.37 | 1.10 | Other Caspian countries would support Russia against Iran. |
| The Other | 2.51 | 1.11 | Iran is a free country. |
| Value | 2.39 | 1.31 | The Caspian Sea is a popular Iranian tourist destination. |
| Value | 2.56 | 1.32 | The Caspian Sea is the only source of natural gas and oil for Iran. |
| Value | 2.50 | 1.41 | It is difficult to extract oil from Iranian territory of the Caspian Sea. |
| Value | 2.60 | 1.44 | It's expensive to extract oil from the Caspian Sea. |
| Religion | 2.71 | 1.56 | Many Russians believe that "religion is the opiate of the masses." |
| Value | 2.75 | 1.67 | The oil resources of the Caspian are limited. |
| Value | 2.86 | 1.78 | The Caspian Sea is a popular tourist destination for Russians. |
| Religion | 2.85 | 1.89 | Russians are not religious. |
| The Other | 2.95 | 2.01 | Iran follows the West. |
| The Other | 3.18 | 2.34 | Russians and Iranians think similarly. |

Figure C4.6-6    Dedoose Features Critical for Analytic Steps

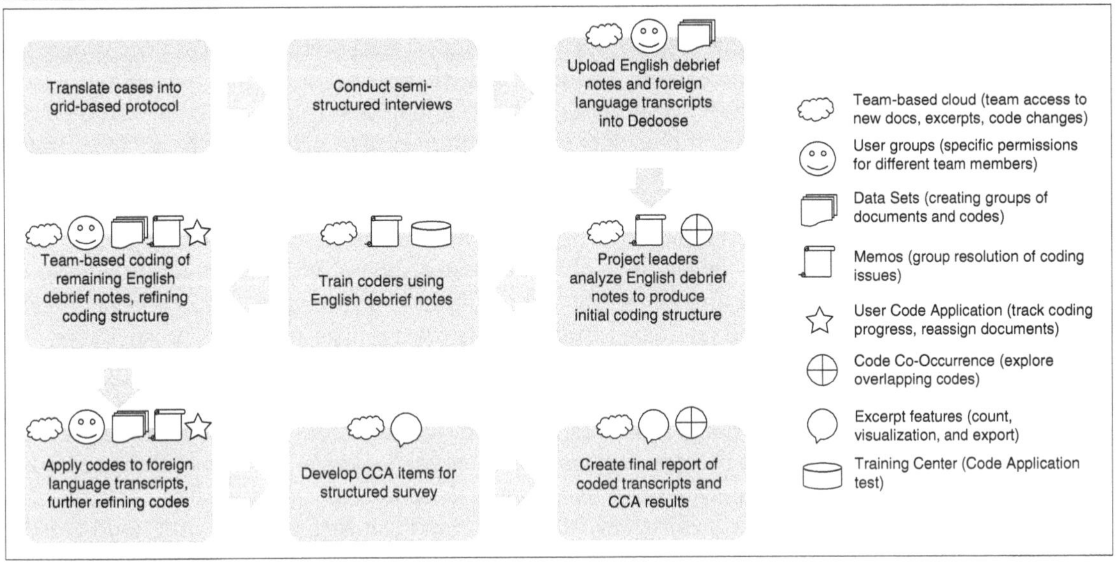

Translate cases into grid-based protocol

Conduct semi-structured interviews

Upload English debrief notes and foreign language transcripts into Dedoose

Team-based coding of remaining English debrief notes, refining coding structure

Train coders using English debrief notes

Project leaders analyze English debrief notes to produce initial coding structure

Apply codes to foreign language transcripts, further refining codes

Develop CCA items for structured survey

Create final report of coded transcripts and CCA results

Team-based cloud (team access to new docs, excerpts, code changes)

User groups (specific permissions for different team members)

Data Sets (creating groups of documents and codes)

Memos (group resolution of coding issues)

User Code Application (track coding progress, reassign documents)

Code Co-Occurrence (explore overlapping codes)

Excerpt features (count, visualization, and export)

Training Center (Code Application test)

the report consisted of a detailed description of each code, starting with a basic code Description as well as Inclusion and Exclusion Criteria (Guest, MacQueen, & Namey, 2012a). Each code also included one or more "Typical exemplar" and "Atypical exemplar" in both English and the native language (Farsi, Russian, or Spanish as applicable).

This meant that each code (for up to 100 or more codes per country/political party, per case) included a page or more of content. While this might seem like a daunting task, the way in which we processed the data in Dedoose allowed us to create our code definition and example excerpt content quite quickly. As described in the previous sections, we developed detailed code definitions as we coded the content for each case and recorded definitions as well as inclusion and exclusion criteria in the code definition field and/or ancillary memos within Dedoose. After porting this information into our report, all we needed to do was to find typical and atypical exemplars. The simple point-and-click interface provided by Dedoose allowed our coding teams to quickly search coded output for these examples, vet exemplars with other team members, and transfer them into our report. To create a quick reference guide for the codes in each case, we created descriptive names for our codes that were included in our Table of Contents. Furthermore, the Table of Contents included a percentage for each code corresponding with the percentage of respondents who mentioned the code (i.e., percentage of documents in which the code appeared one or more times).

### 4.6.6 Looking Back

Looking back at the lessons learned on this project, there are three things we would have done differently "if we knew then what we know now." First, as our analytic teams analyzed the various qualitative data sets we collected, we progressively learned more about Dedoose's analytic features, including the ability to use the Data Set feature to subset documents and codes. In retrospect, it would have been possible to combine data sets from protagonists involved in a case (e.g., Iran and Russia for the Caspian Sea case) and use the Data Set feature to delineate team efforts for each protagonist. In fact, we might even have been able to load all our cases into the same project. This would have made cross-cultural comparison for the purposes of developing cultural consensus items and for writing up our conclusions much more efficiently and would have required us to rely less on Excel to synthesize and compare insights across protagonists and different languages.

Second, data analysis for this project took place over a very short time (2–3 months). We began the project with a small team of RAND on-site coders, only later adding coders whom Keystrokes, Incorporated, hired from different places across the country when it became obvious that we needed a bigger labor pool. It turned out that it was very easy to teach and manage these remote coders because of Dedoose's intuitive interface, many team collaboration and management tools, and cloud-based platform for real-time coder management. If we realized that this process would go so smoothly, we would have ramped up our coder hiring process much earlier.

Finally, while we coordinated coding teams within cases, we did not check in with one another across cases as much as we might have. On checking in later in the coding process, we discovered that team leaders had different "styles" of using parent, child, and grandchild coding options. By the time we realized this, it was too late to implement dramatic restructuring to standardize coding styles. As these differences occurred across cases rather than within, cross-cultural comparison within cases was still possible. However, we would have gained efficiencies across the project if we had implemented more top-down management and coordination of coding style across cases.

*Acknowledgments.* This work was possible because of a contract from the Intelligence Advanced Research Projects Activity (IARPA). We thank our IARPA Program Manager, Dr. Heather McCallum-Bayliss, as well as Dr. Carolyn Adger for their tireless support and assistance throughout this project, as well as for their foresight in sponsoring systematic mixed methods research on cross-cultural issues in national security. The IARPA contract was awarded to RAND's Intelligence Policy Center (IPC), within our National Security Research Division (NSRD). We thank John Parachini (director of IPC) and his associate director, Rich Girven, as well as Jack Riley (director of NSRD), for their expert guidance and management on this unique effort. In addition, Hunter Granger and Melissa Bradley provided tireless management assistance for the numerous administrative complexities involved. Senior RAND researchers Dr. Gery Ryan and Dr. Andrew Morral provided peer review and quality assurance throughout the research process. RAND team leaders Dr. William Marcellino, Dr. Joshua Breslau, and Dr. Olesya Tkacheva were instrumental to this effort, as were RAND coders Aziza Arifkhanova, Semirah Ahdiyyih,

Diana Antonian-Israelian, Olena Bogdan, Mary Lou Gilbert, Polina Kats-Kariyanakatte, Hui Kim, Karin Liu, Christian Lopez, Ervant Maksabedian, Eduardo Marquez-Pena, Ahmad Rahmani, Preeta Saxena, and Robert Stewart. We are grateful to Grace Kono-Wells at Keystrokes, Incorporated, for finding, hiring, and managing numerous additional coders with proficiency in Russian and Spanish. Finally, none of this work would have been possible without the creative and diligent work of our subcontractors responsible for data collection, including Mark House and D3 Systems.

### 4.6.7 Information About the Case Study Authors

**Ryan A. Brown** is a senior social and behavioral scientist at the RAND Corporation. His research focuses on health risk behaviors among rural and other marginalized populations, disaster preparedness and response, counterterrorism and national security, and military health and workforce issues. He codirects the Center for Qualitative and Mixed Methods at RAND, which sponsors innovation and development of novel analytic methods for text, social media, and other semistructured data. Brown is currently leading a project that will use interviews with former members of violent extremist groups (and their family members) to provide insights into pathways to radicalization. He is also involved in a mixed methods project that will help design a landslide early warning system in Sitka, Alaska. His other current efforts focus on assessing the effectiveness of family violence interventions among Aboriginal and Torres Strait Islander individuals, as well as designing culturally grounded substance use interventions for urban American Indian and Alaska Native youth.

**David P. Kennedy** is a cultural anthropologist trained at the University of Florida and is currently a senior social and behavioral scientist at the RAND Corporation. He helped establish the RAND Center for Qualitative and Mixed Methods Research and served as one of its first codirectors. He has conducted research on the intersection of culture, social networks, and health and has developed innovative methods for targeting social network and romantic relationship factors in health and behavior change interventions. He is also developing software for the collection of social network data and for use in social network interventions. He has conducted research on various health topics, including mental health (depression, PTSD, and ADHD), chronic and infectious illnesses (breast cancer treatment, HIV/AIDS, diabetes, kidney disease, influenza), and abuse of substances (tobacco, alcohol, and drugs). He has conducted research with a variety of populations in the United States, such as homeless men, women, and youth in Los Angeles and civilian employees of an Air Force Base, as well as international fieldwork in Latin America and Africa.

# 4.7  Conclusion

Dedoose is, at its core, a collaborative platform, and this chapter focused on the benefits of working in teams. These potential benefits, however, come with a number of associated challenges that must be considered and addressed when seeking to work with a group of others with varying skill sets and levels of experience. How best to meet these challenges is both strategic and practical. From a strategic perspective, clear communication and rules of team conduct are fundamental to creating and maintaining a cohesive and high-functioning team. More practically, as described here, Dedoose offers several features to address the inherent variation across team members in excerpting and coding decisions and how to examine and strengthen team consistency toward creating a valuable database. We believe that successful teams take time to consider the teamwork model and life cycle presented here and work through the issues that may arise. Furthermore, taking time to engage in practical exercises when building a strong and well-understood code system that includes adequate documentation will help ensure that all members of a team are prepared to carry out their tasks with high quality. Finally, the case study offers a clear illustration of how Dedoose can be used to manage and interact with the data within a complex cross-cultural project.

# Qualitative Analysis

Qualitative analysis involves an ongoing struggle with ambiguity. Throughout the analysis process, the researcher strives to remain open to the unknown while drawing on multiple meanings from a diverse range of data sources. In addition, qualitative researchers strive to avoid the temptation of pinning down meaning to a single cause or truth (Erickson, 2012). In this regard, the credibility of a qualitative study requires the researcher to adhere to social science empirical practices. For example, while a single observation may appear interesting or important, it remains nothing more than a single observation. The observation is evidence only when it is part of and linked to broader findings and interpretations (Denzin & Lincoln, 2017; Patton, 2015). Given such ambiguity surrounding the process of qualitative analysis, the researcher is continually challenged when drawing credible and trustworthy findings from gathered evidence.

Each qualitative study is a unique analytic thought process of inquiry into social interactions in the natural setting. Such inquiry is not intended to produce generalizable findings, rather, illumination and deeper insights into the focus of the inquiry. As discussed in Chapter 1, the qualitative and quantitative paradigms are both procedurally and philosophically distinct. Furthermore, the use of terminology for each paradigm reflects these differences. For example, the quantitative constructs of *validity*, *reliability*, and *generalizability* are usually considered inappropriate qualitative terminology as qualitative inquiry draws on an ambiguous and fluid process of meaning making. Whereas terms such as *transferability*, *dependability*, *confirmability*, and *trustworthiness* are applied by the researcher to communicate qualitative distinctions (Anfara, Brown, & Mangione, 2002; Denzin & Lincoln, 2017; Kaczynski, Salmona, et al., 2014; Patton, 2015). The key point of this discussion is to draw attention to the procedural and philosophical distinctions that represent each paradigm and the importance of clear communication during analysis.

## 5.1  Qualitative Analysis: Looking for Quality

When conducting qualitative analysis within a mixed methods study, the researcher must respect and promote high-quality empirical practices. Achieving quality involves the demonstration of technical procedural competence and presenting work that offers a substantial contribution of social importance (Moss et al., 2009).

### Table 5.1  Widely Recognized Qualitative Analysis Practices

| | Further Readings |
|---|---|
| Discourse analysis | Phillips, N., & Hardy, C. (2002). *Discourse analysis: Investigating processes of social construction.* Thousand Oaks, CA: SAGE.<br><br>Wooffitt, R. (2014). *Conversation analysis and discourse analysis: A comparative and critical introduction.* Thousand Oaks, CA: SAGE. |
| Grounded theory | Charmaz, K. (2014). *Constructing grounded theory* (2nd ed.). Thousand Oaks, CA: SAGE.<br><br>Corbin, J., & Strauss, A. (2015). *Basics of qualitative research: Techniques and procedures for developing grounded theory* (4th ed.). Thousand Oaks, CA: SAGE. |
| Narrative analysis | Holstein, J. A., & Gubrium, J. F. (Eds.). (2012). *Varieties of narrative analysis.* Thousand Oaks, CA: SAGE. |
| Thematic analysis | Guest, G., MacQueen, K. M., & Namey, E. E. (2012a). *Applied thematic analysis.* Thousand Oaks, CA: SAGE.<br><br>Patton, M. Q. (2015). *Qualitative research and evaluation methods* (4th ed.). Thousand Oaks, CA: SAGE. |

A key component of these practices is analysis—the interpretation of data as credible evidence from which to present findings and meaningful conclusions.

There are a variety of qualitative methods now recognized as credible procedures for conducting qualitative analysis. The choice of a particular approach, however, must appropriately align with the focus and overall design of the study (Creswell, 2017; Salmona, Kaczynski, & Smith, 2015). Table 5.1 highlights four of the more widely recognized qualitative analysis practices and provides recent references for further readings. Schwandt (2015) provides a brief overview on each of these four methods.

The following five subsections of this chapter discuss (1) the potential pitfalls from theory bits, (2) the role of technology in visualizing multiple relationships within data, (3) strategies to report multivariate findings, (4) using great quotes as an analytic filter, and (5) recommendations for credible qualitative analysis. Combined, these five subsections are intended to provide a foundation from which to draw important lessons in the use of Dedoose analytic functions. The case study at the end of the chapter provides further examples on data analysis.

Before further discussion into the analysis process, it may be helpful to give consideration to potential errors that researchers may encounter. There are always potential pitfalls that qualitative and mixed methods researchers may encounter when selecting the best evidence to use when building a compelling argument. One such potential pitfall is the identification and use of theory bits. Looking at what something isn't often helps clarify what it could look like. In the following section, theory bits are used as an example of what isn't good analytic practice when researchers prematurely draw conclusions in the analysis process.

## 5.1.1 Theory Bits

The potential misuse of theory bits during the data analysis process provides an excellent example of how credible research can be compromised. Theory bits are unsubstantiated points of meaning that the researcher has deductively drawn from a fragment of data (Patton, 2015, p. 589). Meaning from this fragment may distort analysis because a fragment can grab the researchers' attention and sound and feel so correct. Qualitative research practices promote inductive inquiry that strives to avoid such premature deductive pitfalls in the interpretation of meanings. Through the adoption of sound qualitative practices, the researcher is better positioned to promote improvements in the reporting of credible evidence.

It is important to clarify that this discussion of the potential pitfalls of using a theory bit is different from the use of a great quote identified during data analysis. In essence, the theory bit stands alone and apart, whereas the great quote is supported by a larger body of related evidence from the raw data. Section 5.1.4 provides a more detailed discussion of these distinctions and offers steps on how to label, or tag, text as "Great Quotes" for future retrieval and reporting.

More than 50 years ago, Glaser and Strauss (1967) introduced the concept of a theory bit as a potential issue of concern for qualitative researchers when adopting grounded theory analysis techniques. As the founders of grounded theory, they maintained that building meaning on a theory bit was a misuse of grounded theory methodology.

This analytic concern has continued to grow for Glaser (1999, 2002, 2010) as qualitative research has expanded and integrated the applications of grounded theory techniques broadly into qualitative inquiry. In essence, grounded theory techniques include (a) inductive open coding, (b) axial coding to build meaning-making patterns, (c) constant comparative thematic theory building, and (d) saturation, when no new data are emerging (Corbin & Strauss, 2015; Patton, 2015; Saldana, 2013). These steps are presented as a simple representation of a coding sequence and are not intended to represent a full discussion of grounded theory methodological practices. Of importance here is the increasing acceptance of grounded theory coding practices that have now extended beyond qualitative researchers to "those quantitative researchers who adopt it in mixed-methods projects" (Charmaz, 2014, p. 12). Given this growing appeal to adopt elements of grounded theory practices in various qualitative and mixed methods applications, greater awareness of potential analytic mistakes is all the more important.

As shown in Figure 5.1, theory bits are no longer of unique concern solely to grounded theory. The common practices of qualitative data analysis involving stages of open coding followed by building code structures are now evident in a wide range of qualitative theoretical orientations. As the researcher engages with the raw data, the analysis process moves from the identification of disconnected points of interest to building increasingly interrelated connections within the data.

Figure 5.1   Theory Bit and Qualitative Approaches

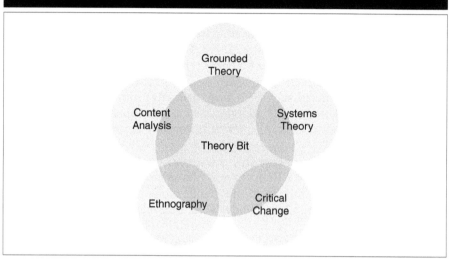

The theoretical orientations shown in Figure 5.1 may adopt variations of a four-stage process involving elements of (1) open coding, then (2) initial groupings of axial codes, followed by (3) advanced pattern building of axial coding, and finally (4) the identification of patterns and themes of related meanings. The point of this discussion is to show that theory bit pitfalls are of concern to many qualitative theoretical orientations.

Glaser (2010) contends that it is increasingly likely that "theory bits will be used almost unconsciously" (p. 11). When used incorrectly, theory bits may distort analysis because they grab our attention and prematurely shape our perception. Since they sound so correct, theory bits may cause several pitfalls, including (a) inappropriately labeling a person or situation badly, (b) providing an analytic shortcut to emergent fit, (c) encouraging an attraction to intuitive findings lacking evidence, and (d) having the ability to thwart further analysis. As Glaser (1999) cautioned,

> The danger, of course, is that they might be just plain wrong or irrelevant unless based in a grounded theory. Hopefully, they get corrected as more data come out. The grounded theorist should try to fit, correct, and modify [theory bits] even as they pass his or her lips. (p. 844)

In practice, this misuse of limited data during analysis represents an incomplete process of low-level analytic thinking. The resulting lack of supporting evidence causes the analysis process to fail in the building of credible complex relationships.

High-quality qualitative data analysis involves uncovering and constructing credible connections between the research questions and data. Data analysis is defined by Schwandt (2015) as "the activity of making sense of, interpreting, and theorizing data" (p. 57). Qualitative analysis is considered both art and science and, thus, is demanding and potentially problematic for the researcher. The focus of a qualitative study aides the qualitative researcher by guiding methodological decisions and providing structure to meaningful analysis. As Patton (2015) explains, "Qualitative analysis ultimately depends on the analytical intellect and style of the analyst. The human factor is the great strength and the fundamental weakness of qualitative inquiry and analysis—a scientific—two edged sword" (p. 522).

The qualitative researcher is therefore confronted with distilling knowledge that can be utilized by the intended audience. It is no wonder that a researcher may unconsciously be drawn to theory bits. Clearly, strategies to respond to this potential analytic mistake from theory bits are needed to strengthen practice.

## 5.1.2 Technological Advances in Visualizing Meanings

Advances in the use of computer technology has expanded adoption of data analysis applications (Davidson & di Gregorio, 2012). As a result, the field of qualitative research continues to advocate for methods to improve the visualization of credible research findings. With the progressive adoption of technological tools in research analysis, data visualization increasingly offers the means to deconstruct complex multivariate relationships that enhance the qualitative analytic process (Cisneros Pubela, Davidson, & Faux, 2012; Evers, Mruck, Silver, & Peeters, 2011; Salmona & Kaczynski, 2016). Visuals serve as powerful analytic tools that expose evidence and stimulate insights into the unexpected. This, in turn, inductively opens the researcher to new thoughts. As suggested earlier, visuals are built on the larger body of data from a study, not from a single key bit of data. By looking at phenomena in depth, the researcher is thus positioned to tell those broader stories.

The application of data visualization during the analysis process supports the construction of larger meanings and the reporting and transference of credible results. This potential to visually share and transfer dense meanings to a larger context is an effective way to identify and report complex patterns in data. It is important to note that, given the challenges of working with qualitative data, visualization can also serve as a risky two-edged sword. It is imperative that the researcher avoids being drawn prematurely to unsubstantiated patterns. Robust qualitative analysis must ensure that meanings are not just figments of the researcher's imagination. As Schwandt (2015) suggests, trustworthiness criteria assist the researcher by linking findings and interpretations to authentic evidence. The sharing and transferring of meanings to a larger audience involves the transferability of evidence-based qualitative findings that are credible and trustworthy. Thus, visualization is a way of looking into the analysis process and exploring higher level connections that may not otherwise be seen.

In essence, visualization, using technological tools, enhances the researchers' ability to see more complex patterns and connections of evidence. A potential methodological weakness, however, is that the researcher may stop thinking and lose analytical lines of inquiry as technology increases the use of visualization. As a result, we may grab hold of the visual message and fail to see what is behind the visualization. Regrettably, lessons learned regarding the dangers of theory bits have the potential to be repeated as the analytic use of visualizations increase.

## 5.1.3 Improving the Reporting of Multivariate Findings

As social science research adopts innovations in data visualization, new methods continue to emerge that can aid in recognizing potentially flawed theory bit analysis. When a study fails to adequately analyze complex relationships, the visual reporting of evidence exhibits a lack of multivariate findings. In this discussion, the term *multivariate* is intended to capture the qualitative analytic exploration of multiple relationships and relevance to the social problem under investigation. Qualitative methods normally do not use the commonly recognized quantitative terminology of multivariate analysis. The concept of multiple variables, however, shares common ground with the qualitative recognition of relationships and multiple meanings. Multivariate findings are qualitatively defined in this discussion as a means to visually investigate complex layers of evidence comprising multiple meanings.

An efficient way of reporting linkages and processing relationships among complex layers of evidence is through visual displays. For example, charts, graphs, tables, and mind maps are increasingly applied in both qualitative and quantitative visual reporting (Anfara et al., 2002; Kaczynski, Salmona, et al., 2014; Martelo, 2011; Richards, 2015). Using technological tools for visualizing qualitative evidence supports and advances this growing practice of investigating complex layers of evidence comprising multiple meanings.

Qualitative software relational databases allow researchers to build connections through a set of relationships in which every piece of information is connected: from media to descriptors, excerpts to media, and codes/tags and tag weights/ratings to excerpts (Dedoose, 2017). These relationships allow software analytic features to use any and every piece of information by enhancing how the data are displayed, filtered, analyzed, and exported. Examples include word clouds, concept maps, sociograms, and bubble plots sized by frequency, which are built on natural connections around themes.

- *Code Co-Occurrence*—code-by-code frequency matrix
- *Code Weight Descriptor Bubble Plot*—perceptual map of average code weight associated with the application for three codes across selected descriptor field subgroups
- *Code Frequency Descriptor Bubble Plot*—perceptual map of application frequency for each of three codes by selected descriptor field subgroups

Note: Refer to the online Dedoose *User Guide* for further assistance using these functions.

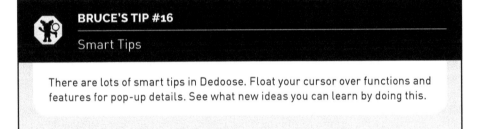

**BRUCE'S TIP #16**

Smart Tips

There are lots of smart tips in Dedoose. Float your cursor over functions and features for pop-up details. See what new ideas you can learn by doing this.

## 5.1.4 Using Great Quotes in Dedoose

High-quality analysis requires knowing the difference between a great quote and a theory bit. This distinction is a critical point. As previously discussed, theory bits are worrisome. Great quotes, on the other hand, hit the nail on the head for the researcher. During the analysis process, the researcher searches for evidence that expresses meanings in the voice of the other—that is, bringing the voice and perspective of the research population to life. These great quotes succinctly contextualize meanings through an authentic voice beyond what the researcher may construct.

As shown in Figure 5.2, great quotes are supported and connected from multiple sources of data. The great quote thus represents a vivid example from a much larger body of evidence.

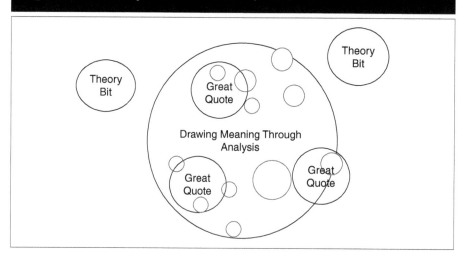

**Figure 5.2   Theory Bits and Great Quotes**

Dedoose allows the researcher to label, or tag, text as "Great Quotes" for future retrieval and reporting. As the researcher codes data, meanings and labels are imposed. The researcher identifies important bits of data. In doing so, the researcher reduces the volume of raw data by filtering and condensing the raw data into these important bits or excerpts, which are then labeled. Some of these excerpts carry more weight and meaning than others. At times, the researcher finds a great quote, a segment of text that the researcher determines is better expressed by the respondent than by the researcher. The researcher codes these respondent nuggets for future consideration and then moves on. Moving on is an important step to take in the context of a reflective process. When analytically filtering, the researcher needs to continue to dig for more meanings and not get distracted by a potential theory bit and disengage from further critical analysis.

As the researcher inductively and deductively shifts back and forth through the data during the analysis process, alternative explanations are considered and different paths of inquiry are explored. Making sense from findings involves the researcher's interpretations of the evidence. For the researcher, the selection and reporting of great quotes is an important element in this process. Inductive–deductive shifting allows the researcher to reflect on their role as researcher in the analysis process and make clear their contribution in attaching meaning during interpretation.

It is important to point out that reflexivity, as such, is not an attribute that should be used to categorize qualitative researchers into novice or experienced. This discussion concerning the differences between a great quote and a theory bit is relevant to all qualitative researchers, regardless of the level of expertise.

Qualitative researchers strive to promote high standards of empirical inquiry through practices such as researcher as instrument, data triangulation, multiple meanings, staying inductive, and respecting the other voice. Reflexivity draws on these practices and drives efforts to apply and enhance analytic skills. In this sense, personal awareness is key to distinguishing between a great quote and a theory bit. Promoting personal awareness requires remaining open to recognizing that the analysis process includes knowing that much remains unknown.

## 5.1.5 Recommendations

The following practical strategies are suggested to promote visualization and enhance the integration of multivariate findings into the qualitative analysis process.

1. Include a disclosure statement in the discussion of analysis procedures when visualizing and reporting great quotes. As Glaser (2010) explains, "A responsible grounded theorist always should finish his or her bit with a statement to the effect that 'Of course, these situations are very complex or multivariate, and without more data, I cannot tell what is really going on'" (p. 12). Using great quotes in the reporting of findings should include this same practice.

2. Acknowledge that a great quote is only one form of compelling evidence. Do not build the findings around a great quote. Rather, use the great quote to succinctly exemplify findings that are supported with triangulated evidence from multiple sources of data.

3. Ongoing creative use of, and advancements in, the visualization and reporting of multivariate findings are recommended. As discussed earlier, multivariate findings are qualitatively defined as a means to visually investigate complex layers of evidence comprising multiple meanings. The continued growth of technological applications will require methodological alignment as we increasingly analyze complex layers of evidence comprising multiple meanings.

4. Be clear when using research terminology, such as *valid* or *significant*, when discussing mixed methods principles. Use of common quantitative language when discussing qualitative concepts may inadvertently imply linear statistical analysis, causal links, or hypotheses testing. Although such qualitative usage may be somewhat contentious, "validating here refers more to a checking out of interpretations with participants and against data as the research moves along" (Charmaz, 2014, p. 48).

5. Throughout the analysis process continue to reflect on who is making evidence great. Member checking and empowering participants to choose and weight the quote will aid the researcher in the deconstruction of multivariate findings. This practice will also enhance better understandings of the deeper subtext beneath evidence.

These five strategies are offered as a starting point to promote further methodological discussions on the joining of qualitative methodological practices with the growing role of technology in research practice. Rapidly expanding use of technological tools has the potential to distract researchers from qualitative methodological principles that guide and shape inquiry. Researchers must remain diligent in the use of new tools and to continually acknowledge that the researcher drives the inquiry, not the tool. Such safeguards will assist in promoting credible findings and reporting trustworthy research to larger audiences.

## 5.2   Working With Codes

Section 4.2, "Collaborative Interpretations," discussed building and applying a code system from a team perspective. Section 4.4.1, "Team Coding and Establishing Consistency in the Dedoose Environment," more specifically discussed creating and tagging excerpts and team coding. The following sections draw on this foundation with a practical discussion about how to code your data and how to code well using Dedoose. Features will be highlighted that show the dynamic and flexible nature of code trees in Dedoose. Given this flexibility, it is important to note that thoughtful use of code definition and weighting systems and the structure of a code tree is central to the value and credibility of any research.

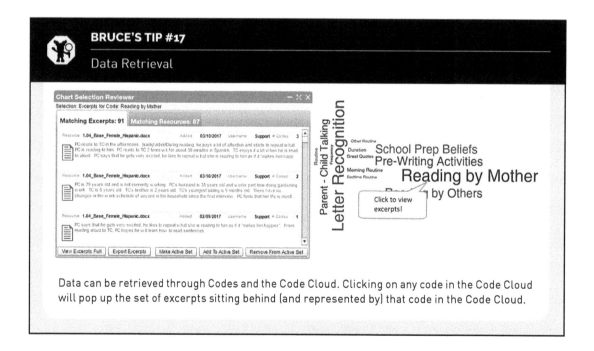

**BRUCE'S TIP #17**

Data Retrieval

Data can be retrieved through Codes and the Code Cloud. Clicking on any code in the Code Cloud will pop up the set of excerpts sitting behind (and represented by) that code in the Code Cloud.

Figure 5.3   Unlocking a Document for Editing

Document: 19.04 Post

## 5.2.1 Creating Connections

Before beginning to code data, let's take a moment to understand how you can work with your qualitative data in Dedoose.

### 5.2.1.1 Editing Documents

Once you have imported your documents into Dedoose, you can unlock, edit, and save documents without any impact on excerpting or memoing by clicking the Unlock Document button seen in Figure 5.3.

- Cross document and cross excerpt text searching. Check into your Media or Excerpts Workspace, type into the search field, and the list will be filtered to only those records, "hits," that contain the text.

- Customize your code and excerpt region colors. You can customize your code tree and excerpt regions by using the controls in the document and code tree settings panels.

### 5.2.1.2 Excerpts

When you create a new excerpt, Dedoose enters excerpt editing mode where the selected section is highlighted in a bolder green color, a bracket appears in the margin defining the excerpt boundaries, colors on other excerpts will be faded, and the "Selection Info" panel header will change from blue to orange as an indicator you are in editing mode. You can click anywhere in the document or media file to exit editing mode.

Figure 5.4 shows an excerpt in editing mode (which you can reenter by clicking the bracket that marks the excerpt boundaries) in which you can add codes, add memos, and set a new excerpt start or end location with a right click of the mouse.

## Figure 5.4 Editing an Excerpt

PC feels that all parents should teach their children to be wel
elders and teachers. PC feels teachers should teach kids th
mannered, and to not act badly with other children. The teach
happy faces, regular faces, and sad faces to demonstrate ho
never received a sad f <>  Add Code(s)    d tells PC when ;
with amusement at hc                says, "Mami, oy J
ultima cara". "Mom, tc ⌀  Add Memos(s)     e has the last fa
TC proper social behɛ                is name, numbɛ
but already from pre-k <  Set Excerpt Start  achers taught hir

The child did well in th >  Set Excerpt End   He behaved wel
more activites with TC                bets, recognizinɡ
asked PC if she's doiɪ ⊘  Exit Editing      the child since th
that she is. PC didn't                omework. Now ;
cutting and pasting, with the alphabet, and recognizing letters

**BRUCE'S TIP #18**

Quick Code Widget

The fastest way to create and code text excerpts is with the Quick Code Widget.

The Quick Code Widget seen in Figure 5.5 allows the use of keyboard short-cuts to maximize efficiency when coding text documents.

### 5.2.1.3 Steps to Use the Quick Code Widget

1. Highlight the text you would like to code.

2. Hit your keyboard space bar or right-click on highlighted region and select "add codes" to open the Quick Code Widget.

3. To apply an existing code, do the following:

   a. Type name in search field or scroll to an existing code with your arrow keys.

   b. With code highlighted, hit Enter key or double-click the code to create excerpt and apply code.

Figure 5.5 Quick Code Widget

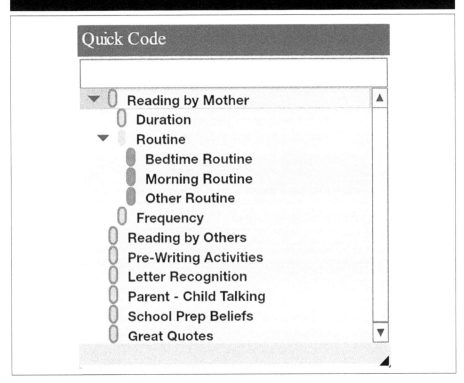

4. To create and apply a new code, do as follows:

   a. Type the name of the new code in the search field.

   b. Hit Enter key to create excerpt, add code to code tree, and apply code to excerpt.

When you apply a code with the Quick Code Widget, once the first code is applied, the "Selection Info" panel in the upper right corner will change to orange as an indicator that you are in excerpt editing mode and information about the excerpt will appear. Finally, note that the Quick Code Widget is a movable and sizable panel and can be left open for subsequent coding so that it does not need to be reactivated for each excerpt or document you are coding.

## 5.2.2 Codes

From a technical and mechanical point of view, coding in Dedoose is easy. You can either use the Quick Code Widget, codes can be applied by double-clicking a code in the "Codes" panel, or by dragging and dropping a code into the "Selection Info" panel. Code weights/ratings (see Section 5.2.4) can be set after the code is

**Figure 5.6  Code Smart Tip**

Codes

Reading by Mother

Du  Reading by Mother
    Mother reading activities with child
Rc  Ratings represent quality.

Frequency

Reading by Others

Pre-Writing Activities

Letter Recognition

applied (if applicable). You can delete codes from the excerpt by clicking the "X" next to the code in the "Selection Info" panel. Any information in the "Description" field or related to any activate code weight/rating will show up in a smart tip when floating over the code in the code tree as in Figure 5.6. This is a great place to store reminders about when and how to use the code.

When you create a new code, it is important to write a short description. Code descriptions must capture your analytic thinking and allow you to appropriately use the code as additional excerpts are identified. Remember, this description process is fluid, in the sense that descriptions evolve as your study progresses. Thus, these changes and modifications to code descriptions represent deeper advances in your qualitative analysis and thinking.

In the following sections, we discuss the steps for creating and modifying codes and the overall code tree. NOTE: Code and tag are used interchangeably (identical meaning) in Dedoose even though they may be distinguished in practice.

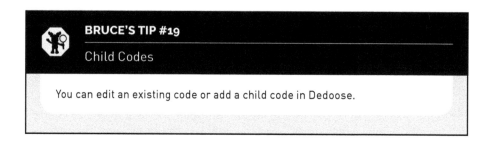

**BRUCE'S TIP #19**

Child Codes

You can edit an existing code or add a child code in Dedoose.

Figure 5.7  Code Editing Options

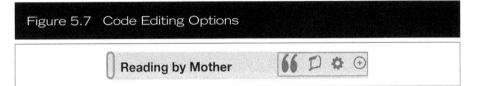

Reading by Mother

To edit a code, float your cursor over an existing code in the tree to reveal controls for editing that particular code and other activities as seen with the Reading by Mother code in Figure 5.7.

### 5.2.2.1 Steps for Editing a Code

- Click the Edit Code/Tag button to modify the code/tag.

- Click the Add Child Code/Tag button to create a subordinate code/tag.

- Enter the details for the new code in the Add New Code pop-up (click Enable Code Weighting if relevant).

- When defining codes weights/ratings, enter the specifications, which include minimum, maximum, and default weight values, then click Submit.

- Click Exit Editing button, and all new code tree specifications are ready for use.

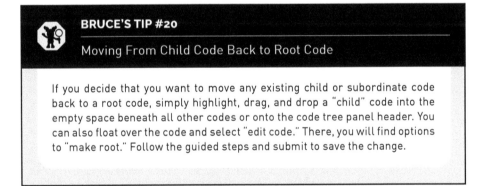

**BRUCE'S TIP #20**

Moving From Child Code Back to Root Code

If you decide that you want to move any existing child or subordinate code back to a root code, simply highlight, drag, and drop a "child" code into the empty space beneath all other codes or onto the code tree panel header. You can also float over the code and select "edit code." There, you will find options to "make root." Follow the guided steps and submit to save the change.

## 5.2.3 Code/Tag Tree Structure Modification

Again, the code tree in Dedoose is flexible and dynamic. Features and functionality are designed to allow for modification as the code system itself evolves by expanding vertically (adding new codes), expanding horizontally (by changing the code hierarchy), and contracting (by deleting or merging codes). These modifications represent the natural evolution of a code system as you become more intimately engaged with your data. This process also encourages further discovery

**Merge Codes**

Here two codes can be combined into one along with all associated excerpt code applications. Please select a primary and secondary code. Upon clicking submit, the secondary code will be merged into the primary code—leaving only the primary code.

Primary Code:    | Parent - Child Talking | ▼ |

Secondary Code: | Pre-Writing Activities | ▼ |

Cancel    Submit

and increased awareness of nuanced meanings. Remember that your code tree will ultimately become the conceptual framework you will use when organizing the meanings you discover in your data. Furthermore, effectively communicating the results of your research findings to your research audience will draw on this well-articulated conceptual framework.

Figure 5.8 shows Merge Codes function.

### 5.2.3.1 Steps to Merge Codes

- Highlight the code you will wish to merge into another and select Edit code. Click Merge in the lower left portion of the pop-up.

- Select the Primary code—the code you want to keep—and the Secondary code—this will default to the code you are editing but can be changed—and follow the guided steps to complete the merge. Again, keep in mind that any applications of the secondary code to excerpts will be recoded with the primary code, and the secondary code will be permanently removed from the code tree.

Delete codes by highlight the code and selecting Edit code. Confirm the code deletion instructions shown in Figure 5.9 to remove the code entirely. Note that deleting a code will also remove it permanently from any excerpt to which it had been applied.

To show the Show Actions Panel, hover over the ! icon at the top of the code panel. Then click on Reorder Codes, and the Reorder code window will appear as shown in Figure 5.10. Now you can reorder and sort your codes.

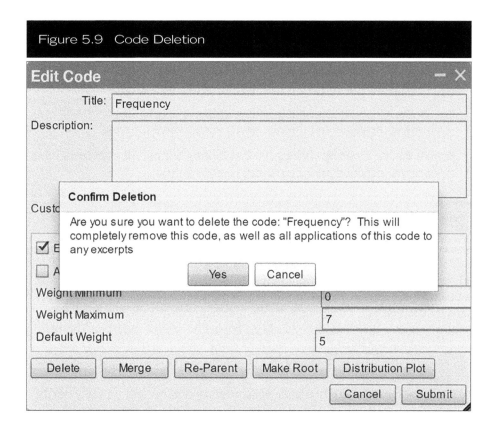

Figure 5.9    Code Deletion

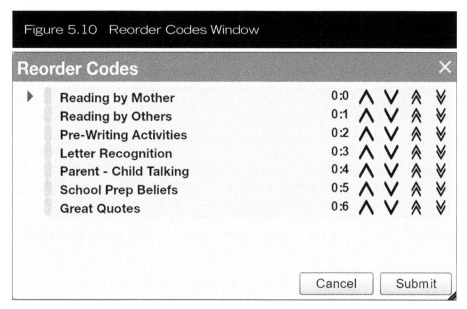

Figure 5.10    Reorder Codes Window

### 5.2.3.2 Steps to Reorder Codes

- Customize vertical ordering of codes by clicking the Reorder Codes button for Reorder Codes pop-up. Use the arrows to move the codes up or down in the tree.

- Use the Sort Alphabetically button to toggle between an alphabetical listing of the codes and the custom user-determined ordering.

- Exit editing mode by clicking the Exit Editing button. All changes to the code tree structure are saved, and it is ready for use.

## 5.2.4 Code Weights/Ratings

Code weights/ratings can be a powerful approach to look at your data in new ways by introducing new and unique dimensions to your database. You can define and apply code weights or ratings to indicate anything that can be represented on a numerical dimension, including quality, sentiment, importance, or any other characteristic that you understand can be indexed or distributed in some mean- ingful way where the same code has been applied to sets of excerpts. The basic purpose of code weights/ratings is to allow commonly coded qualitative content (e.g., excerpts that have been tagged by a common code) to be indexed along some meaningful dimension.

It is important to note that code weight/rating systems will typically not be used until you are familiar with your data. For example, at the beginning of a project, you may imagine that a 10-point scale is needed to index a code across some dimension. However, as you progress further into a study, you might decide that 3 points are sufficient. As such, when a final decision has been made, you can simply edit the code to activate the weight/rating system and set the parameters accordingly. Note that there are a set of charts in the Dedoose analytics that are specifically designed to examine these dimensions in relation to the excerpting and coding activity within the project as a whole and as a function of various subsets of data.

As an example of how these dimensions can be used, imagine interviewing mothers about what it looks like when they read to their preschool-aged child. You might also ask them to self-report on a 5-point scale (1 = *poor* to 5 = *excellent*) what they would consider as the quality of their reading. An important distinction between these self-reports and investigator-imposed ratings is that the mothers only know how they read and, perhaps, how a few others read. Furthermore, self-reports are subject to a social desirability bias where research has shown that people tend to overreport on positive characteristics or behaviors and underreport on negative ones. As investigators, however, we see all excerpts where mothers talk about reading to their child. This perspective lets us see the full range of what reading looks like across the entire research sample and allows us to distribute all the excerpts across a rating scale that we have defined to index reading "quality."

Figure 5.11    Defining a Code Weight and the Parameters Specified

**Add Code**    — ✕

Title: Reading Quality

Description: Mother reading activities with child
Ratings represent quality.

Custom Color: ■

☑ Enable Code Weighting

☑ Allow decimal weight

Weight Minimum  1

Weight Maximum  5

Default Weight  5

Cancel    Submit

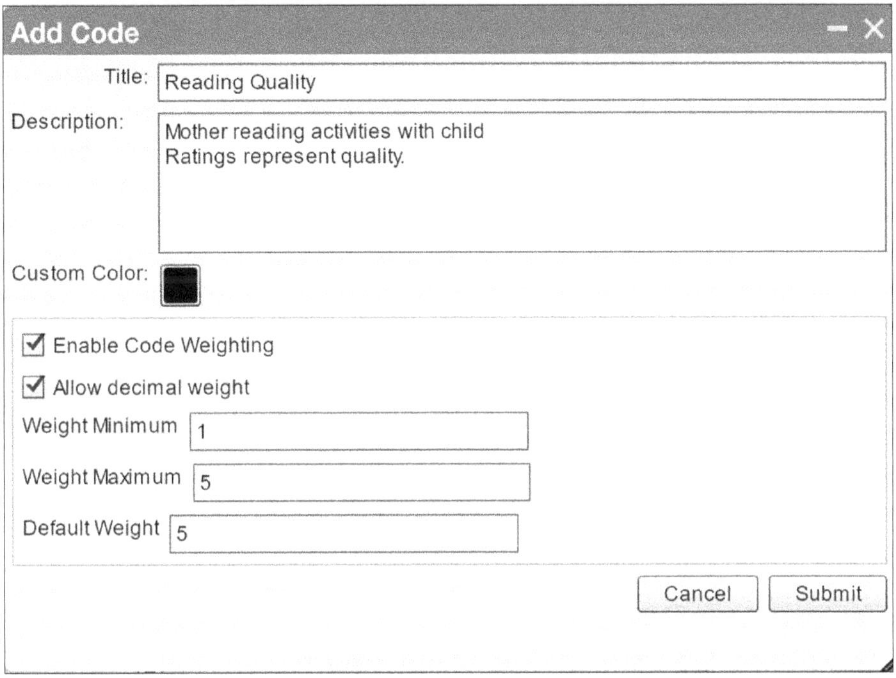

Ultimately, when you can use this feature, you have another set of numbers in your project to incorporate in your data visualization and analysis. Finally, note that these code weights can represent discrete points on a scale, as with reading quality or as purely continuous data across a wide range of values (e.g., $0 to $5,000,000 spent on an intervention program). See the snapshot in Figure 5.11 for an example of defining a code with a weight system active and the parameters specified.

As a reminder, here are a few things to keep in mind as you consider using code weights/ratings:

- Under most circumstances, code weighting is not considered until the team has become intimately familiar with the data under investigation. That is, it is not until a substantial level of familiarity has been achieved that decisions about the range of a scale can be determined. For example, is there sufficient and clear variation to apply a 3-point rating system to index "high," "medium," or "low" or a 10-point system to indicate variation across a broader range?

- Once activated and defined, these weights are typically applied as a second pass through the relevant data. This second pass can be done very efficiently in the Dedoose environment.

- Not all codes will readily lend themselves to the use of this feature but many can, and these weight systems can be used in creative ways to index dimensions such as quality, strength, salience, beauty, sentiment, and value.

The code system feature has a number of other options that may be useful to you and others on your research team. Here are some examples:

- You can import and export codes to research team members or other stakeholders.

- You can customize the color scheme to modify how the excerpts appear in context.

- You can activate an "upcoding" feature that will automatically apply parent and any other superordinate codes when a child is applied to an excerpt.

- You can change the order of codes in how they are presented in the tree.

Finally, remember that you can find more details about all these functions in the Dedoose *User Guide* and other support services on the Dedoose website.

## 5.3 Case Study: Using Dedoose for a Multisite Study

The following case study demonstrates many of the main points raised so far in this book. The study shows how a team of researchers used Dedoose to effectively manage and analyze multiple data sources from a large, multisite study. It describes and discusses data management procedures and how to manage teams through different Access Groups in Dedoose. It also begins our discussion about using charts in Dedoose, which is discussed in more detail in Chapter 7.

---

**THINK ABOUT, AND ANSWER, THESE QUESTIONS AS YOU READ THE CASE STUDY**

1. How will you manage your data in your project?

2. How will you start your coding?

3. What steps will you take to manage your ongoing and developing code tree?

---

# Using Dedoose for a Multisite, Mixed Methods Project on Sexual and Gender Minority Adolescent Health

Kathryn Macapagal, Margaret Matson, & Brian Mustanski

This case study describes how Dedoose is used to manage and analyze data from a large, multisite, mixed methods study on ethical issues in sexual health and HIV prevention research with sexual and gender minority (SGM) adolescents (Fisher, Arbeit, Dumont, Macapagal, & Mustanski, 2016; Macapagal, Coventry, Arbeit, Fisher, & Mustanski, 2016; Mustanski, Coventry, Macapagal, Arbeit, & Fisher, 2017). A brief overview of the study is provided followed by discussions of data management procedures, analysis, reporting, and a conclusion with lessons learned through using Dedoose. This case study will help readers learn how to identify and select appropriate Access Groups for different users by creating and saving multiple data sets for different manuscripts. The utilization of mixed methods charts in Dedoose is applied to identify, interpret, and report findings from mixed methods studies in publications. We also provide some lessons learned, including ways in which we could have utilized different types of mixed methods charts to look at more nuances in the data, considerations for mixed methods research with smaller samples, and thoughts about utilizing other features of Dedoose to facilitate communication between individuals working on multisite projects.

## 5.3.1 Setting Up the Project

SGM adolescents are at greater risk for adverse sexual health outcomes, such as sexually transmitted infections and HIV, compared with their cisgender and heterosexual peers (Centers for Disease Control and Prevention, 2015, 2016). One reason for the paucity of research essential to reducing sexual health disparities for SGM adolescents is a lack of consensus among investigators and institutional review boards about study risks and benefits and appropriate ethical procedures for protecting SGM adolescents' research rights and welfare, especially when parental permission is waived. However, youth's and parents' perspectives are noticeably absent in this dialogue, and decisions about youth involvement in sexual health research and whether to waive parental permission are often based on opinion rather than guided by empirical evidence. Our study sought to give a voice to these crucial stakeholders by using online surveys, online focus groups, and interviews to explore SGM adolescents' and parents' perspectives on parental permission, risks and benefits, and attitudes toward sexual health and HIV prevention research with SGM adolescents.

This project's mixed methods approach enabled us to gain insight into youth's and parents' reasoning about sexual health and HIV prevention research and examine how these perspectives might differ by certain key characteristics. For example, we hypothesized that youth's perspectives on research risks, benefits, and parental permission would differ by "outness" (i.e., disclosure of their SGM identity) to parents, and parents' perspectives may differ according to whether their child was heterosexual or a sexual minority, as well as other attitudinal variables such as social conservatism.

Our study team members were based at Fordham University in the Bronx, New York, and Northwestern University in Chicago, Illinois. We chose Dedoose for mixed methods data management and analysis given our long-distance collaboration, as investigators and research staff from both sites were involved in data coding, reliability testing, analysis, and manuscript preparation.

## 5.3.2 Data Sources

In spring 2015, we conducted six asynchronous online focus groups with 74 SGM adolescents in the United States using a secure forum website hosted by Northwestern University (Fisher, Arbeit, Dumont, Macapagal, & Mustanski, 2016; Macapagal, Coventry, Arbeit, Fisher, & Mustanski, 2017; Mustanski, Coventry, Macapagal, Arbeit, & Fisher, 2017). Parental permission was waived for this study. Participants chose usernames distinct from those they used outside of the study to protect privacy. Two research team members moderated each focus group, which took place over 3 days and consisted of 7 to 13 participants. We posted questions on the forum each day, and participants typed replies to the questions and to one another's responses at their convenience. The semistructured focus group guide contained questions about perceptions of three main ethical issues (parental permission, research risks, and research benefits) for three different types of studies with adolescents (sexual health survey research, HIV behavioral surveillance and testing studies, and clinical trials testing adherence to preexposure prophylaxis [PrEP] medications for HIV prevention). Participants answered questions based on their experiences with this study's surveys and based on two brief videos describing procedures for a hypothetical HIV surveillance study and hypothetical PrEP trial. Youth completed self-report questionnaires, including sociodemographic characteristics (e.g., age, race, ethnicity), sexual orientation and gender identity (including outness), and sexual health and behavior. Our primary research questions were as follows: What are perceived risks and benefits of SGM adolescent participation in each of these three types of studies? What are youth's perspectives on parental permission for these studies? Do these perspectives differ by youth's background or experiences?

In summer 2016, we conducted a substudy involving online surveys and phone interviews with 30 parents of heterosexual and sexual minority adolescent boys in the United States (Mustanski, Macapagal, Thomann, et al., 2018). Similar to the adolescent focus groups, we asked parents about perceived risks and benefits of their sons' participation in hypothetical HIV prevention studies, and whether their perspectives changed if their permission was required or waived for participation. Parents also completed self-report questionnaires about their own and their child's demographic characteristics, sexual orientation identity, political conservatism, and parent–child relationships, among other measures.

### 5.3.3 Data Management

Our team at Northwestern agreed to assume primary responsibility for qualitative and mixed methods data management throughout the study given our prior experience with Dedoose (DuBois et al., 2015; Mustanski, Lyons, & Garcia, 2011). Throughout focus group data collection, the investigative team held monthly conference calls to plan the manuscripts and analyses around the key research questions. These plans informed how we structured the data set within Dedoose—or, how we organized the transcripts, and which descriptor data to upload to Dedoose. As the focus groups generated a large amount of qualitative data focused on several similar areas from which we expected common themes to emerge (i.e., risks, benefits, and parental permission) and the same team of investigators from both sites would be involved in data analysis and manuscript preparation, we created one Project in Dedoose for all the data, then used filters to create smaller data sets for each manuscript. To do this, we used the Data Selector feature, which we accessed by clicking on "Data Set" from the main menu. In Data Selector, we primarily used the "Descriptors" and "Codes" tabs to narrow down our data sets as our analyses often focused on a specific subgroup of youth (e.g., sexual minority girls) or codes (e.g., codes pertaining to parental permission). We then checked off the codes in the "Codes" tab and/or filters in the "Descriptor" tab applicable to our analyses, returned to the "Dataset" tab in Data Selector, and clicked "Save Current Set" to enable us to reuse this data set later. We followed similar procedures for the parent interview data gathered later.

For the focus group study, we gave each team member involved in data management, coding, analysis, or reporting an account with access commensurate with their role. The project director had full administrative access (i.e., Full Access), whereas others involved in only coding and analysis had more limited access (e.g., Project-Wide Assistant; Project Manager with Restricted Excerpts). Any requests for additional users across both sites went to the project director. All investigators on the parent interview study were granted full access to the data set given the limited scope of the project. We recommend discussing at the outset the role and level of access needed for each staff member involved in the project given the scope of the project.

At the beginning of this project, we encountered minor challenges with identifying an appropriate Access Group for users involved in only coding and analysis. For example, we granted these users more restricted levels of access in the beginning and gained familiarity with the parameters of different Access Groups through trial and error. We recommend referring to descriptions of the Access Groups on Dedoose's website, then assigning users to different Access Groups in a practice project to gain a clear understanding and familiarity with each Access Group's parameters before granting users access to actual data in the project, which can also increase data security.

*Creating Media Files.* Media files consisted of Word documents containing group-level and individual-level transcripts. Group-level transcripts included all posts, comments, and replies from participants involved in a focus group.

Individual-level transcripts for the focus group included all posts by one participant and any conversations they had with the moderators and other participants, whereas those for the parent interview study consisted of the interviewer and parents' conversation. Group- and individual-level transcripts were included in Dedoose for different reasons. As group-level transcripts included the entire narrative across 3 days, this transcript provided more context, which enabled identification of emerging themes and patterns in the data during the preliminary stages of coding. We linked individual-level transcripts with each participant's corresponding descriptor data to conduct mixed methods analyses for the focus group and interview studies.

After each focus group ended, we copied all the typed responses from the focus group website into Word documents to create a group-level transcript, then we extracted each participant's responses from the group-level transcript to create individual-level transcripts. Each individual-level transcript included the number assigned to each focus group and dates on which the focus group took place, the focus group's questions for each major topic, participants' replies to those questions, and moderators' and other participants' probes, clarification questions, or discussions involving that participant. We included the participant's username and relevant demographic information in the file name of each individual-level transcript we saved, which facilitated quicker identification of participant characteristics when citing quotes in manuscripts and easier linkage of individual-level transcripts with corresponding descriptors (Figure C5.3-1). All transcripts were uploaded using the Import Data function.

*Creating Descriptor Files.* The descriptor file included participants' usernames to facilitate linkage with each individual transcript and background characteristics and key descriptors that were planned for mixed methods analyses. We dichotomized descriptor variables used in mixed methods analyses (e.g., out to parents vs. not out to parents; socially conservative vs. socially liberal) and included multiple versions of some variables used both for mixed methods analyses and to characterize the sample (e.g., one variable reflected participants' age on an interval scale [14, 15, 16, 17] for descriptive analyses, whereas another categorized age into "younger" and "older" adolescents). We entered variable labels (e.g., "man," "woman") into the descriptor file, rather than raw values (e.g., 0, 1), wherever possible for ease of interpretation of the charts and mixed methods graphs we created in Dedoose.

### 5.3.4 Analysis Processes

*Coding.* Our initial codebook consisted of a priori codes based on our research questions. These higher-level themes (e.g., parental permission for surveys, for HIV surveillance, and for biomedical HIV prevention studies; risks of participating in surveys, in HIV surveillance studies, and in HIV prevention medication studies) were each assigned parent codes, which were applied to excerpts in each individual-level transcript by two coders. During this initial coding process, the coders also began generating lists of themes that emerged from the data.

Filename: Participant1_17_M_Gay_Out.docx
Username: Participant1
Focus Group #5, Day 2 (4/1/15), TOPIC 4: Weighing the pros and cons of being in a PrEP study

Moderator1

1. Discuss with each other some reasons you might WANT to be in a PrEP study like this.
2. Discuss with each other some reasons you might NOT WANT to be in a PrEP study like this.
3. How would knowing about the side effects of PrEP (nausea, diarrhea, small risk of lower bone density)
   influence your decision to participate?
4. How would you feel about coming back for an interview with researchers 3 months after the study starts
   if you DIDN'T take PrEP like you were supposed to (every day)?

Participant1

I would want to be in the study because I could benefit from having pills that prevent HIV. Even though I
only have one sexual partner, it's always better to be safe than sorry. The only reason I would not want to
be in the study is if my parents found my pills. After hearing that the nausea and diarrhea go away after my
body gets used to the pill, I would be completely fine with it. My only concern would be the pill affecting my
bones, but in the video they said that there would be check-ups every couple of months so I would always
make sure to ask how my bones were doing. I would feel ashamed going in for the check-up knowing I had
not taken the pills every day.

Participant2

I would want to be in a PrEP study because prevention against HIV on a daily basis would really help put
me and any partner that I might have at ease. Reasons why I wouldn't want to be in the study would be
side effects & having to ask for my parents' permission. I am prone to nausea so that being one of the
side effects might greatly influence my decision, but if it does go away after the body adjusts, I think I
could deal with it for a little bit of time. I would probably feel guilty and disappointed if I wasn't able to
take it everyday, the same thing happened with some antibiotics I was supposed to take but I could never
remember.

Moderator1 commented

Thanks @Participant1 & @Participant 2! Is there anything else that would affect your willingness to
participate?

Participant1 commented

I agree with Participant2, taking PrEP would put me and my partner at ease. On Question 2, asking my parents
for permission to be in the study would also be a reason for me why I would not participate in the study.

*Note:* PrEP = preexposure prophylaxis.

The coders had regular meetings to ensure consistency in coding procedures (e.g., size of excerpts—words or phrases, sentences, entire paragraphs; inclusion of only an individual participant's words in the excerpt vs. what the moderator and other participants said in response as well), then they started to reduce and refine their lists of themes. Next, the entire investigative team agreed to prepare three manuscripts based on our primary research questions on risks, benefits, and parental permission for (1) survey research, (2) HIV behavioral surveillance and testing research (both led by Northwestern), and (3) clinical trials testing PrEP for HIV prevention (led by Fordham). For each manuscript, the lead site would be responsible for completing the remaining steps of coding, qualitative and mixed methods analysis, writing, and consulting with the other site as necessary. Using the list of themes generated by the two coders, each site worked in parallel to iteratively refine and finalize codes specific to each manuscript.

We used Dedoose's Code Co-Occurrence chart to identify which codes to consider collapsing due to high degrees of overlap in number or meaning. Our plan to conduct mixed methods analyses also informed our code-naming conventions. For example, rather than having only a broad "parent permission" code and unpacking the variety of attitudes toward parental permission in the text of a manuscript (which we might have done had we planned only qualitative analyses), we subdivided the excerpts under this parent code by creating child codes such as "willing to get parents' permission," "unwilling to get parents' permission," and "unsure." By indicating the valence of these excerpts with different codes in Dedoose, we were able to create easily interpretable mixed methods charts and graphs.

*Analysis.* We used the Training Center to establish interrater reliability ($\kappa \geq .80$), then we analyzed the qualitative data thematically (Braun & Clarke, 2006). By this point, there were numerous codes across all three manuscripts, so we used filters to create and save separate data sets reflecting only those codes and excerpts relevant to the specific manuscript we were preparing. Then, we used Mixed Method bar charts to explore group differences. For the focus group data, we generated Codes × Descriptor bar charts to explore differences in code application frequency by participants' outness to their parents, their age-group, race/ethnicity, and gender identity (see Figure C5.3-2, for an example).

We then reviewed the excerpts from each group by clicking on the corresponding bar in the chart, which enabled us to determine whether those groups discussed the codes in meaningfully different ways. We also used Code Count × Media charts to examine the number of times codes were applied to each participant's transcript (Figure C5.3-3a) and then Code Application matrices (Figure C5.3-3b) to identify whether any participants had a disproportionate impact on how often a particular code emerged. Together, these functions aided in interpreting the data and selecting quotes for manuscripts.

We applied the same mixed methods analytic approach with the parent interview data, but it was not as fruitful, as our sample of 30 parents was too small and homogeneous to make meaningful between-group comparisons. Thus, we took a different approach to mixed methods by reporting parents' responses to quantitative survey measures as a complement to the qualitative data, instead of using the quantitative data to make direct comparisons between groups of parents.

Figure C5.3-2   Codes × Descriptor Bar Chart Showing Differences in Willingness to Get Parent/Guardian Permission by Youth Outness

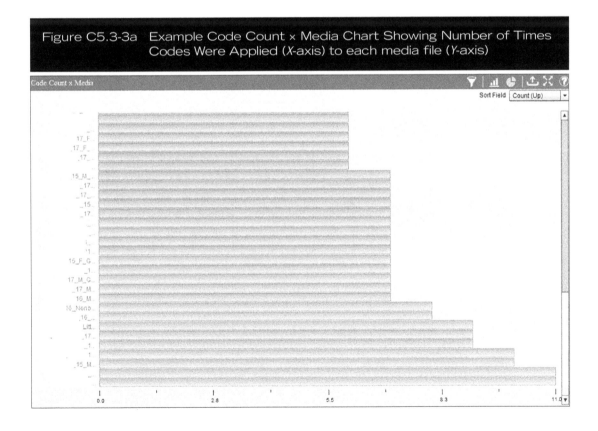

Figure C5.3-3a   Example Code Count × Media Chart Showing Number of Times Codes Were Applied (X-axis) to each media file (Y-axis)

## Figure C5.3-3b Example Code Application Matrix Showing Number of Times Each Participant (*Rows*) Endorsed a Particular Code (*Columns*)

**Code Applications**

| Media | Survey participation - no benefits | Survey participation - no discomfort | Other or coder unsure | Comfort/No Reaction (for | No specific negative | Comfort with survey topics | Private/trustworthy | Survey participation – were there | Made a contribution | ID gaps in knowledge (for | Identified gaps in | Identified topics to discuss | Emotional/psychological | Other or coder unsure | Personal reflection about | Survey participation – were there | Other or coder unsure | Discomfort about past | Concern disclosing illegal | Pressure to give right | Privacy/confidentiality | Totals |
|---|---|---|---|---|---|---|---|---|---|---|---|---|---|---|---|---|---|---|---|---|---|---|
| _14_F_Bi_Out.docx | 1 | 1 | | 1 | | 1 | | | | | | | | | | | | | | | | 4 |
| .17_F_Gay/ | | | | | | | | 2 | | | | | | 2 | | 3 | 2 | 1 | | | 1 | 11 |
| .15_M_Gay_Out.docx | 1 | 1 | | 1 | | 1 | 1 | 1 | 1 | | | | | | | | | | | | | 7 |
| .16_F_QQ_Out.docx | | 2 | | 1 | 1 | 1 | 1 | | | 1 | 1 | | | | | | | | | | | 8 |
| .15_F_GayLes_Not.docx | 1 | 1 | | 1 | | 1 | | | | | | | | | | 1 | | | 1 | | 1 | 7 |
| _17_M_Gay_Not.d | 1 | | | | | | 1 | 1 | | | | | | | 1 | | | | | | | 4 |
| _17_M_Gay_O | 1 | | | | | | 1 | 1 | | | | | | 1 | | | | | | | | 4 |
| _17_M_Gay_Out.docx | 1 | | | 1 | 1 | | | 1 | | 1 | | 1 | 1 | | 1 | 1 | | | | | 1 | 10 |

**BRUCE'S TIP #21**

Frequencies in Dedoose Tables Indicated by Color

Frequencies in all Dedoose tables are mapped to the color spectrum, with lower-frequency cells shaded toward the blue end of the spectrum and higher-frequency cells shaded toward the red end of the spectrum.

## 5.3.5 Reporting the Project

Qualitative and mixed methods manuscripts are sometimes criticized for not showing evidence of methodological rigor. As such, we attempt to address these issues in several ways in our methods and results sections. First, we are explicit about our coding procedures, including the steps we take, the individuals involved, and the reliability testing process in Dedoose in the methods section. In terms of reporting qualitative findings, each time we provide a quote in the manuscript, we label it with the participant's number and relevant demographic characteristics to ensure that a diversity of voices are represented in our results. Relatedly, we utilize a parent code named "Great Quotes" during the coding process, which is not included in any reliability tests, but this enables us to note any particularly illustrative, impactful, or humorous excerpts for use in later publications or presentations and avoid having to search for good examples of quotes for each code after the fact.

In terms of reporting mixed methods findings, we consider group differences as meaningful if (a) those codes are endorsed by a minimum of five different participants and (b) there is at least a 20% difference between groups (Greene, Andrews, Kuper, & Mustanski, 2014; Magee, Bigelow, Dehaan, & Mustanski, 2012). The Codes × Descriptor bar charts make it easy to see whether these criteria are met. We also report group differences using the normalized percentages provided in the bar charts—a function that mathematically accounts for differences in group size. In addition, we typically integrate the mixed methods findings into the qualitative results section to provide context (e.g., "85% of youth who talked about emotional discomfort at the prospect of asking a parent for permission to participate in an HIV research study were not out to their parents. One participant who was not out said . . ."").

Finally, regarding figures and tables, we often provide a table with our coding scheme and definitions, and the number of participants who mentioned each code and/or the number of times participants referenced that code, which we export from Dedoose. The latter number enables readers to see if the frequency of a particular code is driven by multiple mentions of the same code by one or more participants. We also export data from the Descriptor Ratios and the Codes × Descriptor charts into Excel spreadsheets to create tables or figures for publications or presentations.

### 5.3.6 Looking Back

Looking back, there are a few things we might have done differently. We only used a limited number of Dedoose's features for this project. For example, although there is a Memos feature, each team member had their own method of memoing off-line. In the future, it may be useful to keep track of the coding team's thoughts about the data in one central location. In addition, the Project Chat feature enables one to communicate with team members in real time. However, as our coding team was fairly small, there was often only one coder in Dedoose at a time, so having conversations about the data over the phone or in person was more practical for this project. Finally, we could have utilized other mixed methods charts, such as the Descriptor × Descriptor × Code bar charts, to explore more nuanced interaction effects in code endorsement. For example, we could have examined whether the frequency with which certain codes were mentioned were driven by a particular subgroup or differed across subgroups (e.g., Was the number of excerpts coded with "lack of discomfort during survey participation" and "benefits of survey participation" driven substantially more by male youth who were out to their parents versus other youth, like male youth who were not out, or female youth who were out?) This feature could have been useful in focus group study, which had a sample size that might have been large enough to examine such interaction effects.

### 5.3.7 Case Study Conclusion

The interdisciplinary field of SGM adolescent health research is rapidly growing and evolving, and it often requires collaboration with research partners from multiple institutions and from a distance. Moreover, using qualitative and mixed methods enables marginalized populations to have a voice in research that informs their health and well-being, helps researchers better understand the issues faced by contemporary samples of SGM adolescents, and sheds light on how perspectives within this group may differ. For these reasons, Dedoose has been an indispensable tool for our work in SGM adolescent health over the past several years.

*Acknowledgments.* The authors' time and the research described in this case study were supported by a grant from the National Institute of Minority Health and Health Disparities to Brian Mustanski and Celia B. Fisher (R01MD009561).

### 5.3.8 Information About the Case Study Authors

**Kathryn Macapagal**, PhD, is a research assistant professor in the Department of Medical Social Sciences and Institute for Sexual and Gender Minority Health and Wellbeing at Northwestern University. Her research has focused on relationships, sexual health, and HIV prevention among adolescent and young adult men who have sex with men using qualitative, mixed methods, and Internet-based research methods.

**Margaret Matson**, MPH, is a research project coordinator in the Department of Medical Social Sciences and Institute for Sexual and Gender Minority Health and Wellbeing at Northwestern University. Her work has focused on sexual and gender minority adolescent and young adult sexual health and HIV prevention research, intimate partner violence and sexual assault, and qualitative methods and data analysis.

**Brian Mustanski**, PhD, is a professor of medical social sciences, psychiatry and behavioral sciences, and psychology at Northwestern University, Director of the Northwestern University Institute for Sexual and Gender Minority Health and Wellbeing, and codirector of the Third Coast Center for AIDS Research and Center for Prevention Implementation Methodology at Northwestern University. The majority of his research focuses on the health and development of sexual and gender minority youth and the application of new media and technology to sexual health promotion and HIV prevention. His work spans the translational spectrum and includes epidemiological studies, longitudinal cohort studies focused on developmental trajectories and risk/protective mechanisms, the development and testing of HIV interventions, and dissemination/implementation science.

## 5.4 Conclusion

After spending some time thinking about the qualitative piece of your study, now it is time to move on to mixing your study. The next two chapters discuss the challenges in designing and mixing your study design and data analysis to produce meaningful and trustworthy findings.

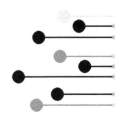

# CHAPTER 6

# Designing Mixed Methods Analysis

## 6.1  Identifying Analysis Strategies

Mixed methods is an emergent research methodology that advances systematic and intentional integration, or "mixing," of qualitative and quantitative data within a single inquiry. When qualitative research or quantitative research limits or hinders your full understanding of a problem, this integration allows a more complete investigation than separate qualitative and quantitative studies. To be successful, you must be knowledgeable and confident in conducting both quantitative and qualitative analyses techniques. Alternatively, collaboration with others who have complementary methods skills can be a successful strategy. You must also know how to mix and even embed these analyses, so that the findings from each component allow you to combine inferences coming from both sets of analyses into one coherent whole (Onwuegbuzie et al., 2009; Tashakkori & Teddlie, 2003). By having a positive attitude toward both qualitative and quantitative methods, researchers are well placed to use qualitative research to inform the quantitative portion of research studies, and vice versa (Onwuegbuzie & Leech, 2005).

Using mixed methods analysis allows you to create a more complex design that seeks more comprehensive understanding of the study focus. When you mix, you get more than just a qualitative and quantitative study; you get a much richer view of the problem under investigation. You collect, analyze, and integrate both quantitative and qualitative data in a social problem under inquiry to address your study focus. This section considers how results can be merged, or integrated, for comparison; how qualitative data explain the quantitative results; or how quantitative results can help explain the qualitative results. Furthermore, what we may learn from qualitative or quantitative analysis can help guide us into the other type of data in ways that may not have been initially apparent to ask potentially new and important questions.

In this chapter, we show you how to use Dedoose to help you discover and explore patterns in your mixed methods data. Using the different tools available in the application, you can drill down into your data to better understand the rich qualitative stories that live beneath the surface.

Assuming that your research problem or question warrants a mixed methods study, we think the core characteristics of a well-designed mixed methods study must include the following:

1. Framing the inquiry using a strong theoretical framework

2. Designing both qualitative and separate quantitative components

3. Designing how to mix these qualitative and quantitative components—for example, either nested, sequential, or concurrent mixed methods designs, as discussed in Chapter 1, which combines the strengths, and overcomes the weaknesses, of a single method design

4. Using systematic and rigorous data gathering and analysis techniques appropriate to the chosen framework

5. Gathering both qualitative and quantitative data

6. Integrating the data during gathering, analysis, and/or discussion

7. Presenting findings drawing on both the qualitative and quantitative components

To help you with your analysis strategies, first list your quantitative and qualitative data sources. Having a clear idea of the data you will be dealing with and what you hope to accomplish as you enter your analytic process will help frame the overall picture of how things will unfold. Then think about the steps you will take to prepare and conduct your analysis: preparing your data, preliminary analysis, and steps to conduct and complete the analysis. While you are thinking about this, consider the skills, time, and resources you have available, and really challenge yourself to be realistic!

**BRUCE'S TIP #22**

Create Diagrams About Your Research

It can be very helpful to draw a diagram of your research design (how you plan to mix your studies), including data gathering, theoretical framework, and analysis strategies. Make sure to keep key research questions and goals in mind throughout the process. *Remember to include the date and save each diagram as your study progresses.* As you find your way through your analysis, it can be very helpful to review this developing thinking.

Regardless of when you gather and analyze your data, Table 6.1 shows some starting points for you to think about as you move into your analysis.

When you have analyzed your data from both the qualitative and quantitative segments of your study, you must integrate the data in an appropriate way to fit with your study design. Integrating your data will allow you to maximize the strengths of each approach, while minimizing weaknesses. Effective integration points can occur during data collection, data coding and analysis, and drawing

### Table 6.1 Working With Your Data

|  | Qualitative Data | Quantitative Data |
| --- | --- | --- |
| Preparing your data | Organizing your data, document management, preparing data for import into data application | Coding your data and assigning numeric values where necessary, preparing data for analysis in data application |
| Exploring | Reading data, memoing, coding | Descriptive analysis, looking for trends and distributions |
| Analyzing | Coding data and assigning labels, looking for related themes, use of data application | Using appropriate statistical tests, using statistical analytic features in Dedoose where applicable or other software, recording of confidence intervals |

meanings or interpreting your data. Successfully integrating your data is how you are able to draw comprehensive conclusions from your work.

At this point, you are probably thinking: "How do I do this?" "Where do I start?" The following discussion shows you a variety of ways to approach these challenges. For now, be thoughtful about your goals, be flexible in thinking how to integrate and analyze your data, and remain focused realistically on the arguments you hope to communicate and can support.

To help you continue your developing thinking about mixed methods, here are some common analytic strategies for the integration of qualitative and quantitative data (Bryman, 2006; Caracelli & Greene, 1993; Onwuegbuzie & Teddlie, 2003):

- *Embedding the Data*

  Using this strategy, here you have to make some choices. Which data set do you consider to be the primary source? Once you have made this decision, the second set of data can be embedded in the first one. For example, the primary data in a project may relate to quantitative data gathered during a clinical trial. You may also have gathered qualitative narrative responses to enhance your data set. These narrative responses can be embedded in your primary data set.

- *Connecting the Data*

  When you are connecting your data, you analyze one set of data and you use your results to guide subsequent data gathering. In this way, you make a connection between the two data sets, but you are not directly comparing the results. This strategy can be used in two-phase projects where data are collected and analyzed sequentially, for example, an action research approach.

- *Data Reduction*

  Here, you reduce the dimensionality of the qualitative data (e.g., via memoing and exploratory thematic analysis) and quantitative data (e.g., via descriptive statistics, exploratory factor analysis, cluster analysis, and transforming data from sets of items to scale scores and from continuous variables to categorical variables).

- *Data Transformation, Consolidation, or Merging*

  Often researchers transform one data set so that it can be compared with the other data set. This conversion or transformation of one data type into the other allows you to then analyze both together:

  o Qualitative data are converted into numeric codes (which can be done using code weights in Dedoose) that can be included with quantitative data in statistical analyses.

  o Quantitative data are transformed into narrative data and included with qualitative data in thematic or pattern analysis.

  o Qualitative and quantitative data are jointly reviewed and consolidated into numerical codes or narrative for purposes of further analysis.

  For example, you might assign numeric codes to the narrative data collected in a qualitative study to enable comparison with the quantitative results. This joint review of both data types allows you to create new or consolidated variables or data sets, which can be expressed in either quantitative or qualitative form. You can then use these consolidated variables or data sets for further analyses.

- *Extreme Case Analysis*

  Identifying extreme, or deviant cases, is a sampling strategy that occurs within the context of and in conjunction with other sampling strategies. "Extreme cases" are unusual cases in the study or cases that are considered outliers. They are identified after some portion of data collection and analysis has been completed. These cases appear to be the "exception to the rule" emerging from the analysis. Once identified, these cases can be investigated through further data gathering or analysis to extend your understanding of any initial explanation for the extreme cases. By seeking out extreme or deviant cases, you can develop a richer, more in-depth understanding of a phenomenon and further strengthen your account of your research and what you are learning.

Good mixed methods studies have distinct, and well-developed, qualitative and quantitative components that are integrated or connected in some intentional way with a sound rationale for doing so. Each strand has its own questions, data, analysis, and interpretations. Data gathering for both components is rigorous using advanced analytic techniques. Meaningful inferences are made from the results of each strand, and procedures promoting trustworthiness of the work are reported (e.g., member checks, triangulation, threats to internal validity, etc.; Creswell & Tashakkori, 2007). Trustworthy mixed methods research integrates or links the strands and describes how this integration has occurred, so it is clear how the conclusions drawn from the two strands provide a fuller understanding of the phenomenon under study. You might integrate your work by comparing, contrasting, building on, or embedding one type of conclusion with the other (Creswell & Tashakkori, 2007; O'Cathain, Murphy, & Nicholl, 2008a).

Having discussed what makes a good mixed methods study and how you might go about mixing your data, it is now time to think about using Dedoose to help you manage your data and carry out your analysis. Basically, the ways in which any REDA assists mixed methods analysis (other than general strategies for the qualitative component) are by

a. allowing contents of a range of different sources to be brought together (using coding) to facilitate complementary analysis;

b. facilitating importing quantitative data, for combination with qualitative data, usually to facilitate comparative analyses based on values of those quantitative variables;

c. identifying and exploring patterns that may draw on qualitative and/or quantitative aspects of the database; and

d. allowing for export of coding information for each case (or source, depending on the structure of the software) as a case by variable table, which can then be imported into statistical software for further processing (Bazeley, 2017).

## 6.2   Using Descriptors

Using descriptors in your analysis can be of great value, but remember, you are not required to use them in your research. While people use different terms for *descriptors*, this term is preferred in Dedoose because they are essentially information that "describes" a research participant or groups of participants and helps the researcher to distinguish between them. For example, ask everyone in the room to answer some questions (i.e., fields or variables). What is your gender? How old are you? What color is your hair? How much do you agree with items like, I love cars, I love dogs, I love Chinese food? Your answers will be unique to you—your descriptor. Furthermore, some of your answers will be the same as others in the room and different from some others in the room. Put them all together, and you have a descriptor set that you can use to group and compare subgroups based on how people responded to the questions.

**BRUCE'S TIP #23**

Using Descriptors

You may not always use descriptors, but it is good to think about whether or not they might strengthen your analysis before you begin.

As a powerful tool, descriptors allow you to break out your qualitative work across demographic and other survey type data for greater insights. When using descriptors in your qualitative data analysis, in addition to being able to analyze media files, you are able to break out the information that describes the sources of your media files to see things from different perspectives and introduce new dimensions to your analysis. Since Dedoose allows for multiple sets of descriptors, you can add as many levels of analysis as your study needs.

As discussed earlier, descriptors are the characteristics of the participants in your research (e.g., individuals, dyads, families) but can also be descriptions of settings in which observations are made (e.g., stores, schools, neighborhoods, cultures). In Dedoose, "Descriptors" are sets of information you use to identify and describe the sources of your media (e.g., documents, video, audio, images).

Descriptors are information that describes the source of your data (e.g., research participants, families, schools, other settings) at a particular level of analysis. The descriptor fields or variables (the term *fields* is used in Dedoose) that constitute each descriptor set may include demographic information, census data, dates, scores from survey measures, test results, and any other information you gather that is useful in describing and distinguishing the source of your media/data—essentially your level(s) of analysis.

- *Topical scope:* statistical study (breadth, population inferences, quantitative, generalizable findings), case study (depth, detail, qualitative, multiple sources of information)

- *Research environment:* field conditions, lab conditions, simulations

- *Descriptive studies:* Who? What? When? Where? How much? Descriptions of population characteristics allow for estimates of characteristic frequency and the discovery of associations among variables.

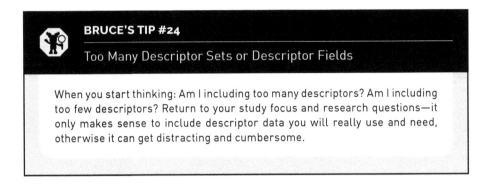

**BRUCE'S TIP #24**

Too Many Descriptor Sets or Descriptor Fields

When you start thinking: Am I including too many descriptors? Am I including too few descriptors? Return to your study focus and research questions—it only makes sense to include descriptor data you will really use and need, otherwise it can get distracting and cumbersome.

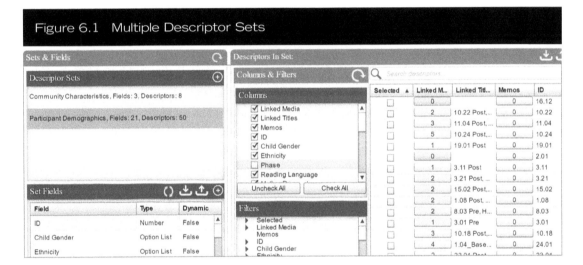

Figure 6.1 Multiple Descriptor Sets

Figure 6.1 shows a study with multiple descriptor sets, one for each different level of the data. Here, some of these descriptor sets can be consolidated into a single set. However, if your research questions only focus on data at the participant level, then the study is more complicated than it needs to be.

For instructions about how to create descriptors, see Section 8.1.1 of Chapter 8.

## 6.2.1 Multiple Descriptors

The use of multiple descriptor sets is ideal for studies that address question(s) that look across different levels of analysis. For example, if a study is comparing student outcomes across different school districts, there might be three levels of data: (1) the district, (2) the schools within each district, and (3) the students within each school. Commonly, different sets of descriptor fields/variables would be collected to distinguish the cases at each level (i.e., district-level fields might include average family annual income, square miles of capture area, percentage of rural vs. urban neighborhoods; school-level fields might include size of student population, student–teacher ratio, percentage of children on free lunch program; and student-level fields might include age, gender, grade level, size of family, language spoken at home, and standardized test scores).

Furthermore, imagine that the study's data come from interviews with parents about the home educational environment. Under these circumstances, each interview could be linked to three descriptor fields or sets: (1) the one specific to their child, (2) one for their child's school, and (3) one for their school district. Dedoose allows exploration of qualitative data and coding activity across multiple descriptor levels. Thus, in a study like this, variations in the qualitative data and coding activity could be explored as a function of district, school, or student fields and combinations of fields across these levels.

## 6.2.2 Dynamic Descriptors

If you are doing a longitudinal study gathering data from the same sources at multiple time points, dynamic descriptors are how you will be separating and organizing these time points. By assigning a field as dynamic, you are allowing it the flexibility of having multiple values based on what media file it is linked to.

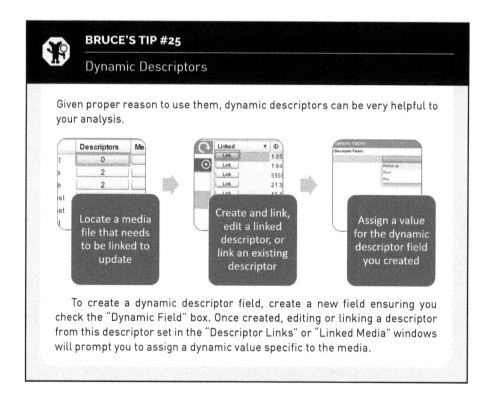

**BRUCE'S TIP #25**

Dynamic Descriptors

Given proper reason to use them, dynamic descriptors can be very helpful to your analysis.

Locate a media file that needs to be linked to update

Create and link, edit a linked descriptor, or link an existing descriptor

Assign a value for the dynamic descriptor field you created

To create a dynamic descriptor field, create a new field ensuring you check the "Dynamic Field" box. Once created, editing or linking a descriptor from this descriptor set in the "Descriptor Links" or "Linked Media" windows will prompt you to assign a dynamic value specific to the media.

Most descriptor data are static, in that the characteristics of research participants usually do not change over the course of a study. Dynamic fields are primarily designed to track change in your data over time in a longitudinal study. Dynamic fields are typically used sparingly, and the values for these fields are set each time a user is linking or editing a static descriptor to media (one-to-many relationship). Once properly linked and assigned to your media, these fields are able to be analyzed as any other static field would be, the main difference being that media linked to the same descriptor can fall into different categories. For example, when analyzing the preinterview option of a given dynamic descriptor field, you would only be viewing analysis sourced from media in the preinterview phase of your study, as opposed to all media linked to a specific participant's descriptor.

In this section, we have talked about strategies for mixing your research design and analysis and about descriptors. Using descriptors takes you beyond coding and allows the researcher to categorize their data in different ways. You may not always use descriptors, but it is good to think about whether or not they might strengthen your analysis before you begin.

## 6.3   Topic Modeling

Rapid advances in technology continue to challenge the role of the researcher in the analysis process. To support these changes, Dedoose is developing an interactive topic modeling engine prototype. This approach to analysis is driven by human interaction with the algorithmic model, both training and leading the inquiry. This new functionality will likely be embedded and integrated into the Dedoose environment in 2020. Although this function is not yet available, the following discussion about using topic modeling as your approach to mixed methods data analysis offers valuable insight into how you might develop your analysis thinking. Also, by giving thoughtful consideration to how you approach topic modeling analysis, you can better assess your overall skills in mixed methods research.

This different type of analysis develops through the research supervising iterative interactions with the topic model algorithm that produces the data analysis model. The researcher can then evaluate the model and give feedback about the analysis, which the algorithm then integrates into its processes and presents a new model for review. The researcher can keep running these iterative cycles until they are satisfied with the results. See Section 6.3.4 for more details on this interactive process.

### 6.3.1 Background

Qualitative and mixed methods researchers are increasingly using data apps with the intention of improving the quality and efficiency of analysis. Early attempts by developers to respond to this growing interest has introduced a range of technology tools. Examples include word frequency count, auto-code by theme, auto-code by sentiment, and automatic grouping of similar sentences for cluster extraction.

Caution is warranted, however, when using any automated app function such as these to analyze data en masse. Despite its attractiveness and convenience, automation may distance or remove the researcher from the analytic process. One consequence of this distancing or removal is the limitations placed on the researcher's ability to monitor or evaluate results. This critical limitation would possibly allow the introduction of various coding errors being introduced into the project data. The challenges and pitfalls of these tools are therefore of serious methodological concern.

Discussed here are some concerns about what technology can provide from the perspective of sound qualitative and mixed methods design, implementation, and rigor. Despite their possible shortcomings, there are many reasons a researcher may desire a technological assist. Efficiency in managing large amounts of data and calls for transparency and quality in analysis are at the forefront of this trend. As a result, efforts have been made by some developers to provide this functionality. For example, qualitative data products such as NVivo, QDA Miner, Max QDA, and Atlas.ti offer features for sentiment analysis, topic detection, language detection, keyword extraction, and entity extraction. Web-based services such as MonkeyLearn also offer text analysis with machine learning to turn tweets, emails, documents, webpages, and more into actionable data. They promote a business model for automated processes intended to save hours of manual data processing.

How well these features work depends on the nature of data involved, which can include sets of open-ended narrative interviews, responses to more structured survey questions, social media streams, news and other articles, and archival documents. What do these features do well and what limitations exist? How does such activity affect the quality or depth of one's analysis? What may be coming next?

Software developers are continuously exploring new ways in which digital tools can immerse the qualitative researcher in a deeper, more personal, connection with the data. Technology offers pathways of connecting a wide range of senses with the analysis process. Imagine hearing the voices and seeing the setting from multiple views while you code the text.

Developing an informative and comprehensive code system for a project is central to producing rigorous and valuable research or evaluation project findings. Under most circumstances, and certainly historically, this was a person-based process and there are a variety of approaches to identifying themes in qualitative data that will best serve a project's goals (Ryan & Bernard, 2003). However, with the advent of technologies to support this work, developers have searched for ways to automate this process as much as possible, removing the manual burden of reading text, identifying themes/codes, determining meaningful segments, and then applying codes. The first efforts to address this challenge focused on the ability of computer systems and programs to identify keywords, entities, and sentiment in natural language. In general, this coding process is one of classification. That is, researchers try to group what is found as meaningful information contained within qualitative data into a pattern or theme that helps in understanding the multiple meanings represented in the data. Attempts to automate this process rely on the capabilities of computer-based classification systems, often referred to as text mining, machine learning, and natural language processing. Much of this work relies on the identification of word and word phrase frequencies and probabilities. While this work shows great promise, it is generally understood that natural language is complicated when considering how words are used in different contexts, for example, sarcasm, local vernacular, and the use of metaphor introducing complications that can be lexical, syntactic, semantic, and pragmatic (Anjali & Babu Anto, 2014). In describing the relative effectiveness of existing tools, "looking at these products it is clear that any sort of truly automated processing of text is in the future, except in some highly restricted domains where controlled vocabularies can be used" (Blank, 2008, p. 547).

## 6.3.2 Modes of Inquiry

As an illustration of the utility of these tools, this section presents the results of a pilot project using MonkeyLearn as a tool to critically explore features for keyword, key phrase, and entity extraction, sentiment analysis, and subsequent auto-coding. A review of the current state of these automated functions frames the discussion with particular attention on the use of these features, what they can offer the end user, and where they might be misused.

For this pilot project, MonkeyLearn (https://monkeylearn.com), a web-based services for text mining and automatic categorization, was integrated into the Dedoose data management and analysis environment. A total of 17,389 *American Journal of Public Health* abstracts were processed and auto-coded in Dedoose. The results included 2,178 codes, which represented 240 entities (137 locations, 10 people, and 93 organizations), 1,934 keywords (or key phrases), and 4 sentiments. These "codes" were automatically applied 72,725 times to 27,896 independent excerpts. Without question, this was a tremendous processing feat that was completed within a matter of minutes. However, from the perspective of what represents high-quality and rigorous qualitative research methods, the results were far from satisfactory and of little immediate usefulness.

A preliminary examination of the results revealed, for example, that among the 1,934 keyword or key phrase codes identified, each needed to be found three or more times in the total corpus to emerge. Thus, auto-coding provided a reasonable job of word, entity, person, and sentiment classification (Namey, Guest, Thairu, & Johnson, 2008) based on the presence, or absence, of words and word phrases. However, results from the pilot study show that an efficient process is needed to reduce the overall number of codes into a useful and manageable system.

The pilot project also examined meanings based on context and related thematic decisions about code definition and application. Results identified 27,896 excerpts with one or more codes that required further analysis. Coding based on only the presence of words or word phrases is likely to classify an overwhelming number of excerpts into a system where a human would not be fully satisfied with the results from a contextual perspective. Thus, to thoroughly "clean" the data set, each excerpt must be reviewed, and any inappropriate codes removed.

That said, there are certainly many controls, like stop word and synonym lists, and minimal criteria for defining codes based on words or word phrases that could have been put into place prior to data processing that would have significantly improved the initial automated results. Nonetheless, from a purely qualitative methodological lens and consideration of the complexity of natural language, the research community must take care when conclusions are drawn from findings where auto-coding is based on keywords, entity, and sentiment extraction alone.

### 6.3.3 Recent Developments

Fortunately, there is promise in more recent developments within the computer science community around topic modeling in qualitative research. Topic modeling is a rapidly developing area in machine learning, text mining, and natural language processing. Particularly at a time when researchers are looking to harness the value of "big data," there is a great deal of exploration into how these models can be used in many areas of inquiry, including the social sciences. Topic modeling aims to automatically identify "topics"—that is, organizational (semantic) structures within a corpus of documents (or set of excerpts from documents)—that reveal key themes around which the corpus can be understood (e.g., Latent Dirichlet Allocation; Blei, Ng, & Jordan, 2003). From a technical perspective, the process relies on the probabilities that words co-occur within individual documents in the overall corpus. For example, in a set of summaries about animals, the words "feline," "fur," "lick," and "purr" were often found in the same summaries and the words "scale," "swim," "water," and "fin" often occurred together. A topic model might identify two distinct classes, of which a person might identify one class as including "cats" and "fish." This may seem oversimplistic, but algorithms for learning topic models are designed to exploit these word co-occurrence structures and find the topics that best describe and organize the corpus of documents. The resulting topics are distributions over the entire vocabulary of words but can also be used to obtain a representation of each document as a distribution over topics. Essentially, a text mining approach is to identify, on a probability basis, how likely it is for sets of words to occur within individual documents. Furthermore, while individual documents will often fall into multiple topics, they will do so with greater or lesser probability. Fundamentally, like qualitative content or thematic coding, topic modeling is a data reduction strategy. It seeks to understand and reduce the number of dimensions or themes across an underlying or latent organizational structure categorizing the important meanings expressed through the natural language in documents.

The application of topic modeling in traditional qualitative and mixed methods research is both promising and challenging. The promise includes the possibility of far more rapid organization of "big data" where unstructured text is in play and, perhaps, the ability for an investigator to argue that a less subjectively defined conceptual framework has been discovered given a purely word-based derivation of the classification system. This "out-of-the-box" application of topic modeling is far more sophisticated than auto-coding based on word and entity frequencies or sentiment ratings as can be found in other contemporary software. Furthermore, as these models are mathematically derived and essentially arbitrary with respect to the real "meanings" conveyed in natural language, it is often the case that topics found by the algorithm don't satisfy the needs of the researcher performing the analysis. Another factor is the nature of the data involved. Again, like many mathematical models, the more data there are to build the model, the better the likely outcome. So these algorithms perform better where the corpus of data is enormous. However, in many areas of social science research, data sets are often relatively small. Thus, the challenge of "thinner" data in many academic research projects presents a unique challenge that must be addressed if there will be any confidence in the results of a study using topic modeling.

As work to build a useful topic modeling feature in Dedoose has progressed, both larger and smaller data set circumstances have been kept in mind and guided the design of a modeling engine and interface that will serve a wide range of circumstances. More recently, there have been various developments in interactive topic modeling, an area that explores ways with which the user can shape the resulting topics according to their needs in interactive ways. These developments include the idea of machine learning, supervised learning, and iterative topic modeling. If communities of qualitative researchers consider embracing the use of statistical algorithms in their work, there must be an adequate level of transparency in the procedures and, at best, clear levels of human control. More recent developments into working and refining topics such as "tuning," "splitting," and "removing" topics may offer the researcher this transparency and control, thus instilling the trust that researchers strive to attain to have confidence in the methodological rigor in our work (Gibbs et al., 2002; Patton, 2015; Poulis & Dasgupta, 2017; Salmona & Kaczynski, 2016; St. John & Johnson, 2000).

In short, given the insights that can be provided after running a topic model, researchers, with their unique human ability to interpret meaning in context and avoid the inherent limitations of simple keyword-based or other classification approach (Cambria & White, 2014), can train and tune the model by providing feedback in a variety of forms. The model can then learn from this feedback and be rerun and retuned iteratively until an acceptable, coherent, and interpretable structure has been defined and applied. From that point forward, the researcher can articulate the structure of the model and have confidence in subsequent classification of new data as determined by the algorithm. Topic model processing can provide a variety of information to allow for evaluation and inform areas for tuning and refining the model. For example, a model can be presented that shows top words and documents (excerpts) for each topic as well as the probability a document is well-represented by each topic. These results that both organize the documents and provide insights into the organizational structure of the model are ideal for a researcher to interact with, evaluate, and enhance the model. As the model further tuned and trained, the model itself is taught and can be run again iteratively through an evaluation, feedback, and retraining cycle until it meets the needs of the researcher.

## 6.3.4 Training the Model

From a qualitative data analysis perspective, Namey et al. (2008) remind us of two general approaches to data reduction: content and thematic. Content analysis is focused primarily on the presence and frequency of words and phrases toward understanding meaning in text data. Toward this end, computers have been found very useful in generating word/phrase counts, and appropriate software can be capitalized on to automate the tagging of content based on these counts. However, given the complexity of natural language, this approach has been criticized because it does not take context into consideration. In addition, a great deal of error can be introduced when using automated tagging software features.

In contrast, thematic coding involves investigator development of sets of codes based on implicit and explicit themes discovered and applied to content in the context of the source text. Ideally, both approaches can be used in any analysis exercise. This is often the case as researchers iteratively move from the raw text to the development of more latent ideas/interpretations and back again as a full code system evolves and stabilizes before a full application of the system to the data set takes place.

The interactive topic modeling engine prototype currently being developed for Dedoose includes features for the human "tuning/teaching" as described above. Such capability addresses many of the shortcomings and concerns described and, at the same time, capitalizes both on the power of what the software can offer alongside human input into determining how the model behaves and what it can ultimately produce.

Consider what interactive and iterative topic modeling might look like (see Figure 6.2) and how a topic modeling feature in Dedoose would function. Ultimately, the goal of topic modeling in any form is to serve as an efficient data reduction activity. During Stage 1, the researcher interrogates, interacts with, and trains the model. Once the researcher is happy with the model, it can be run during Stage 2 on the entire data set, where topics and meanings can be extracted.

From a practical standpoint, the first step to using the Dedoose topic modeling engine would be to prepare your text. If using short answers from a survey, your

## Figure 6.2  Topic Modeling: Training the Model

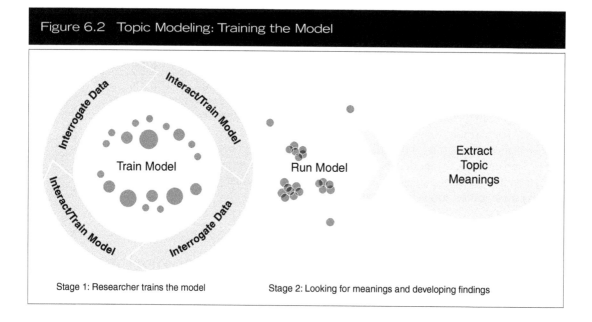

Interrogate Data

Interact/Train Model

Interact/Train Model

Interrogate Data

Train Model

Run Model

Extract Topic Meanings

Stage 1: Researcher trains the model          Stage 2: Looking for meanings and developing findings

data are already prepared and can be imported directly to the system. If not, some criteria for parsing running text needs to be defined and then applied to all documents to create the excerpts that will be processed by the model. Once your data are ready and imported, you'll work through the following steps to generate and train your model:

1. Select an initial number of topics to be generated.

2. Explore top words, salient words, and top documents for each topic, and then take steps to train the model. This training can include the following:

   a. Removing words and/or documents (excerpts) and rerunning the model with those items excluded

   b. Splitting topics, which allows you to create some number of subtopics through a manual assignment of documents (excerpts) from the topic being split onto the subtopics, and then rerunning the model accordingly

   c. Reviewing removed words/documents and determining if they can be returned to an active role

   d. Merging topics

   e. Manually moving documents from one topic to another without the need to split

3. Run the final version of the trained model, export your results (at least until the engine is fully integrated into Dedoose), name your topics, and have all excerpts automatically coded based on the defined criteria.

Using topic modeling in data applications is still in an early stage. Look at the Dedoose website to find updates about how this has been integrated into Dedoose.

## 6.4 Case Study: Integrating Mixed Data in a Longitudinal Study

**THINK ABOUT, AND ANSWER, THESE QUESTIONS AS YOU READ THE CASE STUDY**

1. How did this research team use descriptors to help manage longitudinal, multisource data sets? What are some ideas that you might use in your study?

2. How did the research team members integrate their data? What are some strategies for integrating (managing and analyzing) qualitative and quantitative data across time points that you might use in your study?

*(Continued)*

(Continued)

3.  In a database that has multiple sources of data over time (i.e., different types of data, different reporters), what are some strategies you can use to manage the data to facilitate analysis across data sources?

## Integrating Qualitative and Quantitative Data in a Longitudinal Study of Youth–Adult Relationships: A Practical Example Using Dedoose

### Nancy L. Deutsch, Haley E. Johnson, & Mark Vincent B. Yu

In this case study, we begin with an overview of the Youth–Adult Relationships (YAR) study and describe how we set up a database in Dedoose to manage the data. We discuss the ways in which Dedoose was used to facilitate qualitative and mixed data analysis, reflect on the strengths and challenges of the application for our purposes, and consider what we may have done differently in retrospect. We focus on some of the challenges of integrating our data, such as their longitudinal, multireporter nature; the volume of data, and number of researchers and analytic projects; choices about how to use quantitative data in relation to the qualitative data; and the use of codes for both organizational and interpretive purposes.

YAR is a longitudinal, mixed methods study of adolescents' relationships with important nonparental adults. Spanning more than 3 years, a variety of quantitative and qualitative methods, and multiple researchers, the study seeks to understand the role of supportive youth–adult relationships (aka VIPs) in adolescent development. We focus on five areas of inquiry: (1) understanding how youth develop and sustain relationships with nonparental adults, (2) the characteristics of those relationships and adults whom youth identify as important, (3) how relationships with different adults provide different types of social support, (4) whether and how youth's relationships with adults in one setting influence youth's interactions in other contexts, and (5) whether and how relationships with important adults are associated with youth outcomes over time.

### 6.4.1 Setting Up the Project

The YAR research team is multilevel and over time has included one faculty and two postdoctoral investigators, three project managers, and multiple doctoral, masters, and undergraduate research assistants (RAs). Although we are located in a single geographic space, we bring different lenses to the project and work from different computers, making the teamwork features of Dedoose critical. Data collection occurred across more than 3 years, analysis is ongoing, and researchers cycled in and out of the project, making documentation and training procedures essential. Furthermore, YAR has multiple data sources (interviews, surveys, social network maps), types of participants (youth, parents, VIPs), and time points (five total). The data set includes a total of 311 interview transcripts from youth, parents, and VIPs as well as quantitative data from surveys taken before each interview (data are described further below). Dedoose was used as the primary tool for organizing and analyzing our interview data, which was uploaded as transcripts in text form, and for mixed methods analysis.

After interviews were transcribed, the transcripts were prepared for upload into Dedoose. To reduce the need for editing transcripts individually in Dedoose, we used a three-step process to format transcripts prior to upload:

1. First, we checked transcripts for accuracy.

2. Second, we de-identified transcripts. Dedoose's platform is HIPAA (Health Insurance Portability and Accountability Act of 1996) compliant and meets the security standards for data storage required by institutional review boards, but we replaced names with pseudonyms both for ease of analysis and for an extra layer of protection.

3. Third, we ensured that there were no extraneous spaces between sentences. This avoids difficult to read output when exporting data from Dedoose into Microsoft Word and Excel.

A consistent naming process was used for all transcripts to organize the data: "Participant pseudonym-Time point-Participant Code#-Date." For parents and VIPs, a "P" or a "V" was included after the Participant Code number to denote that it was a parent or VIP interview (e.g., Frau-T1-7678464-V-7.1.14). A project manager was responsible for cleaning and uploading all transcripts to ensure consistency.

We used one Dedoose project to house both the overall study and individual researchers' analyses. Our coding and descriptor structures differentiate project-wide data and categories from those generated for individual researchers' projects (see Figure C6.4-1). When a user adds codes or descriptors to Dedoose for an individual project, the first level (i.e., "parent") code or descriptor category is labeled with the researcher's name or project title (e.g., "Yu Dissertation").

Researchers use Dedoose's "Database" feature to select only the codes or media that they need for their project or analytic task. Users can access any analysis done to date and still screen out unneeded information. This is key for a longitudinal project with multiple time points, sources of data, researchers, and topics of inquiry.

## 6.4.2 Data Sources

The YAR study had two phases of data collection (see Figure C6.4-2). Phase 1 was a survey of 289 youth from which we selected a subsample of 41 youth (20 middle schoolers and 21 high schoolers). In Phase 2, we followed those 41 youth for 3 years. Here, we focus on Phase 2, the phase that included longitudinal, mixed methods data, and for which we utilized Dedoose.

Figure C6.4-1   Excerpt of the Coding Structure of the YAR Study

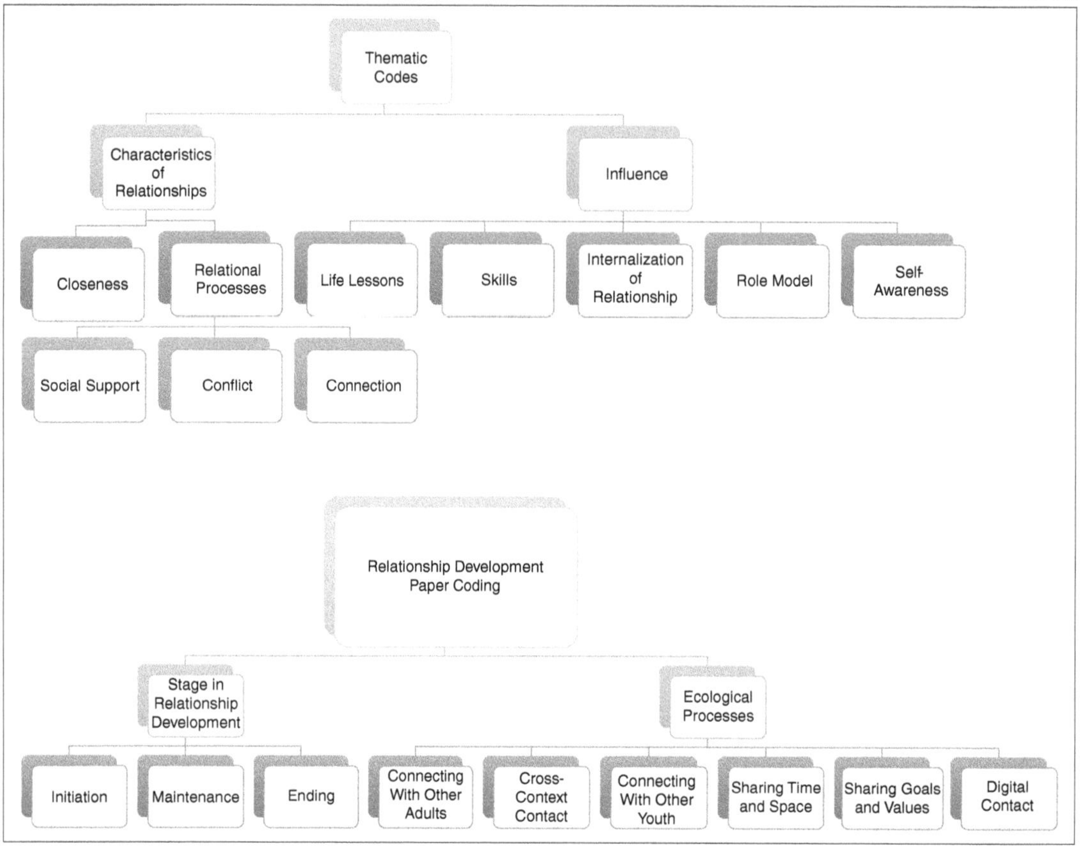

*Note:* Hierarchical nature of code system as shown. YAR = youth–adult relationships.

We surveyed and interviewed the 41 youth five times over the 3 years. Preinterview surveys were administered to participants online through Qualtrics. They included basic demographic information, presence of and closeness to VIPs, and a variety of scales, including measures of Positive Youth Development (PYD; Geldhof et al., 2014), social support (Vaux, 1988), relational styles (Experiences in Close Relationship Scale [ECR]; Wei, Russell, Mallinckrodt, & Vogel, 2007), self-esteem (Shoemaker, 1980), and protective factors (Phillips & Springer, 1992). Semistructured interviews included questions about the youth and their relationships with adults. In each interview, we provided a definition of "significant adult" (aka VIP) and asked if the youth had someone in their life who fit that description. If so, the youth was asked a series of questions about that relationship. If youth named a different VIP at a subsequent interview, we also asked about their previous VIP and

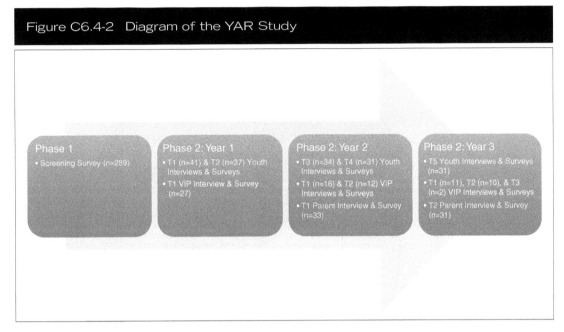

**Phase 1**
- Screening Survey (n=289)

**Phase 2: Year 1**
- T1 (n=41) & T2 (n=37) Youth Interviews & Surveys
- T1 VIP Interview & Survey (n=27)

**Phase 2: Year 2**
- T3 (n=34) & T4 (n=31) Youth Interviews & Surveys
- T1 (n=16) & T2 (n=12) VIP Interviews & Surveys
- T1 Parent Interview & Survey (n=33)

**Phase 2: Year 3**
- T5 Youth Interviews & Surveys (n=31)
- T1 (n=11), T2 (n=10), & T3 (n=2) VIP Interviews & Surveys
- T2 Parent Interview & Survey (n=31)

*Note:* YAR = youth–adult relationships.

why that relationship was no longer significant. At the last time points, we asked youth about their identities and goals and to reflect on all the VIP relationships they had discussed during the study.

During Interviews 1, 3, and 5, youth made social network maps, depicting different contexts of their lives and the peers and adults they interact with in those settings (see Figure C6.4-3; Hirsch, Deutsch, & DuBois, 2011). The maps included both quantitative and qualitative data; youth rated how close they felt to each person and responded to open-ended questions about the relationships on their map. Once during the study, youth made pie charts (illustrating the percentage of their interactions with adults that they would describe as positive, negative, and neutral) and graphs (plotting their relationships with their parents, best friend, and VIP in terms of levels of trust, closeness, and importance over time). The network maps were converted to quantitative data and entered in our master SPSS database. These data may be uploaded to Dedoose as descriptors for mixed methods analysis in the future. The graphs, maps, and pie charts may also be uploaded as images into Dedoose for coding as research questions drawing on those data emerge. Of particular interest will be the ability to link the sections of interviews where youth are describing their maps, graphs, and pie charts with the images themselves.

The social network map is broken up into six "slices" representing different contexts in which youth may interact with adults (e.g., family, school, neighborhood). Each youth writes their name in the middle of the map. They were

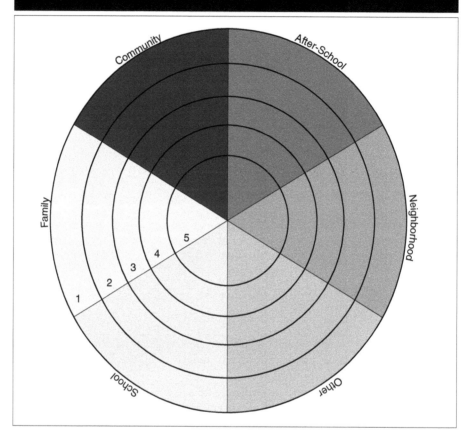

Figure C6.4-3    Social Network Map

then provided with two different colored sticky notes—one for adults and one for peers. Youth were asked to place adults and peers on the map in the context in which they interact with them and at the numbered level that represented how close they felt to the person, with 5 being the closest and 1 being the least close. The names on this image are covered to protect the confidentiality of the participants and the people on their map.

We surveyed and interviewed youth's parents twice during the study and the nominated VIPs up to three times. We followed up with previous VIPs when possible. The surveys were used to assess characteristics of the adults (e.g., self-esteem, self-efficacy, relational style). The open-ended interviews focused on the adults' relationships with the study youth, with youth in general, and their own experiences with mentors.

## 6.4.3 Data Management

We used descriptors and codes to organize and reduce the data, making it easier to navigate the large volume of data and prepare the data for deeper levels of analysis based on specific research questions.

### 6.4.3.1 Descriptors: Organizing Data and Utilizing the Mixed Methods Features

Each transcript, when it was uploaded to Dedoose, was assigned a number of descriptors to categorize and describe the data and the participants (see Figure C6.4-4).

We used three organizational descriptors to facilitate sorting data in different ways: (1) Youth Anchor, (2) Wave, and (3) Participant Type. Because each youth had multiple data sources (up to five youth interviews; two parent interviews; 0–3 VIPs, each of whom was interviewed up to three times), we tagged each interview with the "Youth Anchor" descriptor to identify the youth participant with which it was associated. This allowed us to easily access all the data on a particular participant. For example, if we wanted to review all of Bob's data, we could use the "Youth Anchor > Bob" descriptor to quickly pull all his interviews, all his VIPs' interviews, and all his parents' interviews.

"Wave" referred to the period of data collection, sorting transcripts by time point. This allowed us to look for developmental patterns, something we discuss further below. It also provided quick access to all the data from a particular wave, which is important because different topics were discussed at different time points. For example, at Wave 4, we asked youth about their identity. A researcher who wanted to focus on youth identity could use the wave descriptor to quickly select the Wave 4 transcripts for analysis.

Finally, we tagged interviews by Participant Type (i.e., youth, parent, VIP). This facilitated selection of data from specific types of participants (e.g., all VIP interviews). It also enabled us to use Dedoose's "Codes × Descriptor" analysis function to compare data and codes across participant types (e.g., comparing how youth vs. VIPs talk about "closeness").

Descriptors also provide a tool for exploring interactions between our quantitative and qualitative data. To create descriptors from our quantitative data, we cleaned the survey data in SPSS and imported it into Dedoose. We found that the most effective way to use our quantitative variables in Dedoose was to create "high" (1 *SD* or more above the mean), "middle" (within 1 *SD* of the mean), and "low" (1 *SD* or more below the mean) groupings for each variable. We could then use Dedoose's analysis tools (e.g., the "Codes × Descriptor" chart) to compare patterns across participants more efficiently than with individual mean scores. This may not be ideal for every scale, but we used it as a starting point to examine descriptive patterns. Researchers can then create more nuanced descriptors as needed.

## Figure C6.4-4   Descriptor Organizational Chart and Example Descriptors in YAR Study

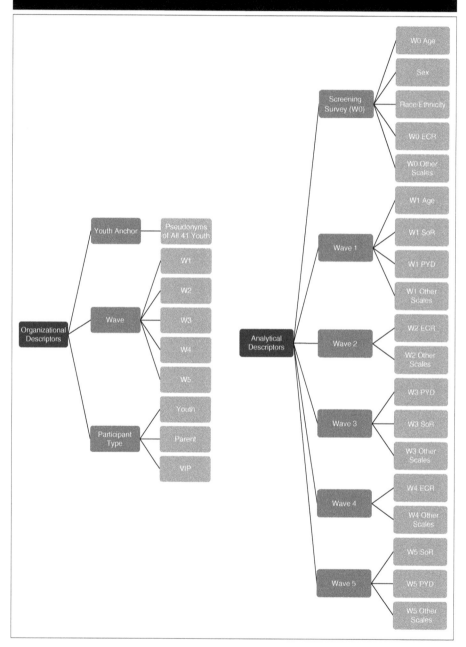

*Note:* YAR = youth–adult relationships.

When a youth interview transcript was uploaded to Dedoose, it was tagged with the descriptors from that youth's screening (W0) survey (e.g., ECR, PYD). These data serve as baseline youth characteristics. Each interview was also tagged with the descriptors from that Wave's survey. For example, a Youth Wave 3 interview would be tagged with both the screening (W0) survey and the Wave 3 survey descriptors. Tagging all youth interviews with baseline and time point–specific descriptors allows us to compare data based on youths' initial or current characteristics and to explore change over time.

## 6.4.3.2 Coding

Our coding structure includes two types of codes (Miles, Huberman, & Saldana, 2014): (1) descriptive codes, which label the topic of an excerpt based on its content (e.g., relationship with VIP), and (2) interpretive codes, which apply meaning to the excerpt in relation to the researcher's conceptual frames (e.g., social support). Initial codes were developed based on our research questions and important constructs from the literature (e.g., adult's relationship to youth; context of relationship; characteristics of the relationship such as closeness, conflict, and types of interactions; characteristics of people; influence and outcomes). We created three categories of codes to organize our data: (1) question codes (descriptive), (2) who codes (descriptive), and (3) initial thematic codes (descriptive and interpretive). We also created codes for "great quotes" (as recommended by Dedoose). These codes served as organizational buckets into which we sorted data for analysis in relationship to specific research questions. We keep track of codes in a codebook in Excel, where each category of code has its own tab with definitions and examples.

*Question Coding.* Coding the data by interview question is useful for data reduction and allows us to easily access all youth's responses to a given question. Each transcript was broken into excerpts using codes representing the interview time point and question number (e.g., T1-Q1). If someone is interested in understanding how youth define closeness, for example, the researcher can start by pulling all the data related to the interview question "How do you define feeling close to someone?" (T2-Q44). The question codes are applied as their own excerpts, separately from thematic coding.

*Who Coding.* The "who" code identifies the person about whom an interviewee is speaking. We coded for both the person's role within our study (e.g., VIP, peer, other adult) and their relationship to the youth (e.g., parent, sibling, school-based adult, nonfamilial peer). Our "who" code tree includes child codes identifying whether an adult is a current or past VIP and the time point at which the VIP was nominated (e.g., Current T1, T2 VIP, etc., see coding table). This facilitates data reduction, allowing researchers to select only the data that are relevant for their questions. For example, if a researcher wants to examine how youth are describing their VIP relationships at Time 3, they can select all the data coded as "Who → Role → Current VIP → Current T3." If a researcher wants to look at how youth at Time 4 describe *past* VIP relationships, they can create a data set of transcripts tagged with the Wave 4 descriptor and select data tagged as "Who → Role → VIP Relationships → T1 VIP and T2 VIP and T3 VIP." This time-specific VIP coding became necessary as we added waves of data and realized that we needed a way to differentiate conversations about current and past VIPs. Like the "question" codes, "who" codes were applied as their own data excerpts to reduce the cognitive load on researchers, who applied the "who" codes in large excerpts during an initial read through of the data. This does pose challenges for searching the data for coding overlap, however, an issue we discuss below.

*Initial Thematic Coding.* Our thematic coding scheme was developed through a series of inductive and deductive practices (see Futch Ehrlich, Deutsch, Fox, Johnson, & Varga, 2016, for more details). Thematic codes were applied to smaller excerpts of the transcripts than the "who" or "question" codes during a second, in-depth reading. We initially planned to train RAs on the coding protocol, ensure intercoder reliability, and have coders individually code the interview transcripts. We set up a coding training in Dedoose, with the principal investigator and the coprincipal investigator as the master coders. However, because of the nature of our coding process (e.g., coding large excerpts with the "who" code before tagging smaller excerpts with thematic codes) and the structure of the Training Center (which offers up excerpts in a random order and doesn't take into account overlapping excerpts), the training infrastructure didn't work for our needs. Instead, we set up a separate project in Dedoose in which new RAs were trained and could practice thematic coding. The training database allowed RAs to become comfortable in Dedoose and with our data, without compromising the master database. RAs could familiarize themselves with our coding norms by going through the transcripts with the coding visible. They could also practice coding by turning off existing coding in the data set selector, creating and coding excerpts themselves, and then comparing them with the existing coding. After reviewing the codebook, reading through existing coded transcripts, and discussing coding at team meetings, RAs would independently code a transcript with the existing coding turned off. Codes would then be compared and discussed at a team meeting. After multiple rounds of whole-team coding training, we assigned two RAs to each interview transcript.

RAs coded transcripts independently, using Dedoose's data set feature to select only themselves as a user so they could not see the other RA's coding. After both RAs coded a transcript, they met and compared their coding, reconciled any discrepancies (see Hill et al., 2005, for discussion of consensus coding), and deleted one of their sets of codes so that each interview had one complete set of coding. Any discrepancies that they could not reconcile through discussion or which they were unsure about were brought to the full team for discussion.

### 6.4.3.3 Naming Protocols in Dedoose: Advice for Facilitating Data Management

Data management is facilitated by clear and consistent protocols for document and code naming. We developed the following suggestions for naming based on our experiences with our database. First, be purposeful in assigning names to your media (i.e., documents, video, etc.) when you upload your data to Dedoose. Using a thoughtful naming protocol can make it easier to sort your media in ways that are useful to your project. For example, we named our transcripts starting with the participant name to allow for easily sorting data by participant, as the participant is the "anchor" in our study and the most common way we want to scan our data. Second, when developing code names, be sure each one is distinct. It becomes difficult to distinguish data if codes share the same name. For example, in our thematic coding, we coded for emotional support a theme that runs throughout our interviews. But we also ask an interview question about emotional support. Because of how we initially labeled the question and thematic codes, when we exported data into Excel, we had two columns labeled "emotional." This was confusing, and as a result, we renamed the codes.

## 6.4.4 Analysis Processes

We began analysis following the first wave of youth interviews and used ongoing reflections and discussions to shape our analysis in response to emerging questions and findings. Our team met weekly to discuss analytic tasks (e.g., coding questions and reconciliation). We had biannual data retreats in which we spent 1 to 2 days looking at data, identifying emerging themes and questions, discussing findings, and planning next steps for analysis. As researchers on our team pursued different research questions, they used the initial coding in Dedoose to select the data relevant to their question and conduct further analysis. Below, we provide three examples of what this looks like in practice.

*Cross-Sectional Mixed Methods Analysis.* Early on in the study, we noticed that youth were not always describing their relationships with their VIPs as "close" in the ways that we expected. We decided to use the T1 interview data to examine how youth define closeness in VIP relationships. To do this, we needed to select all the data that had been coded as both "closeness" and "T1 VIP" from the T1 youth interviews and create a data set with those excerpts. We faced a challenge in this, however, as "who" (i.e., VIP) and "thematic" (i.e., closeness) codes were applied in different excerpts (as described above). To address this, we developed a system to export data and isolate overlapping data excerpts that were coded as both closeness and T1 VIP.

First, we selected the T1 VIP and Closeness codes using the Dataset function. Then, we used the Code Co-Occurrence feature in the Analyze function, selected "include overlapping excerpts," and exported those data to Excel. We read through the excerpts in Excel and deleted any irrelevant data (e.g., large excerpts coded as T1 VIP but not closeness). We then exported relevant excerpts to Word for holistic read-throughs to identify emerging themes. This was a stylistic preference on our part. This read through could have been done in Dedoose, but the researchers conducting the inductive analysis felt more comfortable reading through data in Word or on paper to develop the codes before applying codes in Dedoose. After the themes were identified and defined, RAs returned to Dedoose and coded the data for those themes. Finally, we used the "Code × Descriptor" function to examine patterns of difference in youth's descriptions of closeness for youth who were high, average, and low on connectedness, one of the scales from the T1 survey (see Futch Ehrlich et al., 2016).

A similar type of analysis was conducted by the third author (Yu et al., 2019), who used descriptors to sort youth into groups representing more positive and more negative attachment styles (based on their ECR scores from the screening survey). He then compared the groups on the prevalence of five types of social support (Wills & Shinar, 2000), as coded for in the interview transcripts. He found differences in the prevalence of emotional and validation support between youth with more positive and youth with more negative attachment styles. Therefore, he selected data excerpts coded for emotional and validation support and worked with a team of RAs to read through the data and identify themes, for which they coded in Dedoose. Youth with positive and negative attachment styles were again compared, this time on the prevalence of the themes identified within emotional and validation support.

*Longitudinal Data Analysis With Between- and Within-Youth Comparisons.* Currently, we are analyzing youth perspectives on the development, maintenance, ending, and impact of relationships across time. We began by selecting all the youth interview data, from all five time points, that have been coded as Story of Relationship. We developed an initial codebook based on the literature and our knowledge of the data and refined it through three researchers reading the data, discussing the codes, and separating and merging codes until agreement was reached on a final set of codes and definitions. We then attempted to apply the codes in Dedoose. In doing so, however, all three researchers agreed that because excerpts appeared in a random order for coding, we were losing the developmental narrative of the relationships, which was part of the question we were seeking to investigate. Therefore, we exited Dedoose, returned to the raw transcripts, and cut and paste from them to create a Word document for each youth with all their VIP data, color coded by time point. We then created a second Word document for each youth–adult relationship with separate sections for initiation, maintenance, ending, and impact, into which relevant data from the first document was copied and pasted with the color coding intact. This allowed us to (a) read holistically, for each youth–adult relationship, the story of how the relationship began, was sustained, ended, and the influence the youth felt it had for them, and (b) examine patterns of change and stability in those over the 3 years of the study. Finally, we created a third Word document for each relationship in which we applied the previously identified codes to each section of the narrative (i.e., beginning, maintenance, ending, impact), selecting excerpts of data as evidence of each code that is present and writing a brief narrative summary of the relationships. This allows us to look for thematic patterns within youth over time, within youth across relationships, and across youth within relationship stages (Arbeit, Johnson, Grabowska, Mauer, & Deutsch, in press). This analysis could have been done in Dedoose by coding for the relationships stages and then for the emergent themes. We preferred, however, to read the data holistically in Word rather than as excerpts.

Using Dedoose in combination with Word in this example facilitated the process of data reduction (Miles et al., 2014) in conjunction with a more narrative approach to analysis (Josselson, 2011). Because the data were tagged with time points in Dedoose, we were able to retain that tagging in Word to ensure that a developmental lens was applied to the analysis. As we continue, we will be able to use the mixed methods charts in Dedoose to explore patterns within and across youth over time by examining the prevalence and content of codes in relation to scores on the quantitative measures.

## 6.4.5 Looking Back

Dedoose was critical to our ability to organize and manage a large amount of multimethod, multisource, longitudinal data. Yet we also identified places where Dedoose was limited given our aims. For example, we would like to be able to create data sets within Dedoose based on descriptors in the same manner that you can create data sets by other organizational categories (e.g., users or codes). There are also tasks that we would approach differently now that we have been working with the data. For example, we split our organizational and thematic codes into different excerpts, as described earlier. Yet because the architecture of Dedoose relies on excerpts as building blocks for its analytic functions, searching data for coding overlap is most efficient if all codes are applied within a single excerpt. Although you can tell Dedoose to include overlapping excerpts in its searches, this approach was not optimal for our project. If we had it to do over again, we would probably put all codes into single excerpts. In addition, we found that when we wanted to look at the data more holistically or use a narrative approach to analysis, the best approach for us was to utilize Dedoose's organizational functions to identify the data we needed and then to export the data. This allowed us to read it in blocks of shared narrative meaning or structure instead of small excerpts or entire transcripts. Sometimes, we returned to Dedoose for additional coding and analysis after that step, and at other times, we did not. Thus, sometimes we used Dedoose as the main analysis software, conducting both qualitative and mixed methods analysis within the program. Other times, we drew on it primarily as a data organization and reduction tool to allow for analysis outside of the program. Yet in all cases, the program allowed us to manage and access a large amount of longitudinal data in different ways. Our lab motto is "encourage the platypus," a reference to looking for the unexpected and maintaining a creative and open mind-set when analyzing mixed methods data. Dedoose facilitated this mind-set by allowing us to look at our data in different ways and to explore a variety of combinations of qualitative and quantitative patterns in the data.

*Acknowledgments.* This research is supported by a grant from the William T. Grant Foundation, whom the case study authors would like to thank for their support. We would also like to acknowledge Youth-Nex: The UVA Center to Promote Effective Youth Development, which has supported our work. Youth-Nex is supported by a grant from Philip Morris, Inc., an Altria Company. The work of Youth-Nex is solely determined by itself, and Youth-Nex does not represent the official views of the sponsor.

### 6.4.6 Information About the Case Study Authors

**Nancy L. Deutsch,** PhD, is a professor at the University of Virginia's Curry School of Education and director of Youth-Nex: the UVA Center to Promote Effective Youth Development. Her work focuses on how settings can best meet adolescents' developmental needs, with a focus on out-of-school time programs and relationships with mentors and other nonparental adults. Her expertise includes the use of rigorous qualitative and mixed methods in developmental research, an emphasis that she brings to bear in her work as editor of the *Journal of Adolescent Research*.

**Haley E. Johnson,** MEd, is a doctoral student in the applied developmental science program at the University of Virginia's Curry School of Education and a former research specialist at Youth-Nex. Her research focuses on how youth's relationships with adults can create safe spaces for identity exploration, expression of authentic self, and education in ways that promote social change and dismantling of structural inequalities.

**Mark Vincent B. Yu,** PhD, is currently a National Science Foundation SBE Postdoctoral Research Fellow at the University of California, Irvine School of Education. Utilizing qualitative and mixed methods, his research interests focus on socioecological and strengths-based approaches to youth development. He is particularly interested in understanding how ecological assets such as supportive nonparental youth–adult relationships (e.g., with teachers, mentors, extended family members) and settings (e.g., schools, afterschool programs, communities) can be optimized and designed to capitalize on youth's strengths.

## 6.5   Conclusion

Chapter 6 addressed important questions about the challenges of mixed methods enquiry and identifying appropriate analysis strategies. There was a lengthy discussion about descriptors and how they can help you when working with your data. Remember that it is not a requirement to use descriptors; only use them if it makes sense to you. The subject of topic modeling was also covered, as an introduction to the field. Check out the Dedoose *User Guide* to see more about topic modeling in Dedoose. The case study then described an ongoing project as a practical example using Dedoose. Now Chapter 7 continues this theme and delves deeper into complexity in mixed methods.

# Managing Complex Mixed Methods Analysis

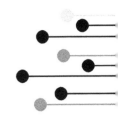

Chapter 5 discussed qualitative research and analysis, and it was followed with a discussion in Chapter 6 about the use of descriptors and topic modeling as mixing analysis strategies. Here in Chapter 7, the discussion goes further into the mixed methods analysis process by exploring a range of complex issues that may be encountered when conducting social science inquiry. More specifically, where does this complexity come from? What are some strategies you can use to further develop your thinking about interpreting data and producing relevant and credible findings?

A range of charts in Dedoose are highlighted in this chapter showing how to analyze both qualitative and quantitative data. When using these analysis tools, the researcher must remain in charge of interpreting meanings from the data to appropriately mix results. Mixing requires following a plan of action based on the original research design as discussed in Chapter 1. For example, the choice of implementing a sequential, concurrent, or nested study design each requires a different approach to when and how data are mixed.

A good place to start this discussion is to review your mixed methods study design and identify decision points where mixing occurs. It is hoped that you will find mixing decision points in the focus statement of your study as well as in the key research questions that define the scope of your study. As the study progresses, additional mixing decision points will continue to occur. Each point represents an important step forward in the overall study. Connecting and weaving these decision points together with justification supporting the use of mixed methods research strengthens the credibility of the study and aids in managing complexity.

## 7.1 Recognizing and Managing Complexity in Analysis

Complexity comes in a variety of forms. In a complex and rapidly changing social world, relationships between peoples' characteristics, values, beliefs, and behaviors and the ideas they communicate are often obscured. Ideally, study designs are sufficiently developed to allow researchers to better understand these relationships and gain clarity on the phenomenon of interest. By helping organize, connect, and navigate through raw data, Dedoose assists in the discovery and exploration of important patterns in qualitative and mixed methods data and facilitates representation of important deep meanings in these rich data. Furthermore, it is important to keep in mind that when investigating the complexity of the natural world, thoughtful and intentional steps are taken to ensure the reporting of credible findings and recommendations. Before launching into how mixing can take place at design, data gathering, data analysis, and interpretation stages, let's consider some methodological foundations and related implications for social science research.

Figure 7.1 illustrates a continuum of theoretical orientations anchored by a quantitative perspective of logical positivism and logical empiricism on the one end and a qualitative perspective of postmodern critical theories on the other (Hofer & Bendixen, 2012; Loseke, 2017; Patton, 2015). Each of the different views represented on the continuum have their strengths and limitations, and a history of particular research methods for gathering different types of data, sampling strategies, and, accordingly, analytic approaches. When engaged in social science work, any inquiry is positioned somewhere along this continuum. Awareness of this positioning is essential for ensuring that the theoretical orientation of a study is appropriately integrated throughout the design. As researchers position themselves on the continuum, they may also note that the research design may support intentionally shifting to different theoretical perspectives in response to different types of data and/or changes in perspective to the problem of interest.

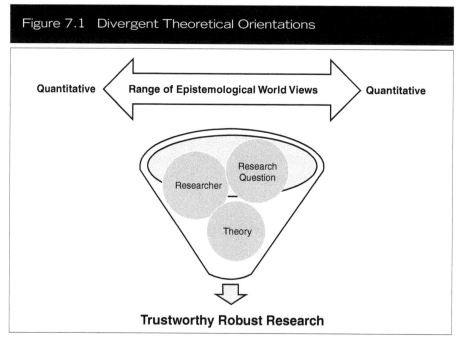

**Figure 7.1   Divergent Theoretical Orientations**

Quantitative — Range of Epistemological World Views — Quantitative

Researcher — Research Question — Theory

**Trustworthy Robust Research**

*Source:* Adapted from Kaczynski, Salmona, and Smith (2014).

As the study progresses, such refinements may be considered to further shape and strengthen the overall inquiry. With mixed methods research, it is important to remain respectful of other philosophical approaches during this process and take note of shifts and mixing of orientations throughout a project. Of particular interest to this discussion, a mixed methods design often involves the mixing of theoretical orientations. Accordingly, it must be recognized that such mixing introduces a new level of complexity to design thinking and conducting the proposed work in the interest of producing valuable and informative findings.

Two important points can be drawn from this discussion. First, qualitative and quantitative paradigms stand very much apart on an epistemological continuum. Second, trustworthy robust research is dependent on acknowledging these distinctions and providing constructive design strategies when conducting a mixed methods study. Figure 7.2 builds on these two points by emphasizing the importance of carefully thinking through the research design before starting the study. By taking into consideration each step of a study design, the researcher can build a visual model. The model visually represents the mixing process and aids in sorting through the unique challenges of conducting a mixed methods study.

## Figure 7.2   A Mixed Plan: Thinking About Levels of Mixing

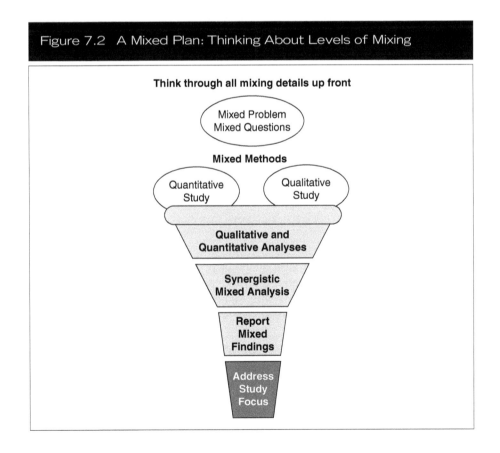

Avoid viewing the mixing process as a single step of placing everything into a blender to see what emerges. Rather, credible mixing involves due diligence throughout a study and awareness of decision points throughout the mixing process. An important point to draw from Figure 7.2 is that mixing occurs throughout a study: from defining the problem, to designing the study and sampling decisions, to data gathering, and, then, to data analysis. For the purposes of this chapter's discussion, this includes several levels of mixing that must take place even before mixed methods analytic mixing begins. Only after this up-front thinking occurs can strategies be considered for reporting combined results.

When thinking about your own study, begin with a complex key research question that drives the decision to adopt a mixed methods approach. Next, consider how the study employs mixed methods that draw on some variation of mixing both qualitative and quantitative methods. The mixing process continues with mixed analysis. Finally, the study reports distilled findings combining both qualitative and quantitative data. An important final step is to ensure that the conclusions address the original complex key research question.

From a practical perspective, a lack of mixing is essentially the same as designing two independent studies—one is qualitative and the other is quantitative. Each study can be conducted and described separately. As a result, findings can be reported independently of the individual study designs. Such a practice is not mixed methods research. The mixed study is reported as a whole rather than as its individual parts. For a successful mixed study, the findings from more distinct traditional perspectives are the starting point for integrating and looking to mix and report mixed methods findings.

## 7.2  Data Complexity in Your Project

Before turning to how Dedoose can assist in your mixed methods data integration, consider the various types of data that may be used in a project, how they may be important in your analysis, and how they may be connected within a Dedoose project.

The following example considers where and how qualitative data are analyzed and then moved into integration with quantitative analysis. Remember that data can be mixed in other ways as well. Figures 7.3a–c show how this analysis can be developed using Dedoose, starting with Figure 7.3a, which presents a starting point to think about mixed methods data in a study and how they may be treated in traditional ways.

Column A illustrates a simple depiction of qualitative data gathering, identification of key themes within those data, building and refinement of code systems, applying codes to excerpted content, and then searching, filtering, and retrieving. These steps allow the researcher to better understand the meaningful content within qualitative data, especially in the phases related to the identification of themes and the evolution, stabilization, and application of a useful code system.

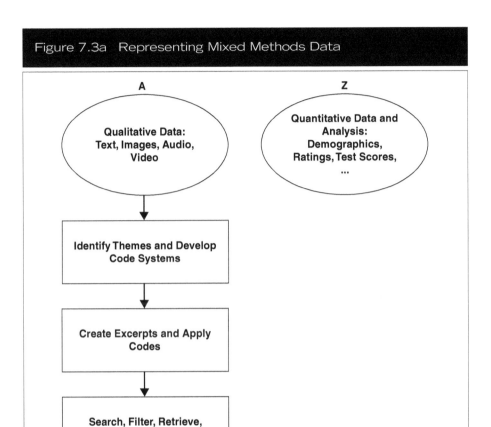

**Figure 7.3a  Representing Mixed Methods Data**

A
Qualitative Data: Text, Images, Audio, Video

Z
Quantitative Data and Analysis: Demographics, Ratings, Test Scores, ...

Identify Themes and Develop Code Systems

Create Excerpts and Apply Codes

Search, Filter, Retrieve, Interpret, and Present

Qualitative practices frequently revisit the raw data throughout the analysis process. Dedoose supports these purely qualitative data interactions and activities, and there is more that can be accomplished when the mixed methods features in Dedoose are applied.

Oval Z represents the quantitative data in a study and how findings might be discovered through traditional quantitative analysis. Note that qualitative analysis is a more iterative process, while quantitative results are commonly produced in a more linear manner such as using standardized measures as per analysis plans that are often determined prior to data gathering in a more structured manner. That is, with quantitative data, analysis plans are usually based on the study's hypotheses and can be set before data are gathered.

Moving to a more complex mixed methods approach, consider capitalizing on the Dedoose code weight/rating feature. Arrow B in Figure 7.3b shows where code weights and/or rating dimensions can be added to mixed methods data. For more details on code weights, refer back to Section 5.2.4.

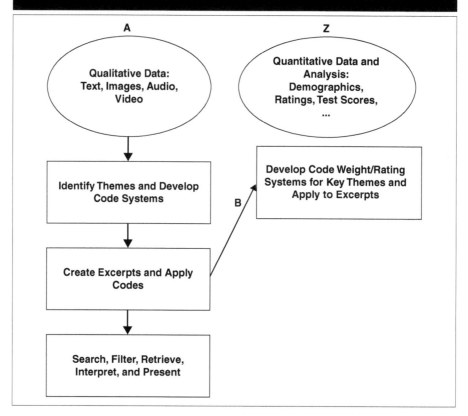

Figure 7.3b Introducing Code Weight/Rating Dimensions to Mixed Methods Data

Code weights can be an illuminating data reduction strategy producing data that can be analyzed in terms of looking at simple distributions or, as illustrated by Arrow C in Figure 7.3c, integrated and analyzed alongside other quantitative data in the study. Arrow D in Figure 7.3c illustrates how insights drawn from the qualitative data can be transformed into other continuous or categorical data and then integrated and analyzed with other quantitative data.

Let's consider a real-world example of transforming qualitative findings into categorical data. A mixed methods study was conducted to examine how working poor families might benefit from access to resources beyond those typically available as they navigated their lives with young children. These resources included access to financial, educational, child care, vocational training, and other supports. Early quantitative analyses failed to find significant program impacts for the experimental families for whom the additional resources were available and the control families who only had access to standard community

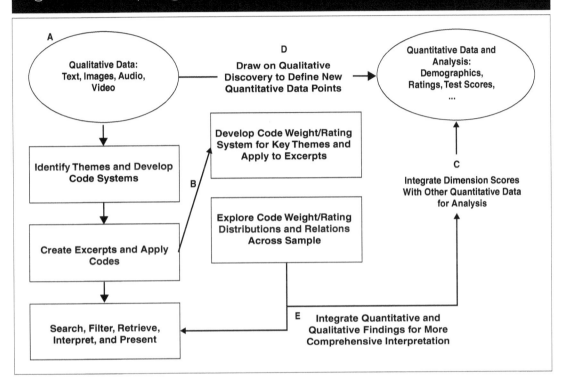

Figure 7.3c  Completing the Mixed Methods Conceptual Model

A
**Qualitative Data: Text, Images, Audio, Video**

D
**Draw on Qualitative Discovery to Define New Quantitative Data Points**

**Quantitative Data and Analysis: Demographics, Ratings, Test Scores, ...**

**Identify Themes and Develop Code Systems**

B

**Develop Code Weight/Rating System for Key Themes and Apply to Excerpts**

C
**Integrate Dimension Scores With Other Quantitative Data for Analysis**

**Create Excerpts and Apply Codes**

**Explore Code Weight/Rating Distributions and Relations Across Sample**

**Search, Filter, Retrieve, Interpret, and Present**

E  **Integrate Quantitative and Qualitative Findings for More Comprehensive Interpretation**

supports. However, it was discovered from interview content that for experimental families experiencing two or more major stressors (i.e., domestic abuse, special needs child, and drug addiction), life was too unstable for them to take advantage of the added available supports. From this finding, a new descriptor field was created to distinguish experimental families with one or fewer stressors from those with two or more stressors. Using this new variable to compare these groups alongside the control group allowed the research team to more precisely understand the actual impact of the intervention from a quantitative perspective than was possible by simply comparing the control versus experimental groups (Bernheimer, Weisner, & Lowe, 2003; Huston et al., 2005; Lowe, Weisner, Geis, & Huston, 2005).

Finally, we return to Figure 7.3c, where the full set of pathways in a mixed methods data conceptual model are complete. The path for Arrow E illustrates how a research study can flow from informed quantitative results back into the qualitative findings that triangulate and integrate the mixed results toward more comprehensive understanding of the phenomenon under investigation. By recognizing that quantitative results only tell part of a story, more can be learned by having connections to the qualitative findings. This allows an inquiry to follow the quantitative–qualitative connections in informed ways and provide for much deeper consideration of what could be drawn from only examining the surface quantitative results.

## 7.2.1 Setting Up Complex Data in Dedoose

Now moving from the conceptual to the concrete, Dedoose features and functionality are well prepared to support all of how you may wish to transform, integrate, and analyze mixed methods data. Keep in mind that from an analysis perspective, you will want to comingle qualitative and quantitative data in the interest of triangulation and segmentation. Furthermore, when working collaboratively, you will wish to engage and capitalize on the multiple perspectives brought by each member of a research or evaluation team. Dedoose helps meet many of these challenges through the use of descriptors, dynamic descriptors, and the variety of features supporting collaboration and team building. When a project makes full and proper use of these features, the filtering capabilities and mixed methods analytics in Dedoose allow for exploring these data from an endless number of directions. Dedoose provides many charts and tables that are available to shine a lens on variation from a range of perspectives.

To best capitalize on Dedoose features for complex analysis, it is important to understand the different aspects of a database when setting up your project and correctly place your different data in an optimal configuration. To be clear, descriptors are characteristics of your primary qualitative data sources (or "media" in Dedoose; see Section 6.2 for more on descriptors) and codes are characteristics of your excerpts. Another way to think about this is that, while they may seem to have similar purposes of representing characteristics of qualitative data, descriptors and codes are separate objects with distinct functions. Descriptors will be linked to entire media files and codes will be linked to excerpts (portions of your media files). Using REDA allows you freedom and flexibility to move backwards and forwards in your qualitative data via

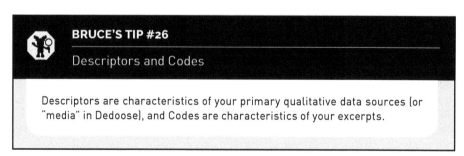

**BRUCE'S TIP #26**

Descriptors and Codes

Descriptors are characteristics of your primary qualitative data sources (or "media" in Dedoose), and Codes are characteristics of your excerpts.

these descriptor and code connections as well as through subsets of commonly coded data based on code weight values.

## 7.2.2 Moving From Qualitative to Quantitative

Before setting up your descriptors in Dedoose (described in detail in Section 6.2), think carefully about your investigation goals. As you move into analysis, new descriptors may emerge from your qualitative investigation. Accordingly, Dedoose allows you to easily create new descriptor data as your understanding of your data deepens and evolves. This flexibility supports moving along the theoretical continuum. Ideally, new descriptor data discovered and defined within the qualitative data can contribute to and expand further quantitative analysis in informative ways as you immerse yourself further and further into your analysis. The real-world example, previously discussed in Section 7.2, further demonstrates this point by showing how information gained from interviews helped distinguish families with different numbers of stressors, which was then used to create new descriptor data that enhanced subsequent quantitative analysis.

## 7.2.3 Moving From Quantitative to Qualitative

The more quantitatively focused analytic features in Dedoose provide yet another way to move along the theoretical continuum. Distribution plots for code weights/ratings and continuous number descriptor data allow for customizable visual display of these distributions with controls for setting the number of segments along the range and all associated distributional data, including mean, range, and standard deviation. As with all other visualizations in Dedoose, you can click through the segments to pull up the underlying qualitative excerpts when seeking to explore deeper meanings.

For example, you might have weighted codes that you used to tag content related to reports of the length of time, 0 to 30 minutes, physicians spent during clinical visits with patients who had a variety of ailments (e.g., influenza, joint pain, skin rash). These excerpts also include content regarding what took place during the visit. Then, from an analytical perspective, you might wish to look at variation in the time spent as a function of ailment; perhaps comparing the qualitative data behind those episodes that were 0 to 10 minutes and those that lasted between 20 and 30 minutes. The code weight distribution plots allow you to pull up excerpts for shorter visits versus longer visits by ailment and provide insight into the physicians' decisions being made about their approach and time spent related to diagnosis, treatment, and counseling—in a sense, using time variation along a continuous numerical variable to gain insights into clinical decisions and behavior from a qualitative perspective.

Similarly, we can use *t* tests, ANOVA, and/or chi-square analysis to identify group differences from a purely quantitative perspective based on code weighting or descriptor field variation. Subsequently, drilling into the underlying qualitative content as distinguished by groupings defined by the quantitative results can help shift our lens on the qualitative based on what was known from the quantitative. This type of investigation capitalizes on Dedoose's integration of these various data sources and allows for dynamic segmentation and unique navigation through the complex data relations. In contrast to the creation of new descriptor data toward guiding new quantitative investigation (as described above), this approach is essentially moving in the opposite direction across the theoretical continuum, from quantitative findings to new qualitative investigation.

 ## 7.3  Using Visualization Tools for Analysis

 **BRUCE'S TIP #27**

Versions of Figures and Charts

Remember to save early (and all) versions of visual figures and charts. These early drafts represent an audit trail of evidence that can be used to explain rigorous stages of analytic mixing.

Data visualization is a powerful way to communicate results to a research or evaluation audience. Dedoose includes a wide variety of customizable and interactive data visualizations that you will find in the Analyze Workspace. All visuals are designed around the tables, charts, and plots that are commonly used to both explore qualitative, quantitative, and mixed methods data and present findings. You can use the visualizations in the Analyze Workspace to examine the general nature of your data, to understand how the code system has been applied to the qualitative content and how code weighting varies by subgroups, and to expose and explore patterns of variation in the qualitative data and coding activity across subgroups. Also, keep in mind that all visuals can be exported to an appropriate format to facilitate the presentation of your research findings. These charts, tables, and plots are designed to be as informative, intuitive, and transparent as possible. You can use them in numerous combinations and adapt them to address your particular research questions. Most visuals have a variety of options that are found in the upper right corner of the display panel, so look for icons and check boxes (as shown in Figure 7.4) to swap display format, expand view, export, include subcode counts, and control other aspects specific to the visual.

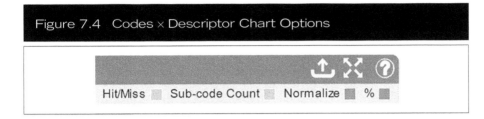

Figure 7.4  Codes × Descriptor Chart Options

Hit/Miss    Sub-code Count    Normalize    %

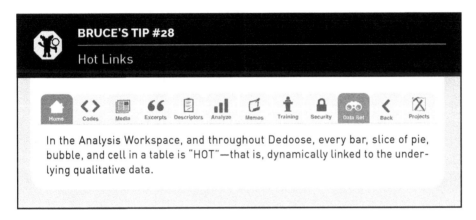

**BRUCE'S TIP #28**

Hot Links

Home  Codes  Media  Excerpts  Descriptors  Analyze  Memos  Training  Security  Data Set  Back  Projects

In the Analysis Workspace, and throughout Dedoose, every bar, slice of pie, bubble, and cell in a table is "HOT"—that is, dynamically linked to the underlying qualitative data.

All visuals in Dedoose are "hot-linked" to the underlying qualitative data. Clicking on a cell in a table or bar in a chart will immediately pull up a chart reviewer that includes the underlying qualitative content. From there, you can explore to more deeply understand the nature of the qualitative content or export for use in a manuscript or presentation preparation.

These chart reviewers presenting the qualitative content allow you to export, explore through filtering (discussed further below), and open the excerpt records for review and/or modification of coding. Note that you can also click through to see an excerpt in its original context. While providing a comprehensive listing and description of all analytic features is beyond the scope of this book (see Dedoose *User Guide* for more detail), we now describe a few to provide a sampling of what you will find when using Dedoose.

## 7.3.1 Descriptor Ratios Pie Chart

In the Analyze Workspace, there is a folder for charts related to Descriptors. Here you will find pie charts that present a quick overview of the percentage of members in each category across all descriptor fields. Clicking any slice on one of the pie charts will pull up all excerpts for members of that category, regardless of the codes that may have been applied, along with all associated media. You can also use these pie charts to produce a filtered subset of your data by category. For example, if you just want to work with data for African Americans in your study, you can click on that slice of the pie in Figure 7.5.

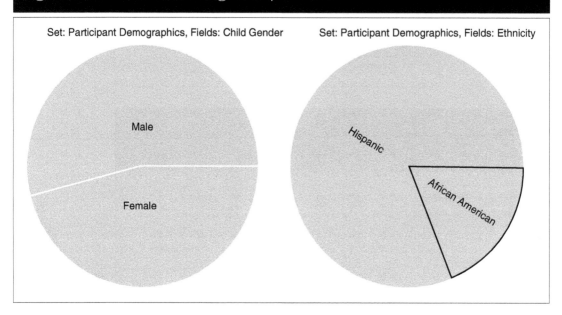

Figure 7.5  Pie Charts Showing Descriptor Ratios

Set: Participant Demographics, Fields: Child Gender

Male

Female

Set: Participant Demographics, Fields: Ethnicity

Hispanic

African American

This will show you all excerpts relating to African Americans, and you can activate a simple filter by clicking on the Make Active Set button. This filter allows you to narrow your analysis to this particular subset of participants without distraction from the data provided by those who do not meet your filter criteria. See Section 7.5 for more on filtering in Dedoose.

Spending some time exploring and becoming familiar with what is available in the Analyze Workspace will help you when conducting analysis. Not all visuals will be of value to you every time, but knowing what is available will make it easier to navigate through the analytics that will best meet your needs.

## 7.3.2 Code Co-Occurrence Table

In the Analyze Workspace, there is also a folder for Qualitative charts. One of the options available here is the Code Co-Occurrence table (see Figure 7.6), which shows the intersections where excerpts have been coded with two codes or, by default, pairs of overlapping excerpts where each has been tagged by one of the codes in question. Accordingly, the cell counts or "hits" include single excerpts that were tagged with both codes in question and pairs of excerpts that have one of the codes on one excerpt and the other code on an overlapping excerpt—one "hit" per pair is represented on the table when it comes to the overlapping excerpts, where overlapping excerpts are those that touch in part or simply are not separated by any space or character in the media file in Dedoose.

Figure 7.6   Code Co-Occurrence Table

| Codes | Reading by Mother | Routine | Bedtime Routine | Morning Routine | Other Routine | Frequency | Entire Paragraph | Positive | Reading by Others | Pre-Writing Activities | Letter Recognition | Parent - Child Talking | School Prep Beliefs | Great Quotes | Totals |
|---|---|---|---|---|---|---|---|---|---|---|---|---|---|---|---|
| Reading by Mother | | 5 | 1 | 2 | 1 | 1 | | 1 | 11 | 6 | 11 | 2 | 3 | 1 | 45 |
| Routine | 5 | | 1 | 2 | 1 | | | 1 | 2 | 3 | 4 | 1 | 1 | | 21 |
| Bedtime Routine | 1 | 1 | | 1 | | | | | 1 | 1 | 2 | 1 | 1 | | 9 |
| Morning Routine | 2 | 2 | 1 | | 1 | | | | 1 | 1 | 1 | 1 | 1 | 1 | 12 |
| Other Routine | 1 | 1 | | 1 | | | | | 1 | | 1 | | | | 5 |
| Frequency | 1 | | | | | | | | 2 | 1 | 2 | | 1 | | 7 |
| Entire Paragraph | | | | | | | | 1 | | | | | | | 1 |
| Positive | 1 | 1 | | | | | 1 | | | | 1 | 1 | 1 | | 6 |
| Reading by Others | 11 | 2 | 1 | 1 | 1 | 2 | | | | 9 | 10 | 1 | 1 | 1 | 40 |
| Pre-Writing Activities | 6 | 3 | 1 | 1 | | 1 | | | 9 | | 7 | 5 | 4 | 1 | 38 |
| Letter Recognition | 11 | 4 | 2 | 1 | 1 | 2 | | 1 | 10 | 7 | | 4 | 1 | 1 | 45 |
| Parent - Child Talking | 2 | 1 | 1 | 1 | | | | 1 | 1 | 5 | 4 | | 1 | 1 | 18 |
| School Prep Beliefs | 3 | 1 | 1 | 1 | | 1 | | 1 | 1 | 4 | 1 | 1 | | | 15 |
| Great Quotes | 1 | | | 1 | | | | | 1 | 1 | 1 | 1 | | | 6 |
| Totals | 45 | 21 | 9 | 12 | 5 | 7 | 1 | 6 | 40 | 38 | 45 | 18 | 15 | 6 | |

The table in Figure 7.6 helps represent how the study respondents are naturally connecting the ideas we are interested in exploring (and have coded as such) as they are responding to our qualitative inquiry. Matrices like these can show sample-wide patterns that would be difficult or impossible to identify without a visual display. For example, connections between these ideas can seem clear when you are reading a small number of interviews, but how such patterns hold up across a larger sample become obscure at the interview-by-interview level. You can think of this as the 30,000-foot view on how the sample as a whole is connecting these ideas on a relatively frequent basis. Finally, frequency here, as in all tables, is mapped to the color spectrum to help quickly identify where the most, or least, "action" is taking place.

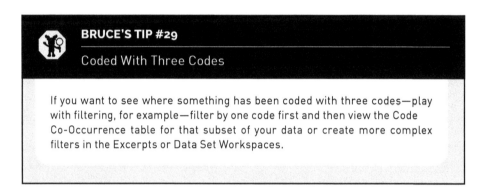

**BRUCE'S TIP #29**

Coded With Three Codes

If you want to see where something has been coded with three codes—play with filtering, for example—filter by one code first and then view the Code Co-Occurrence table for that subset of your data or create more complex filters in the Excerpts or Data Set Workspaces.

### 7.3.3 Descriptor × Descriptor × Code Chart

In the Mixed Methods Charts folder, the Descriptor × Descriptor × Codes chart is a cross-tab display that, by default, presents a set of subgroups based on the descriptor fields selected and, within each, the relative frequency the selected code had been applied (see Figure 7.7).

For example, using the demo project data, imagine you are wondering if mothers report reading to their child more frequently depending on their work status and the gender of their child. You can open the Descriptor × Descriptor × Code Chart, select "Mother Work Status" and "Child Gender" as the descriptor fields, and select "Reading by Mother" as the code. Note that the defaults for this chart include presenting the data in percentage terms within each cluster.

Figure 7.7   Descriptor × Descriptor × Code Chart

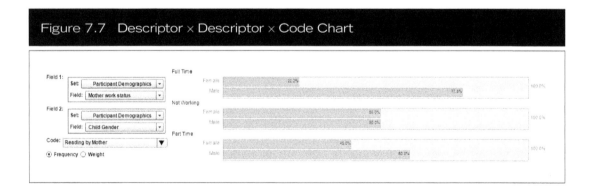

**BRUCE'S TIP #30**

Normalization in Frequency Charts

Where "normalization" is present as a default in any excerpt frequency bar charts, this indicates that a calculation has taken place that automatically adjusts the bar size relative to each other based on the number of participants in each subgroup—so regardless of variation in the sample numbers, the visual is meaningful in terms of "relative" frequency.

If you wish to view raw counts, you can deactivate the percentage option. Furthermore, if your code system is hierarchical, you can click the Sub-code Count option, which serves to collapse up the tree. For example, in the demo project, the "Reading by Mother" code has child and grandchild codes (e.g., frequency, duration, routine, and different types of routines). So if you include subcodes, the bars will represent any excerpts tagged with Reading by Mother or any of the Reading by Mother subcodes. This feature can be handy when you want to look at whole groupings of related excerpts. Finally, this chart also allows you to toggle to a weight chart. For codes with code weighting active, selecting a weight chart presents a different dimension to your data from excerpt frequency. The demo project includes a 5-point rating/weighting system intended to index the quality of reading episodes as interpreted by the research team. Accordingly, the code weight display presents bars representing the average quality of reading episodes these children have experienced as a function of their gender and their mother's work status. Visuals like these expose different dimensions in your data and help you explore and communicate different and unique stories.

## 7.4  Moving Through and Filtering Your Data

Using the Dedoose charts, tables, and plots, exploring and exporting excerpts and/or moving from excerpt lists to excerpts in context allows you to move through your data in unique ways as you seek a greater sense of nuance and understanding, and it is fundamental to the analysis process. Dedoose was designed with these needs in mind, and the functionality is designed around how we understand expert and experienced researchers and how evaluators interact with and move through their data. As you have seen, the actual structure of a database can be very complex, and it is this ability to move through the data as fluidly as possible that supports the

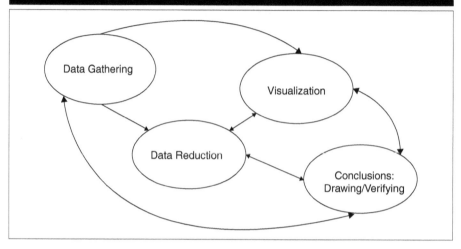

Figure 7.8 The Iterative Nature of Qualitative and Mixed Method Data Interaction and Analysis

*Source:* Adapted from Miles, M. B. & Huberman, A. M. (1994). Qualitative data analysis (2nd ed.). Thousand Oaks, CA: SAGE.

analytic goals and helps make the overall process more efficient. Note that many find this process an iterative one as illustrated in Figure 7.8. Once you have gathered and started working with your data by coding, weighting, and linking to descriptors, there are many paths you can take as you think through what evidence you can glean and what findings you can communicate and support.

Miles and Huberman (1994) brought to light the fluidity of the qualitative data reduction processes. They contended that flexibility during the analysis process promotes better understandings and illuminates deeper meanings. When working in the Dedoose environment, this fluid and iterative process can further strengthen your study, allowing you to enter and exit the process at any point. In addition, moving from visuals to consideration of conclusions to additional data reduction, displaying, gathering, and revisiting allows you to capitalize on everything you have created in your Dedoose database.

There are many reasons why you might want to narrow the scope of your analysis to unique subsets of data in a project as you seek to identify and explore patterns. Refer back to Section 3.3, "Memos as Data," and think about earlier phases of your project where you may already have identified and documented some potentially valuable lines of inquiry. These are directions you want to take into your data analysis in searching for deeper understandings of your data. You might also want to focus your analysis on a subset of data to produce findings specific to particular subgroups of participants or settings. To serve these analytic needs, Dedoose offers powerful filtering capabilities throughout the application. However, remember your analytical needs may be met by simply using the auto-generated and interactive data visualizations available in the Dedoose Analyze Workspace. These visuals make it easy to discover and explore patterns in your data and then drill down to better understand the rich qualitative stories that live beneath the surface. That said, Dedoose offers three basic approaches to defining and activating database-wide filters. This filtering can take place via a Chart Selection Reviewer you may have activated by using one of the charts, tables, or plots in the Analyze Workspace, via the Excerpts Workspace, or by using the Data Set Workspace capabilities. What is most important here is to first have a clear idea of why you are wanting to filter your data and precisely what criteria you wish to use in this filtering. With that plan in mind, you can select the most efficient approach to meeting your filtering goals.

## 7.4.1 Filtering via Chart Selection Reviewer

The simplest way to filter is based on the chart selection reviewer following the activation of a subset of data from one of the data visualizations. For example, say you are working in the Dedoose Sample Project and want to focus your analysis on the data about families reporting having a male child. You can easily pull up all the excerpts for families with male children by clicking the Male portion of the Descriptor Ratio Pie Chart in the Analyze Workspace. Then, by clicking the Make Active Set in the Chart Selection Reviewer, you can activate a filter, so all subsequent analysis will be focused only on excerpts from families reporting having male children (see Figure 7.9).

When such a database-wide filter is active, you can navigate to different Workspaces in Dedoose knowing that you are only working with data from families reporting having a male child.

Note that when a filter is active, there are two visual cues:

1. First, you will see a funnel icon in the panel header for charts and other workspaces that serves as a toggle to switch back and forth between the filtered subset of data and the full data set with a simple click.

2. Second, you will see that the Data Set Workspace button in the main menu bar is shaded red as a visual reminder that a filter is active.

The male child example is a simple one, but keep in mind that you can use the chart reviewer for filtering regardless of the action that activated the reviewer pop-up. Furthermore, you can also add or remove other subsets to/from the active filter by using the "Add to/Remove from Active Set" buttons. This helps you apply greater control and precision in how you narrow and refine your data exploration to best meet your research or evaluation analysis needs.

**Figure 7.9 List of Excerpts for Families With Male Child**

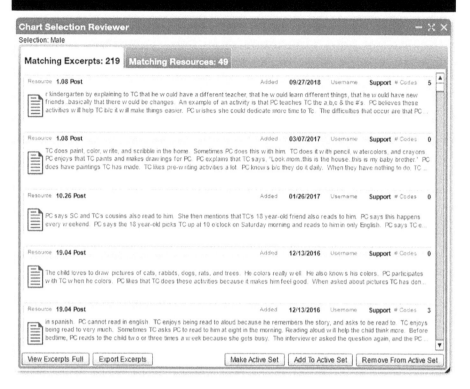

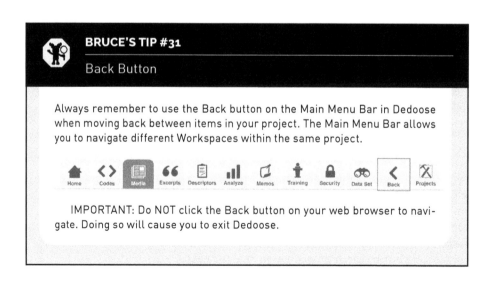

**BRUCE'S TIP #31**

Back Button

Always remember to use the Back button on the Main Menu Bar in Dedoose when moving back between items in your project. The Main Menu Bar allows you to navigate different Workspaces within the same project.

IMPORTANT: Do NOT click the Back button on your web browser to navigate. Doing so will cause you to exit Dedoose.

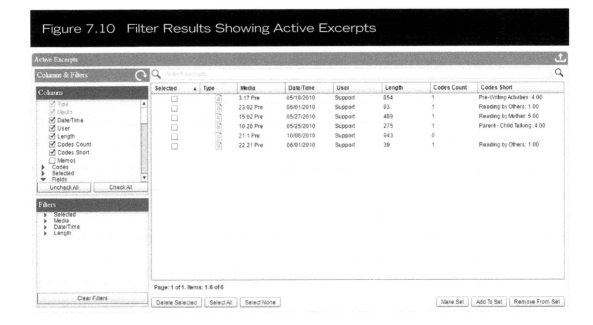

Figure 7.10   Filter Results Showing Active Excerpts

| Selected | ▲ | Type | Media | Date/Time | User | Length | Codes Count | Codes Short |
|---|---|---|---|---|---|---|---|---|
| ☐ | | | 3.17 Pre | 05/18/2010 | Support | 854 | 1 | Pre-Writing Activities: 4.00 |
| ☐ | | | 23.02 Pre | 06/01/2010 | Support | 93 | 1 | Reading by Others: 1.00 |
| ☐ | | | 15.02 Pre | 05/27/2010 | Support | 489 | 1 | Reading by Mother: 5.00 |
| ☐ | | | 10.26 Pre | 05/25/2010 | Support | 275 | 1 | Parent - Child Talking: 4.00 |
| ☐ | | | 21.1 Pre | 10/08/2010 | Support | 943 | 0 | |
| ☐ | | | 22.21 Pre | 06/01/2010 | Support | 39 | 1 | Reading by Others: 1.00 |

**Active Excerpts**

**Columns & Filters**

**Columns**
- ☑ Type
- ☑ Media
- ☑ Date/Time
- ☑ User
- ☑ Length
- ☑ Codes Count
- ☑ Codes Short
- ☐ Memos
- ▶ Codes
- ▶ Selected
- ▼ Fields

Uncheck All    Check All

**Filters**
- ▶ Selected
- ▶ Media
- ▶ Date/Time
- ▶ Length

Page: 1 of 1. Items: 1-6 of 6

Clear Filters    Delete Selected    Select All    Select None    Make Set    Add To Set    Remove From Set

## 7.4.2 Filtering via the Excerpts Workspace: Increasing Complexity

A second way to define and activate a database-wide filter is via the Excerpts Workspace (see Figure 7.10). Much more complex and precise filtering can be accomplished using this approach. Again, it is very useful to make sure you think about what you are trying to accomplish before you begin defining and activating any filters so that you can be confident that you are in control of the process and understand the impact.

Also, it helps to keep in mind that the Excerpts Workspace is fundamentally an organizational space with excerpts being the primary object. Controls are provided for both determining what is in view at a particular moment and filtering to subsets of excerpts based on any variety of criteria.

### 7.4.2.1  Controlling Active Excerpts in the Excerpts Workspace

Entering the Excerpts Workspace, you will find three panels: (1) Columns, (2) Filters, and (3) the Excerpt records themselves. What is checked off in the Columns panel determines which characteristics of the excerpts will be in view in the Excerpt panel. It can be helpful to uncheck any characteristics that are not relevant to your intended filtering. For example, in the demo project, you might wish to filter to a subset of excerpts that are tagged with two particular codes—let's say

"Reading by Mother" and "Reading by Others"—that come from families reporting mothers who are not working or who work only part-time. In this scenario, it is recommended to only check the boxes for the two codes and Mother work status. Once checked, you will then see folders in the Filters panel for each code and the Mother work status descriptor field. When you open the folders in the Filters panel, you will find the filtering controls. As you click the check boxes to select true or false for codes or, more narrowly with weighted codes, codes with specific weight values, and Not Working and Part Time work status in the Filters panel, you will see the list of active excerpts reduced to only those that meet the specified criteria. In this example, an "AND"/"OR" filter was created. That is, reduce the subset to excerpts tagged with both "Reading by Mother" AND "Reading by Others" AND come from families that reported Mother is Not Working OR Mother is Working Part Time.

### 7.4.2.2 Activating Filters in the Excerpts Workspace

Once you have reduced the set of active excerpts, activating a filter involves only two additional steps. First, click Select All in the lower left corner of the Active Excerpts panel to select the excerpts that meet your criteria. Then, click Make Set to activate the database-wide filter. Note that using the filter controls in the Filters panel only reduces the list of active excerpts that are in view in

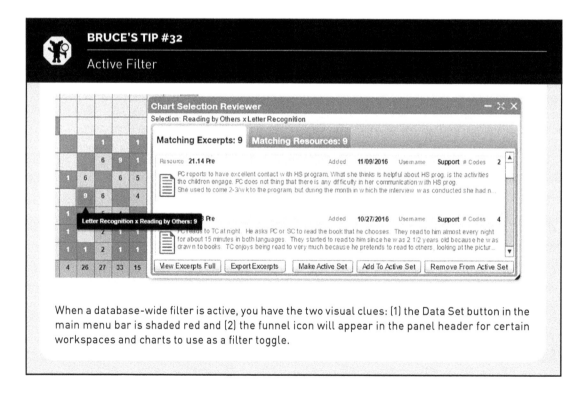

**BRUCE'S TIP #32**

Active Filter

When a database-wide filter is active, you have the two visual clues: (1) the Data Set button in the main menu bar is shaded red and (2) the funnel icon will appear in the panel header for certain workspaces and charts to use as a filter toggle.

the Excerpts Workspace. To activate a database-wide filter, you must take the added step of making what is in view a "set." When this added step has been taken, you can leave the Excerpts Workspace and navigate to other places in Dedoose where only the data that met the criteria in your active set will be accessible. Now that you can define and activate a database-wide filter within the Excerpts Workspace, let's get fancy and look at how to modify the active set further.

### 7.4.2.3 Modifying Database-Wide Filters in the Excerpts Workspace

In this next scenario, you have activated the filter described above in Section 7.4.2.2: Excerpts tagged with Reading by Mother and Reading by Others from not working or part-time working mom families. Perhaps as you explore the filtered data, you decided you'd like to include excerpts that were tagged with Reading Routine, also from not working or part-time working mom families. To do so, you will return to the Excerpts Workspace and click the funnel icon in the Active Excerpts panel header to bring all the excerpts back into view. Following the same steps as before, first filter the visible excerpts to those that meet the new criteria, click Select All, and now select Add to Set. Presto, you've now added another subset of excerpts to the database-wider filter, essentially including another "OR" condition to your filtering criteria! Your new set includes excerpts that come from Not Working OR Part Time Working moms that were tagged with Reading by Mother AND Reading by Others OR were tagged with Reading Routine.

### 7.4.2.4 Advanced Filtering Approaches in the Excerpts Workspace

The Excerpts Workspace facilitates creating filters on the individual excerpt level and allows the creation of filters that cannot be created in any other workspace. As such, a deep understanding of filtering options and some creativity is valuable to make sure you are able to explore any desired niche in your data. Filters based on keywords can be created by using the "Search excerpts" function at the top of the panel. Searching for a specific term pulls up the set of excerpts that contain the term at least once. Figure 7.11 shows the set of excerpts that contain the term *responsible*. Additional terms can be included in the filter by toggling the filter off via the funnel icon, as mentioned before, searching for the new term, clicking Select All, and then clicking Add to Set.

Individual excerpt filtering is another filter exclusive to the Excerpts workspace. You may have noted that any filter created via the Excerpts workspace requires you to click Select All once you have narrowed your view via the Columns & Filters section on the left. Manually checking excerpts instead of using the Select All function lets you fine-tune your data set down to the excerpt level if needed.

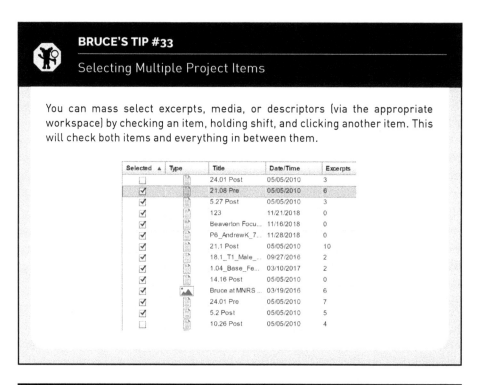

**BRUCE'S TIP #33**

Selecting Multiple Project Items

You can mass select excerpts, media, or descriptors (via the appropriate workspace) by checking an item, holding shift, and clicking another item. This will check both items and everything in between them.

| Selected ▲ | Type | Title | Date/Time | Excerpts |
|---|---|---|---|---|
| ☐ | | 24.01 Post | 05/05/2010 | 3 |
| ☑ | | 21.08 Pre | 05/05/2010 | 6 |
| ☑ | | 5.27 Post | 05/05/2010 | 3 |
| ☑ | | 123 | 11/21/2018 | 0 |
| ☑ | | Beaverton Focu... | 11/16/2018 | 0 |
| ☑ | | P6_AndrewK_7... | 11/28/2018 | 0 |
| ☑ | | 21.1 Post | 05/05/2010 | 10 |
| ☑ | | 18.1_T1_Male_... | 09/27/2016 | 2 |
| ☑ | | 1.04_Base_Fe... | 03/10/2017 | 2 |
| ☑ | | 14.16 Post | 05/05/2010 | 0 |
| ☑ | | Bruce at MNRS ... | 03/19/2016 | 6 |
| ☑ | | 24.01 Pre | 05/05/2010 | 7 |
| ☑ | | 5.2 Post | 05/05/2010 | 5 |
| ☐ | | 10.26 Post | 05/05/2010 | 4 |

Figure 7.11   Keyword Filtering

Q responsible

| Selected ▲ | Type | Media | Date/Time | User | Length | Codes Co... | Cod |
|---|---|---|---|---|---|---|---|
| ☑ | | 19.14 Pre | 06/01/2010 | DedooseAdmin | 713 | 1 | Sch |
| ☑ | | 10.06 Post | 06/15/2010 | DedooseAdmin | 327 | 1 | Sch |
| ☑ | | 19.04 Pre | 06/01/2010 | DedooseAdmin | 731 | 1 | Sch |
| ☑ | | 24.01 Pre | 06/01/2010 | DedooseAdmin | 193 | 1 | Sch |

24.01 Pre                                                                    (2635-2828)

PC states that the teacher should be responsible
for teaching TC numbers, letters and how to read          **School Prep Beliefs: ...**
and write. On the other hand, the PC states that
she needs to teach her TC to behave properly.

Showing 1 of 1 Codes

In the Excerpt Workspace, it is possible to create a filter that will allow you to gather excerpts based on the presence or absence, or combination of presence or absence, of multiple codes. This function allows you to pull up and filter by any

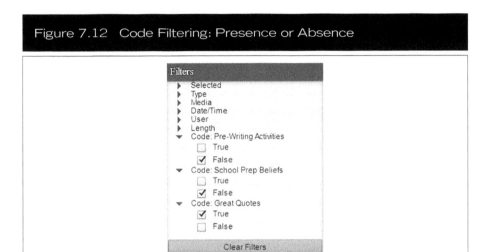

number of codes' application status, where the application status shows whether the code has or has not been applied. Figure 7.12 shows the filter applied that results in a data subset being created of any Great Quotes not related to School Prep Beliefs or Pre-Writing Activities. Like previous filters, this is done via the Columns & Filters section in the Excerpts Workspace.

## 7.4.3 Filtering via the Data Set Workspace

Filtering via the charts, tables, and plots, as described above or via the Excerpts Workspace may meet all of your needs. However, the Dedoose Data Set Workspace (see Figure 7.13) is another place you can create more complex filters, including user information in filters, where you can save filters, and where you can clear any active filters.

In the Data Set Workspace, a filter can be defined based on any object in the database, including descriptors, media, users, and codes. Two important things to keep in mind when creating filters here are as follows:

1.  Excerpts are the focus of all filtering. Remember that the ultimate filtering goal is to reduce your data to a subset of excerpts meeting particular criteria that you set.

2.  When a filter has been activated, it will remain in place until it is changed or deactivated by clicking the Clear Current Set button in the Data Set Workspace or by exiting the Dedoose application.

When you open the Data Set Workspace pop-up, you'll see tabs that let you access Descriptors, Media, Users, and Codes. Filtering here is very similar

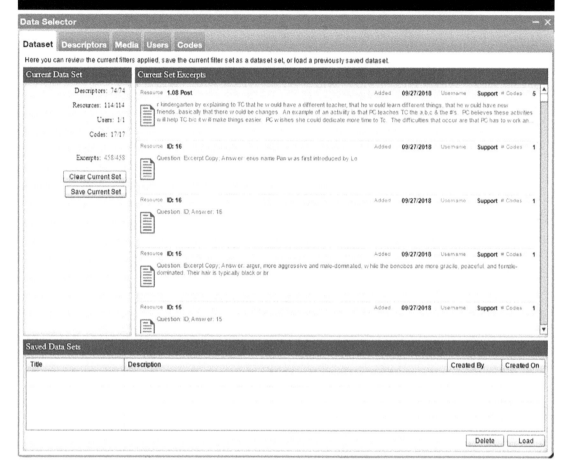

**Figure 7.13** Data Selector in Data Set Workspace

to filtering in the Excerpts Workspace with two noted differences. First, when you narrow the records, for example, for Media or Users, you will need to click Activate All or Deactivate All to activate the filter. Often, it can be easier to work backward by first deactivating all records and then activating only those you intend to focus on. So, for example, let's look at the steps to create filters like the example in the Excerpts Workspace. First, you would go to the Codes tab, click Filter None to clear all check boxes, and then check only those codes you wish to include. Note that in the Data Set Workspace, you can only use codes in an "OR" manner, so we'll check Reading by Mother and Reading by Others in Demo Project example. That is, you cannot narrow to excerpts that have two or more codes applied as can be accomplished in the Excerpts Workspace. Once

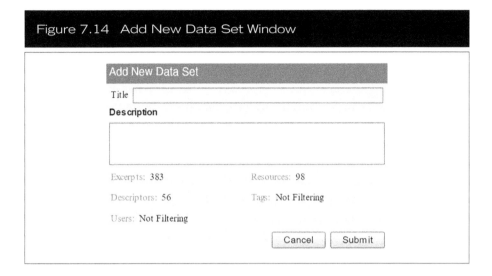
**Figure 7.14** Add New Data Set Window

Add New Data Set

Title

**Description**

Excerpts: 383          Resources: 98

Descriptors: 56          Tags: Not Filtering

Users: Not Filtering

Cancel     Submit

the codes of interest are checked, select the Media tab. Click Deactivate All to essentially turn off all media files. Click Uncheck All in the Columns panel to simplify the view. In the Columns panel, select Mother work status to bring that information into view in the right panel. Open the Mother work status folder that will appear in the Filters panel and select Not Working and Part Time working moms to filter the active records to media files that come from either not working and part-time working mothers. Click Activate All to bring those data back to active status.

For verification that you are only working with filtered data, it is often helpful to click the Data Set tab and look at the details in the Current Data Set panel, where you would expect to see that only a subset of resources and codes are active. Close the pop-up, and you are now exploring only those data that met your criteria—again with the main menu bar Data Set tab shaded red and the funnel toggle icon appearing in various chart and workspace headers.

Finally, regardless of their complexity or how you created and activated filters, you may want to save them to use later. To do so, access the Data Set Workspace while any filter is active, click the Save Current Set button in the Data Set tab view (see Figure 7.14), provide a title and description (to help remember the purpose of the filter), and Submit.

The filter will then be available in your Saved Data Sets library for later use regardless of whether you've added new data to the project. To reactivate, return to the Data Set Workspace, highlight the filter you wish to use, and click Load. Note that there are two ways to deactivate a filter: (1) by accessing the Data Set Workspace and clicking the Clear Current Set button or (2) by closing the Dedoose application.

## 7.5 Case Study: Complex Yet Manageable—the Organizational Genius of Dedoose

**THINK ABOUT, AND ANSWER, THESE QUESTIONS AS YOU READ THE CASE STUDY**

1. What steps are you taking to prepare, and organize, your data for analysis? Think about how you are weaving your qualitative and quantitative worlds together.

2. How will you explore your data? Think about some questions that may be relevant to your study. For example, is there a difference across genders? What about age or location? What are some ways you might filter your data to create different subsets to work with?

3. As you explore connections in your data, ask yourself: Are you using your study focus to frame your inquiry? Don't go down too many unrelated rabbit holes.

### Complex Yet Manageable: The Organizational Genius of Dedoose

#### M. Cameron Hay

Ever have the feeling of drowning in too much data? In this case study, I discuss a mixed methods study with 184 participants with whom we gathered multiple kinds of data during more than 300 events that occurred in a time sequence. Managing such data used to be unwieldy at best, making it extremely difficult to ask a new question of the data after analysis has begun. The same is not true of data entered into Dedoose. Dedoose has enabled us to ask emergent questions of the data—that is, questions that emerged after finishing the initially intended analysis. Often, with a looming deadline such as a grant proposal that needed pilot findings, we were able to extract participants with certain characteristics for further analysis to address a new and emergent question. In this case study, I illustrate this quality of Dedoose with a question that emerged as we were writing a grant proposal for a different study—Could the data from our earlier sample of 184 participants tell us something about adherence? I demonstrate how Dedoose's organizational system enabled selecting subsets of populations for closer and efficient examination. The efficiency of the analytical processes in Dedoose not only facilitated a timely grant submission but also, more centrally, has enabled us to continue to ask questions of this rich data set.

> "Wait, with your data you can explain *why* people do or don't do something?" the physician and colleague asked me.

"Well, yes" I answered, "if we've asked participants about a behavior it's relatively easy, and even if we haven't asked, sometimes people will volunteer information as part of their narrative that will explain why they do what they do."

The physician went on to explain, "In rheumatology we have a problem with adherence. In some studies, the adherence rate is as low as 20% (see, e.g., Waiman et al., 2013), but we don't know why. Any chance in your study there might be some data that we could use as preliminary data in a grant proposal?" And thus, what began as a catching-up chat between colleagues shifted into a conversation exploring a new research project.

## 7.5.1 Setting Up the Project

Flash back to a decade earlier and another conversation, much less relaxed, in the same office. Then, I had been entreating that same physician to allow me to conduct a research project with his patients. I had generous National Science Foundation funding to examine how patient access to online health information shaped patient interactions with their physicians; all I needed was a clinic in a medical specialty that treated chronic diseases and that would allow me to interview patients and audio-record patient–physician clinical interactions. It was a big ask. Multiple physicians in multiple clinics had turned me down. But this physician was listening, interested in the research question, and wanted to know which standardized instruments I was using. I had not planned on using any.

I had envisioned the project as a natural extension of my qualitative, ethnographic research conducted in Indonesia. There, I had examined an egalitarian medical tradition in which everyone had access to the knowledge that could potentially treat a patient. Would the relatively new availability of online health information in the United States offering similarly egalitarian access to medical knowledge result in a similarly egalitarian medical tradition? And would knowledge gained from the Internet really translate into equal power in clinical interactions? My plan was to recruit new patients at their first appointment, interview them before and after each appointment, and audio-record those appointments for 18 months of active data collection.

After the physician's question about standardized instruments and with the encouragement and wisdom of Tom Weisner, Eli Lieber, and Ted Lowe, mentors and colleagues at what was then the UCLA Center for Culture and Health, I redesigned the study to integrate standardized measures such as a pain scale (Wong & Baker, 1988), a learned-helplessness scale (Nicassio, Wallston, Callahan, Herbert, & Pincus, 1985), and a health-related quality-of-life scale (Hayes, Sherbourne, & Mazel, 1993). This redesign, together with the sheer complexity of the research design, meant that I was soon drowning in data. My initial plans for organizing the data were utterly inadequate.

## 7.5.2 Data Sources

The research design was straightforward, allowing me to answer the question, "To what extent and in what ways do access to online health information shape clinical interactions and patient illness experience?" And with supplemental funding from the National Multiple Sclerosis Society, I was able to further explore whether there were differences in the impact of online health information across clinical populations.

The mixed methods study that we ultimately conducted was large in scale. With institutional review board approval and with the protection of a National Institutes of Health Certificate of Confidentiality, I recruited two tertiary medical divisions—rheumatology and neurology—and recruited the new patients of participating physicians working in three clinics. We obtained consent from a total of 184 patients in the waiting room before their first appointment, giving them the standardized measures of pain, helplessness, and functional quality of life, as well as a demographic survey to fill out. Then, using semistructured interviews, we talked with patients before their appointment, asking about their concerns and whether they had gathered any health or medical information from any source prior to this appointment. When called back for the appointment with the physician, we sent them with an audio-recorder to record the interaction—a recording that was later transcribed. After the appointment, we again interviewed patients asking them to reflect on the appointment and answer a satisfaction survey. We also made ethnographic observations in the public spaces of the clinic and, for after each appointment gathered from the physician, a global assessment of the patient's health and disease activity. We repeated this process at every follow-up patient appointment for 18 months (see Figure C7.5-1).

While many patients only had one appointment, our data set includes more than 330 clinical appointments. Thus, this was a complex mixed methods study gathering multiple kinds of data in a longitudinal study with patients and their providers.

## 7.5.3 Data Management

Organizing data was a significant challenge in this study. I had initially conceived of this project as similar to my previous dissertation research and had planned on relying on some version of what I call the "sticky note method." My dissertation research was gathered in hand-written ethnographic field notes in 10 legal-sized composition notebooks and augmented by photographs, videotapes, and audiotapes of everyday interactions. When I initially returned home after my 22 months of fieldwork in a rural hamlet on the island of Lombok in Indonesia, I spent the first 6 months typing all my field notes into a database that was widely used in the mid-1990s that I thought would help me search for key themes. It might have worked had I spent another year cross-referencing all the data, but I had a dissertation to finish. So rather than working in the clunky database, I looked for themes by buying different colored sticky notes, and systematically reading and rereading each of my 10 notebooks, marking themes by

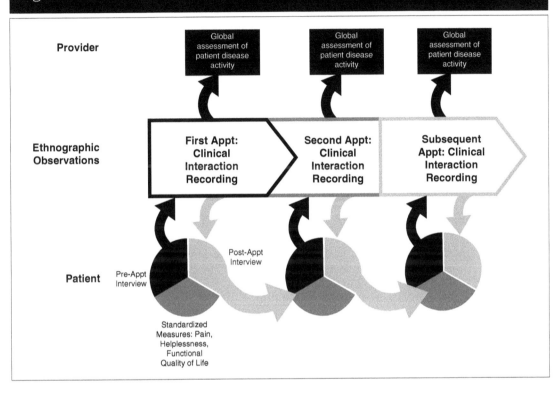

color of the sticky note, and discarding hypothesized themes that didn't hold up. Then, I tested and honed the emergent themes by examining them in light of the videos and audiotapes. Each chapter in my dissertation meant going through the entire process again and again to find, check, and refine themes as well as exemplary data; thus, I walked through the dissertation inch by inch. It was a slow but workable process, in part because all the data were *mine*, I had gathered all of it personally and I was flooded with remembered scenes and experiences as I reread the notes and relistened to the audiotapes.

The sticky note method simply wouldn't work with the online health information project. First, I was not the only person gathering the data: Over the course of the project, three postdocs and two graduate students worked with me to collect data. Second, unlike ethnographic fieldwork in which people's experiences unfolded in a seamless landscape of time and space, here, experiences were disjointed, as we worked across 3 different clinics, 11 physicians, and 184 patients, some of whom came for only one appointment, some of whom had multiple appointments—as many as 10 over the 1.5 years of active data collection. Whereas the data gathered during my dissertation research privileged ethnographic field notes, in this project, pre- and post-appointment semiformal interviews with the patient needed to be mapped onto standardized measures of well-being and the transcriptions of clinical interactions, tracking everything over time.

In looking for a software to manage the project, something affordable and Macintosh friendly, I had few choices in 2002. I initially settled on HyperRE-SEARCH. We entered the data into it, created a coding tree, and hired a small team of researchers to do the coding. However, while the initial training was easy, we realized early on that coding style varied substantially across researchers and maintaining consistency required constant supervision, essentially doubling coding time. After a while, we gave up, and only the postdocs and I did the coding. But even then, we had trouble ensuring that we were all coding the data the same way. In addition, it was cumbersome, and when physicians asked me what I had found (Were patients actually going online and what were they saying about that?), I had trouble finding an answer using our then mostly coded and integrated HyperRESEARCH data.

For our earliest publications, we went back to a modified version of the sticky note method. We'd highlight and color-code quotations from patient interviews with the findings from reviews of each patient's clinical interactions regarding online health information, quantifying those reviews, and turning to SPSS for analysis that we then mapped back onto the interviews. It was an onerous process. And then came Dedoose.

While it is now possible to import coded data from HyperRESEARCH into Dedoose, this was not true at the time of our move. Even so, Dedoose's flexibility, ease of use, and ability to easily ensure high intercoder reliability made it worth the cost of abandoning 2 years of data coding and starting from scratch with Dedoose. So I imported the raw data, refined and cleaned the octopus-like coding scheme we had created in HyperRESEARCH, and started coding. This time, the coding went faster because of the more streamlined coding scheme and the intuitive way of coding in Dedoose. In Dedoose, one codes by highlighting text, clicking your space bar, and double-clicking a code: very easy. When I hired students to help, I could use Dedoose's intercoder reliability tests to easily ensure accuracy.

Moreover, in Dedoose, I could categorize each data entry with what Dedoose calls descriptors and I think of as basic demographic or statistical data. For example, in this data set, I could categorize a data entry (what Dedoose calls "media") with all the stable demographic data (e.g., type of data [interview, transcription], patient ID, age, sex, diagnosis) and by the dynamic data that changed over time but which we captured with our standardized measures such as pain and functional quality of life. Because of the capacity to link descriptors with the data and then sort by particular descriptors, what was once an unwieldy data set became manageable. Using the filtering tools in Dedoose, with a few clicks, I could isolate subsets of subjects, such as all patients with rheumatoid arthritis, and explore previously coded categories that I thought might have captured comments related to adherence. For example, I knew that the data had been coded for how patients narrated their sensations. Thus, when my colleague-physician asked if our data might be able to provide some insights into adherence behavior, I knew I could efficiently answer our new question about adherence using Dedoose.

## 7.5.4 Analysis Processes

In our conversation, we narrowed down our focal group to two very specific disease populations—(1) patients with rheumatoid arthritis and (2) patients with scleroderma. We focused on these groups because these were the two populations with the worst adherence rates (e.g., 20%), or about which next to nothing was known (only one previous study had examined adherence in scleroderma). We also hypothesized that patients may be more likely to discuss issues that might negatively affect adherence with the researcher during interviews than in a clinical interaction with a physician. This meant that to do the analysis, I probably only needed to do additional coding of the interview data (but I could need to check this) from two subsets of the larger sample: the 20 patients with rheumatoid arthritis and the 21 patients with scleroderma.

On the Dedoose project home page, all excerpts are automatically organized into pie charts based on the linked descriptor data. Using these pie charts, I found the descriptor chart for patient diagnosis, selected rheumatoid arthritis, and made that my "active set." An active set is simply the collection of data one wants to analyze; the default is the entire data set, but by using one of the descriptors, I could easily select a subset to examine, for example, only patients with rheumatoid arthritis.

To check our assumption about disclosure, I only needed to look at the interview data. I looked first at the Code Co-Occurrence analytical tool for all the data with rheumatoid arthritis patients. I scrolled through excerpts that had been coded with both "Patient Experience Narrative" and "Sensations" and found excerpts like these:

Doctor: And, you said you're taking Celebrex about twice a week?

Patient: Yeah. Twice a week.

Doctor: And, one pill at a time or two pills?

Patient: No. One—it's a hundred milligrams.

Doctor: Okay. So you're taking about two pills total a week?

Patient: Yeah. A week, so, only like on days I overdo and actually I am anticipating maybe I'll have some pains I can feel a little bit, so I take [it].

It only took one case like this one, of a patient telling the physician that he took his medications as needed for pain or anticipated pain rather than as prescribed, to tell me that our hypothesis was incorrect. Patients might disclose non-adherence in interactions with physicians as well as in the interviews. So it was a bit more work than initially expected: Rather than just looking at interviews, I also needed to look at clinical interactions.

Concerned that the previous codes would not necessarily capture every instance related to adherence, I decided to do additional coding. The data had been coded for a host of other behaviors, including life concerns (e.g., family, work), experienced sensations/symptoms, expressions of uncertainty and help-lessness, and expressions of control. I read through a couple of transcriptions and full interview field notes, jotting down any words that patients or others used that could be connected to treatment adherence: medications, meds, pills, injection, or prescribe. With this initial list of search terms, I searched each media entry in the active set, coding relevant passages that emerged. I repeated this process with "scleroderma" as my active set. Then, I compared charts of high code co-occurrence across the two disease categories.

The Code Co-Occurrence chart is one of my favorite analytical features of Dedoose. This chart counts the number of times there is overlap in two codes for an excerpt, highlighting relatively high code co-occurrence through color coding, with a higher co-occurrence indicated by a warmer (yellow, orange, red) color. The color coding is particularly useful for quick indications of relative areas of conceptual overlap. From there, it is easy to drill down to the overlapping excerpts by double-clicking the highlighted area on the chart. Using this feature, I noticed that adherence was most strongly related to issues of patient control in rheumatoid arthritis and sensations in scleroderma. This is perhaps not a surprising finding because it makes sense that medications are related to things that patients do to manage sensations. Even so, it made me understand that the adherence is a matter of intentional patient sensation management.

Then using the Descriptor × Codes Mixed Methods chart in my analysis, I noticed two things that were common in patients with either disease. First, medications were discussed far more in clinical interactions than in the interviews. This was initially surprising, but when I drilled down to look at how medications were discussed in clinical interactions (by clicking on the line bar and reading through the excerpts), I noticed that mentions of nonadherent behaviors centered on either unwanted side effects or feeling so well that the medication wasn't perceived as needed. In comparison, drilling down to the ways medications were discussed in interviews, patients were far more likely to mention life responsibility reasons, rather than symptom reasons, for not taking a medication. Second, I noticed a substantial difference in the frequency of coding of adherence-related concerns between the male and female patients. Drilling down to the excerpts in the inter-views, by clicking on the respective bars, I was able to round out my understand-ing of patient nonadherence and ultimately answer the physician's initial question.

## 7.5.5 Reporting the Project

In our grant proposal, and later in a published letter to the editor, we reported that overall 50% of rheumatoid arthritis patients were explicitly nonadherent and a total of 70% reported busy life schedules or family concerns suggestive of adherence inconsistences. Similarly, 57% of the scleroderma patients reported stopping or reducing medications without talking to their physicians. In both the groups, women were most likely to report adherence inconsistencies while discussing the busy-ness of their schedules making it, as one woman put it, "Too difficult to keep up with all the meds." Our findings highlighted the relevance of life responsibilities to medication adherence and uniquely suggested that gender roles may need to be intentionally included in studies of medication adherence (Hay & Furst, 2016).

## 7.5.6 Looking Back

In an ideal world, one would know all the analytical questions to be posed to one's data when designing the initial coding tree. In the real world, it is also true that a good data set can be mined over time as new questions emerge. Being able to answer questions that emerge *after* the collection and initial analysis of data—that is, to go back into complex data sets and reanalyze the data with a new question—used to be challenging at best. The genius of Dedoose is in its flexibility, enabling researchers to dive back in with new questions and build on previous coding and descriptors to analyze data with relative ease. For the sticky note method I had previously used, every time I had a new question for the data, I needed to reread it all and apply fresh sticky notes. With Dedoose, I didn't need to reread everything. I just needed to be able to select the subset of data relevant to the question and identify key words I could search for to ease coding. Then, with a click of a few buttons, Dedoose put me on the right track, helping me hone my understanding of adherence as patients talk about it, as a way of managing sensations to enable them to get on with their lives.

## 7.5.7 Information About the Case Study Author

**M. Cameron Hay**, PhD, is professor and chair in the Department of Anthropology and director of the Global Health Research and Innovation Center at Miami University in Oxford, Ohio. She also holds an affiliation with what is now the Center for Social Medicine and Humanities at the University of California, Los Angeles. A graduate of Grinnell College and Emory University, she is a psychological and medical anthropologist interested in the social–cultural processes within which people experience and cope with illness and suffering. Early in her career, she conducted ethnographic research on how Indonesian peasants cope with the fragility of their lives resulting in a book, *Remembering to Live: Illness at the Intersection of Anxiety and Knowledge in Rural Indonesia* (2001). For the past 16 years, she has collaborated on transdisciplinary teams using mixed methods to examine things such as physician medical decision-making, doctor–patient relationships in the age of the Internet, the impact of pediatric chronic illness on child and family well-being, and health inequities in African American birth outcomes, with current projects in the United States, India, and Zambia. Her work has been published in anthropology, psychology, medical, and health policy journals, and in 2016 she was honored with the Miami University's Distinguished Scholar Award. Committed to doing research that contributes to scholarly conversations that transcend disciplinary boundaries, she recently edited the volume *Methods That Matter: Integrating Mixed Methods for More Effective Social Science Research* (2016). An early Dedoose enthusiast, since 2007, all her projects have been analyzed in Dedoose, and she regularly uses Dedoose to teach undergraduates how to organize, analyze, and present data.

## 7.6 Conclusion

This chapter explored a range of complex issues that you may encounter in mixed methods social science inquiry. It has given you some strategies you can use to further develop your thinking about interpreting data and producing relevant and credible findings. Starting with understanding mixed methods complexity and moving through visualization to working with filters to create data subsets, you now have new tools with which you can explore your data.

# CHAPTER 8

# Working With Numbers in Dedoose

## Statistics, Tabling, and Charting for Numbers, Weights, and Option List Field Data

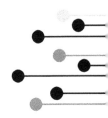

## 8.1  Background/Introduction

Fundamental to Dedoose is the ability to upload and tag qualitative media content, such as text, images, audio, or video. Dedoose, however, is a unique mixed methods tool, which means it is intentionally designed to incorporate numbers and other types of data. Knowing where these numeric and other data come from and how to use them will benefit and enhance your research and evaluation findings. Categorical data can provide insights and deeper understanding into the characteristics of the people, places, and programs being investigated. When writing reports, articles, chapters, and preparing presentations, it is important that these characteristics are clearly presented.

This chapter describes what can be done in Dedoose from a descriptive statistics perspective, which may be sufficient for many Dedoose users. Woven through this chapter is an example taken from data collected in a large-scale online survey. This survey gathered a range of data, including respondents' positive and negative technology beliefs using the Technology Readiness Index 2.0 (TRI; Parasuraman, 2000; Parasuraman & Colby, 2015), which is a way to specifically measure and categorize these beliefs. References to TRI in this chapter are used here for demonstration purposes in the visual display of quantitative results.

*Note that the statistical features now embedded into Dedoose are not intended to replace the more advanced statistical analyses that can be carried out in more sophisticated statistical software.*

In Dedoose, pure numbers are dealt with in two ways: either as descriptor data (refer back to Section 6.2) or as code weights/ratings (Section 5.2.4). Section 8.1.1 describes how to use descriptors to work with quantitative and categorical data. Quantitative descriptor data can be continuous to represent variables such as annual income, age, or scale scores that are used to measure some characteristic related to the phenomena under investigation. Similarly, code weights/ratings can be used to index or distribute coded qualitative data across some dimension to represent variation in quality, importance, sentiment, or anything that can be distributed along a numeric scale. This is not intended to suggest that you have to convert qualitative data to a numeric scale; rather, this feature gives the researcher another tool with which to gain insights into the phenomenon under investigation.

dedoose

## 8.1.1 Descriptors

In Dedoose, descriptors allow the researcher to work with quantitative and categorical data so that, if necessary for the study, the data for each qualitative unit of analysis can be described and distinguished from other qualitative units of analysis.

**BRUCE'S TIP #34**

Creating Descriptors

First create the Descriptor Set—for example, Participant Descriptor Set; then create the Fields—Age, Gender, Location, and so on. When first created, a descriptor field can be defined as one of four types: (1) Number, (2) Text, (3) Date/Time, or (4) Option List.

To use descriptors in Dedoose, you must first create a "Descriptor Set," where you can create, upload, store, and interact with these data. Think of a "set" as a folder where the fields and data reside to differentiate segments about the source of our data like "gender," "age-group," and "country of birth" and/or levels of data like "city," "county," and "state." A descriptor set has two features: (1) the "fields" (Dedoose uses the term *fields* instead of the term *variables*) and (2) the "descriptors"—the data themselves. If the descriptors were set up as a spreadsheet in Excel, the descriptor set would be the name of the spreadsheet, the fields would be the column names, there would be one row for each member of the set, and the descriptors (describing each member of the set) would be found in the spreadsheet cells. See Figure 8.1, which shows how descriptors look in Dedoose.

When first created, a descriptor field can be defined as one of four types: (1) Number, (2) Text, (3) Date/Time, or (4) Option List—these are categorical fields and when defined you also include the valid values (e.g., an option list field called "Ethnicity" might have three valid values: (1) "Hispanic," (2) "White," and (3) "Asian"). "Descriptors" are the actual data for each case (or setting, dyad, family, etc. to represent the level of analysis at which we are working). For example, "ID," "Ethnicity," and "Age" might be the fields and "Person 24," "Asian," and "36 to 40 years of age" would be the descriptor. Figure 8.1 shows the Descriptor Workspace in Dedoose, with fields displayed in the lower left panel (e.g., ID, Child Gender, Ethnicity) and descriptors in the right panel with records for each case and all values for some of the fields in view. Think of the fields as the questions that might be asked to a participant and the descriptors are the answers for each case.

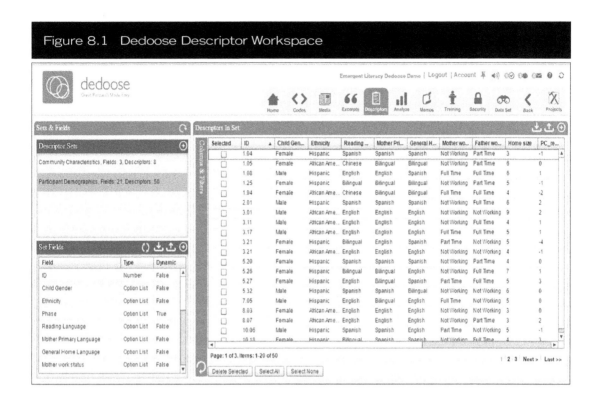

Figure 8.1   Dedoose Descriptor Workspace

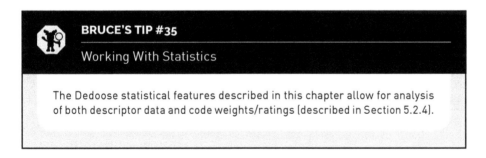

**BRUCE'S TIP #35**

Working With Statistics

The Dedoose statistical features described in this chapter allow for analysis of both descriptor data and code weights/ratings (described in Section 5.2.4).

## 8.1.2 Types of Numeric and Categorical Data

There are two basic types of "numeric" data: discrete and continuous.

Discrete number data essentially distinguish categories and are described in terms of frequencies, for example, data from a 5-point agreement scale where 1 = *strongly disagree* and 5 = *strongly agree*. Data here can only be 1, 2, 3, 4, or 5 (five discrete choices, but the order is important and meaningful across the scale). In Dedoose, these types of data would be stored in "Option List" type fields.

Continuous data are not restricted to any defined specific values—for example, age or height, where people can report across the full range of values. These data occur over a continuous range and are described by a set of descriptive statistics:

1. Central tendency—mean (average), median, and mode

2. Measures of variation and dispersion—minimum, maximum, range, variance, standard deviation, skew, and kurtosis

Categorical data, referred to as "Option List" type fields in Dedoose, are variables that are designed to group cases—for example, ethnicity (where one can be a member of the "Asian," "Hispanic," or "White" group). Categorical data are similar to discrete numeric data in how they can be presented, but the order in which they are presented is not important or meaningful.

In Dedoose, the best tables and/or charts to visualize any data will depend on the number and types of different fields (number or option list) included in your data set. Similarly, the statistics you might wish to use also depend on the number of descriptor fields and field types or code weights/ratings as well what you are trying to discover by employing these analyses.

## 8.2 Charts, Tables, and Plots for Individual Fields or Code Weights

Now that different types of data have been discussed, the next step is to look at common visualization approaches and relevant statistics for individual fields. For illustration purposes, data are drawn from a survey of qualitative and mixed methods researchers investigating their perspectives on the use of technology in their work.

### 8.2.1 Individual Number Fields or Code Weights/Ratings

One set of continuous number data (i.e., a number type descriptor field or code weights/ratings) can be displayed in a distribution plot (see below) and can be described via its central tendency and dispersion characteristics including the following:

a. The number of cases, or count

b. Mean or average value

c. Median (the value that marks the point where 50% of cases fall above and 50% of cases fall below)

d. Mode (the value that appears most often)

e. Minimum value

f. Maximum value

g. Range of values

h. Variance

i. Standard deviation

As you will see below, when seeking to learn if two groups are different in some statistically significant way, it is important to know both how far apart their mean (or average) score is from each other and how the scores are distributed around the mean score (both central tendency and degree of spread).

Simply examining the distribution of descriptor data can tell us many things about our research participants such as the following: Do most report lower levels of income? Does the group lean toward being older? Examining the distribution of code weights/ratings can inform how you have used the weight system for that code across the possible range for all the excerpts tagged with the code. For example, if you had a code for how important training support is in making decisions about choosing software and importance was weighted across a 10-point scale, you might find most training support as moderately important as shown in Figure 8.2.

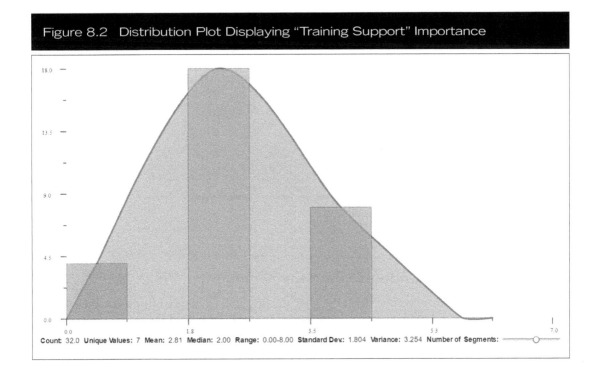

Figure 8.2  Distribution Plot Displaying "Training Support" Importance

Count: 32.0  Unique Values: 7  Mean: 2.81  Median: 2.00  Range: 0.00-8.00  Standard Dev: 1.804  Variance: 3.254  Number of Segments:

Similarly, Figure 8.3 and Table 8.1 show a display and associated set of characteristics for a descriptor number field called Technology Readiness Index 2.0 (TRI).

---

**BRUCE'S TIP #36**

Interactive Visuals

Note that the vast majority of Dedoose visuals are interactive. For example, clicking a segment on a distribution plot will pull up all associated excerpts. Click away!

---

**Figure 8.3  Distribution Plot Displaying TRI Total Score Frequency**

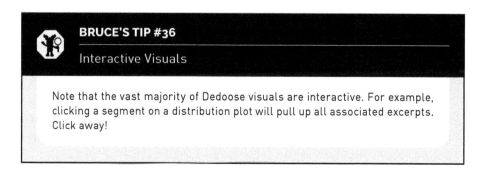

Count: 353.0  Unique Values: 44  Mean: 55.65  Median: 56.00  Range: 22.00-80.00  Standard Dev: 8.415  Variance: 70.808  Number of Segments:

*Note:* TRI = Technology Readiness Index 2.0.

## 8.2.2 Individual Option List/Categorical Field Data

Next, consider two examples dealing with a single option list data field, with discrete data as opposed to continuous. The first example is "Age-Group," which illustrates how often continuous data are converted to categories for the purposes of controlled presentation and analysis. With continuous age data, the data would have to be converted if it was advantageous to analyze and

| Table 8.1 | Distributional Characteristics of TRI 2.0 Total Score |
|---|---|
| *N* | 353.00 |
| Mean | 55.65 |
| Median | 56.00 |
| Mode | 55.00 |
| Standard deviation | 8.41 |
| Variance | 70.81 |
| Range | 58.00 |
| Minimum | 22.00 |
| Maximum | 80.00 |

*Note:* TRI = Technology Readiness Index 2.0.

explore the data as six distinct groups. In this case, a decision would be made about what best defines the groups for the purposes of the research question (see Figure 8.4). The second example is "Gender," which is a type of purely categorical data. It is important to note that with "Age-Group," the order of presentation is important (because the groups represent progressively older people). In contrast, the order of presentation for "Gender" is not meaningful or important.

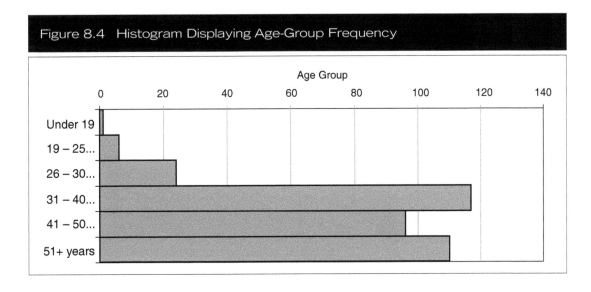

Figure 8.4   Histogram Displaying Age-Group Frequency

Age-Group data can be presented visually in a histogram because this was a converted continuous number field and the order of segments is meaningful. In Figure 8.4, 1 = Under 19 years, 2 = 19 to 25 years, . . . and 6 = 51+ years. The distributional characteristics of the Age-Group data are presented in Table 8.2, where, for example, the mean age is 4.78.

"Gender" data, created in Dedoose using option list fields (often referred to as "nominal," since the order of presentation is not meaningful), can be visually presented as a bar chart (see Figure 8.5) and its characteristics presented in a simple table (see Table 8.3).

| Table 8.2  Distributional Characteristics of Age-Group | |
| --- | --- |
| N | 354.00 |
| Mean | 4.78 |
| Median | 5.00 |
| Mode | 4.00 |
| Standard deviation | 1.03 |
| Variance | 1.07 |
| Range | 5.00 |
| Minimum | 1.00 |
| Maximum | 6.00 |

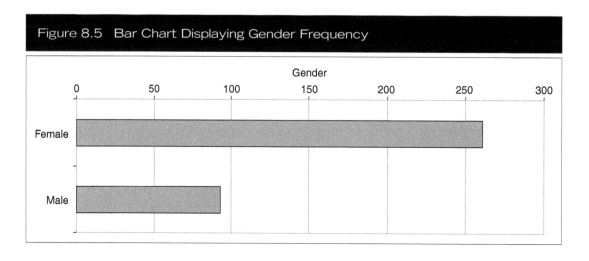

Figure 8.5  Bar Chart Displaying Gender Frequency

| Gender | Absolute Frequency | Relative Frequency |
|--------|--------------------|--------------------|
| Female | 261 | 74% |
| Male | 93 | 26% |
| Total | 354 | 100% |

Table 8.3 Frequency Characteristics for Gender

## 8.3 Charts, Tables, Plots, and Analyses for Pairs of Fields/Code Weights

When looking at more than one descriptor field and/or code weights/ratings, the next step is to turn to more complex visualizations and analyses. What becomes important here is the types of questions to be explored, what types of fields and data are needed to address those questions, and what analysis can be done to generate useful results. First, look at the questions about the relationship between two option list fields, then turn to combinations of an option list field with a continuous number field or code weights/ratings, and finish by looking at combining two continuous number fields or code weights/ratings.

### 8.3.1 Pairs of Option List Fields: Data Interaction

When looking at pairs of option list fields and how their data interact, you are asking questions such as the following: "If you have blue eyes, are you more likely to have blond hair?" or "If you are older, are you more likely to agree to the statement, I have confidence in my qualitative methods skills?" Dependencies like these may or may not exist in statistically significant ways (regardless of what might be expected or believed), and when they do, the relationships might influence or enhance deeper insights that might be drawn from qualitative data.

The comingling or combining of data from pairs of option list fields can be presented in a Contingency Table (see Table 8.4), visualized in a cross-tabulation (Cross-Tab) display (see Figure 8.6), and analyzed via a chi-square test for independence.

A quick glance at these data and the cross-tab display may seem to suggest that the older you are, the more likely you are to agree with the statement, "I have confidence in my qualitative methods skills." The chi-square test for independence can help determine if such a conclusion can be supported from a statistical perspective.

While the actual computational formula can be found elsewhere and such a level of detail is beyond the scope of this chapter, Dedoose generates the result and, in this case, finds a result of 48.12 with 20 degrees of freedom. To determine if this is a statistically significant relationship, you would compare your result with an appropriate critical value. A critical value is the point (or points) on a

| | Under 19 | 19–25 years | 26–30 years | 31–40 years | 41–50 years | 51+ years | Total |
|---|---|---|---|---|---|---|---|
| **Table 8.4** Contingency Table for Age and Agreement With "I Have Confidence in My Qualitative Methods Skills" | | | | | | | |
| Strongly disagree | 0 | 0 | 0 | 0 | 6 | 1 | 7 |
| Disagree | 0 | 0 | 3 | 2 | 10 | 5 | 20 |
| Not sure | 1 | 2 | 3 | 11 | 10 | 5 | 32 |
| Agree | 0 | 4 | 13 | 67 | 39 | 55 | 178 |
| Strongly agree | 0 | 0 | 4 | 34 | 28 | 43 | 109 |
| Total | 1 | 6 | 23 | 114 | 93 | 109 | 346 |

**Figure 8.6** Cross-Tab Display for Age and Qualitative Methods Confidence Agreement

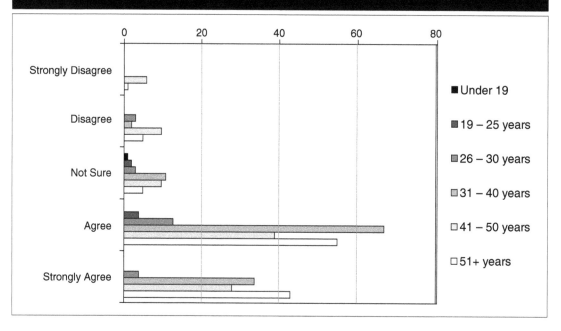

distribution specific to the test we are using. When a result is beyond a certain value, you can conclude that there is a significant relationship between the two fields in questions. Examining the table of critical values for the chi-square distribution, you see that the value exceeds the value of 45.31 ($p < .001$) in the table. Thus, you would reject that null hypothesis and conclude that there is a statistically significant relationship between age-group and confidence in qualitative methods (and you can say so with 99.99% confidence).

## 8.3.2 Tests With Continuous Numbers

### 8.3.2.1 *t* Tests: Comparing the Averages of Two Groups

*t* tests deal with data from one option list field with *only two values* and one number field or code weight/rating. The independent samples *t* test, sometimes called the simple *t* test, tests the null hypothesis that there is no difference between two independent samples. Remember, the null hypothesis is the conclusion when there is nothing going on that can be supported statistically. When statistically significant differences are found, you "reject the null hypothesis" and conclude that there is significant evidence that the two groups differ. For example, if you are looking at the age differences between the males and females in a study and find statistically significant differences, you could say that there is evidence that, for example, the females in the sample are older than the males.

Visually, you can simply present two distribution plots—one for each group along the same *X*-axis. In Figure 8.7, there are three pairs of distributions with the same two mean scores (the lines in the center) but with very different variability. Figure 8.7 illustrates how differences in variability for groups with the same mean

### Figure 8.7   Types of Variability

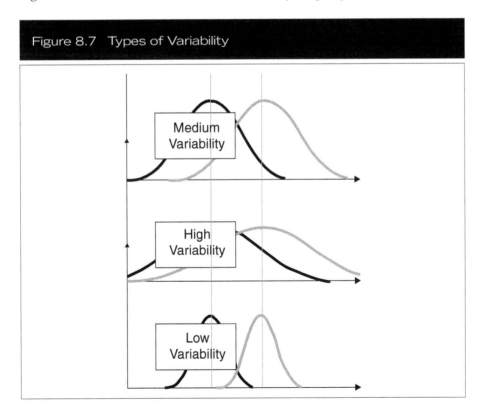

Figure 8.8  Distribution Display for TRI Total Score by Gender

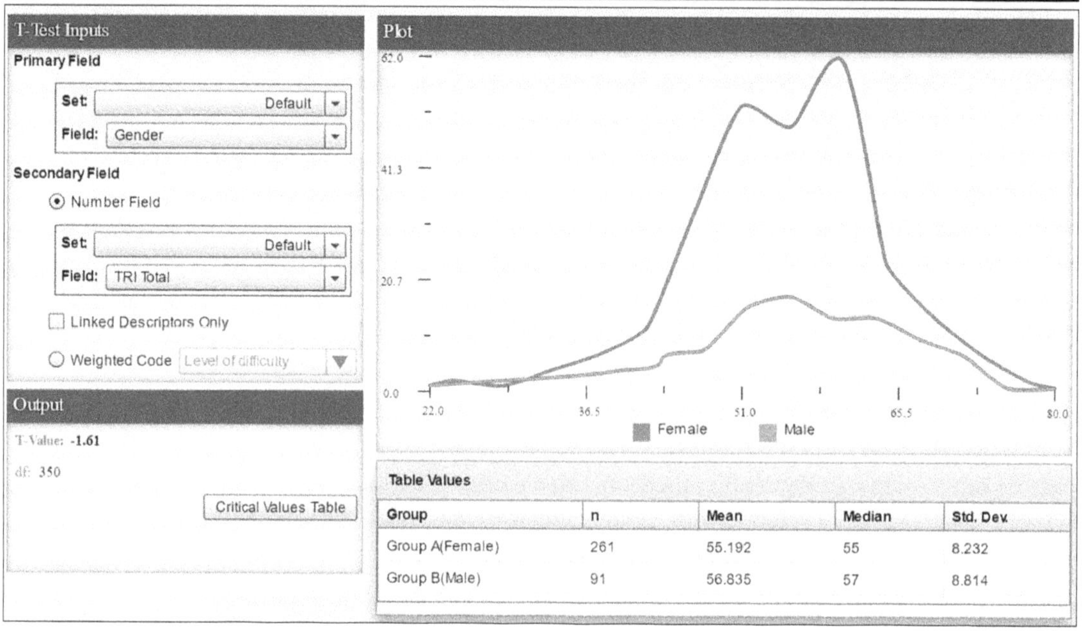

| Group | n | Mean | Median | Std. Dev. |
|-------|---|------|--------|-----------|
| Group A(Female) | 261 | 55.192 | 55 | 8.232 |
| Group B(Male) | 91 | 56.835 | 57 | 8.814 |

*Note:* TRI = Technology Readiness Index 2.0.

value will affect your ability to determine if the groups are really different in their scores. Where variability is high, there is a great deal of overlap in the distribution, and it is more difficult to envision group differences. Yet, where variability is low, group differences are more likely to be found. As such, when calculating $t$ tests and ANOVA, both these factors are taken into consideration in the calculation.

Using our example, the difference in TRI total score between males and females (see Figure 8.8) is examined.

Here, Dedoose computes a $t$ value of $-1.61$, which can then be compared with the critical values of $t$ with the appropriate degrees of freedom (350 in this example). The result here does not exceed a value in the table that would indicate statistical differences, indicating that the average TRI total scores for males and females in the sample are equal. The researcher would then accept the null hypothesis that the two groups are the same.

## 8.3.2.2 One-Way ANOVA: Comparing the Averages of Three or More Groups

ANOVA deals with data from One Option List Field with *more than two values* (e.g., for race: Asian, Hispanic, and White) and One Continuous Field or Code

Weights/Ratings. Very similar questions are being asked of the data as with a *t* test but now involve comparing more than two groups against each other. This example asks if the four TRI total groups differ significantly on the scores for the TRI motivation subscale.

Visually, the data can be presented as overlapping distribution plots with one for each group (see Figure 8.9).

Finally, a comparison can be drawn between the value of the *F* computed in this analysis and the critical value of *F* in a table of critical values for the *F* distribution. With an ANOVA, you look up the critical value by using the degrees of freedom both between and within group: in this case, the $df_b = 3$ and the $df_w = 349$. The critical value of *F* for an alpha of .01 is 3.78. Since the obtained *F* greatly exceeds this value, you would reject the null hypothesis and conclude that there is a significant difference between the groups. You would then report the result as follows: $F_{(3,349)} = 130.24$ ($p < .01$). Thus, you can conclude that with 99% confidence, there are differences between two or more groups.

The tricky part of ANOVA is that when a statistically significant result is found, you still don't know which groups are statistically different from each other. That is, an ANOVA test can tell you if the results are significant overall, but it won't tell you where those differences actually exist. For example, two

**Figure 8.9  Visualizing Distributions for TRI Motivation by TRI Total Subgroup**

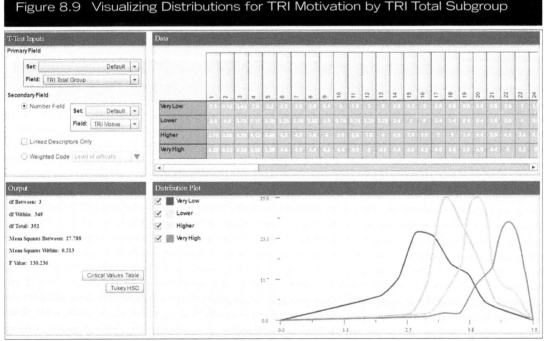

*Note:* TRI = Technology Readiness Index 2.0.

groups might be the same but the third and fourth are different. Or all four groups might be significantly different from all others. To answer these questions, you need to do what is called post hoc tests. While there are different post hoc tests to select from, in Dedoose, the Tukey's Honestly Significant Difference (HSD) test is used.

### 8.3.2.3 ANOVA Post Hoc Tests: Which Groups Are Different

When a significant ANOVA result is found, the researcher must conduct these tests for every pair of groups (called pairwise comparisons) in the ANOVA test. As mentioned earlier, while there are statistically significant results, you don't yet know which groups are statistically different from each other.

Note that when you run these tests, $q$ and $MS_w$ will not change for the different pairs, but the number of cases $n_k$ in the group might.

Once you have the HSD value for each pair, the rest is simple. If the difference between the means of the two groups exceeds the benchmark HSD, the groups are considered "honestly" significantly different.

Remembering that you found an overall ANOVA significant result at the .01 level, you now turn to Tukey's HSD. For this example, you look to the Critical Value Table for $p < .01$ with four groups and 349 degrees of freedom and find the value to be .05. You need to compare the mean scores of the groups against each other to see if any of the differences exceeds the .05 HSD value (see Figure 8.10).

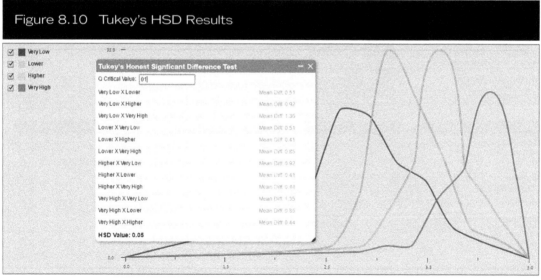

Figure 8.10   Tukey's HSD Results

*Note:* HSD = Honestly Significant Difference.

Results indicate that with the exception of the TRI Total "Lower" and "Higher" pair of groups and the "Higher" and "Very High" pair of groups, all differ at statistically significant levels.

## 8.3.2.4 Correlations Between Two Continuous Fields and/or Code Weights/Ratings

Finally, consider how Dedoose can help you analyze two continuous number fields and/or code weights/ratings. This may involve asking questions about whether numbers from two fields or code weights tend to increase or decrease with each other, or one increases when the other decreases, or are entirely unrelated to each other. For example, do people who score higher on the TRI total scale also score higher on the TRI motivation subscale (a positive relationship—when one increases, so does the other)? Or do people who score higher on the TRI total scale score lower on the TRI motivation subscale (a negative relationship—when one increases, the other decreases). To measure the strength of these relationships, Dedoose uses the Pearson product–moment correlation as a statistical indicator of the degree of linear relationship between two numbers that are both provided by the study participants.

Visually, these types of data can be displayed in a scatterplot with each dot representing a single case (see Figure 8.11).

As you can see in Figure 8.11, Pearson's correlation coefficient can range from 1 to –1 to represent both the nature of the relationship (positive or negative) and the strength of the relationship.

For the example in this chapter, you will find a strong positive relationship between the TRI total score and TRI motivation subscale score of 0.8 (see Figure 8.12).

You can then compare the obtained value to the table of critical values for $r$ with the appropriate degrees of freedom (in this case, $df = 351$). If you assume an alpha of .01, the critical value of $r$ is .148 for a one-tailed test, because 0.8 exceeds the critical value of $r$, you conclude that there is a statistically significant positive relationship between the two variables (TRI total score and TRI motivation subscale score) in the group of respondents to the survey.

### Figure 8.11  Variation in Scatterplots for Correlation Analysis

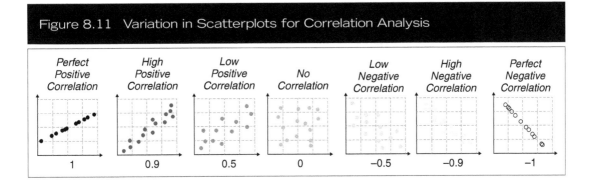

| Perfect Positive Correlation | High Positive Correlation | Low Positive Correlation | No Correlation | Low Negative Correlation | High Negative Correlation | Perfect Negative Correlation |
| --- | --- | --- | --- | --- | --- | --- |
| 1 | 0.9 | 0.5 | 0 | –0.5 | –0.9 | –1 |

Figure 8.12   TRI Total and TRI Motivation Subscale Scatterplot

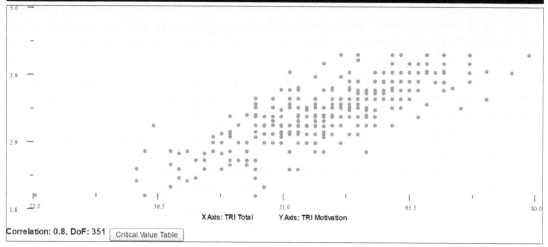

*Note:* TRI = Technology Readiness Index 2.0.

---

## 8.4  Summary

As a brief recap, Dedoose was designed from its outset to support the research needs of both qualitative and mixed methods investigators. The statistical analysis features now embedded in Dedoose allow for seamless movement from findings in qualitative data analysis into the quantitative data, what might be discovered there, and vice versa. In mixed methods investigation, there is potentially great value in the complementary nature of what these various perspectives can bring to research through the facilitation of mixed methods features in Dedoose.

# Reporting Credible Results and Sharing Findings

You are now likely at the point where you want to share findings with others. Sharing involves producing something of value to a particular audience, and it can be important to consider what particular audiences are best prepared to consume in terms of format and detail. To maximize the potential of your research effectively reaching decision makers and promoting social change, it is important to communicate the results in ways that are appropriate for the intended target audience. Reaching your audience with compelling research encompasses drawing on the research foundations you put into place during Part I of this text and your analysis work from Part II.

An example that draws on the previous chapters is the use of images to communicate and report complex evidence. Images, charts, graphs, and other forms of visualizations offer clear connections to central research questions, all of which facilitate the articulation of the full richness contained within a project. Data visualizations can be helpful both in the exploration and analysis of data and in the dissemination of findings by communicating broad surface patterns in familiar forms. Reporting and sharing a valuable product is thus enhanced through such a process.

Dedoose offers a wide variety of data visualizations, or ways to explore complex meanings and presenting the jigsaw pieces from social science inquiry to form a complete picture. The charts, tables, and plots in the Analyze Workspace will likely meet all your needs in terms of presentation graphics, filters, and other tools for the syntheses of your research findings. These visualizations are tools to examine the general nature of data and expose patterns of variation in the data and coding activity across subgroups. The visuals can be exported to facilitate the presentation of research findings and as filters or paths of further inquiry to drill deeper into findings. Charts, tables, and plots are designed to be as informative, intuitive, and transparent as possible. In addition, these visual tools can be used in numerous combinations and be flexibly adapted to address particular research questions and effectively communicate findings to the intended audience.

# CHAPTER 9 — Reporting Your Findings

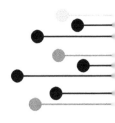

## 9.1  Reaching Your Audience

As discussed throughout the book, mixed methods research practices can be supported and strengthened through the use of Dedoose. The various chapter case studies have demonstrated specific strategies that enhance the interaction and relationships within data and the transformation and integration of evidence through analysis. This chapter moves forward with a case example that demonstrates strategies to reach your audience by reporting meaningful findings and conclusions using Dedoose.

Reporting meaningful findings requires the presentation of credible evidence that supports a compelling message. The utilization of credible evidence by others involves you drawing on your skills in helping the reader understand your message. Reporting therefore entails connecting each step of the research design starting with the positioning of the social problem to your intended audience. Your audience needs to buy into your research by seeing the problem as an issue of social importance. They need to appreciate the "so what" factor at the heart of your research. Your goal is to help your audience see why your research matters.

How do you connect your research with your findings and then connect to your audience? With this connection in place, your design needs to collectively weave the purpose, focus, and research questions together. Once this thread is crafted into a firmly established argument, reporting becomes a matter of connecting the supporting research literature and evidence into the findings and recommendations.

Using your research design as a road map for reporting provides a valuable structure for both you and your audience (Creswell & Clark, 2011; Patton, 2015). This structure frames your story. It helps your audience follow your thinking as it develops into a story and relates back to your research purpose, focus, and key questions. As you have worked through your analysis and found meaning(s) in your study, you have taken a circuitous, iterative path. Set aside time to reflect on this journey and present it in a linear developing format that your audience can follow. Unless the audience can follow your developing thinking, you have lost them before you start to present your findings.

You may find it helpful to review data management of your Dedoose project. Data management involves the identification of data and getting data prepared for analysis. Reporting the steps taken to set up your Dedoose project may help your audience connect with your findings and recommendations. As discussed in Section 3.3, memos are data and must be included in data management reporting. Remember, the memos are an audit trail of the journey taken through your research project.

## 9.2   Mixed Methods Procedural Checklist

The following checklist may be a useful means to further strengthen the reporting of your study results. When using a checklist, it is important to recognize that every study approaches a social issue in a unique way with the use of methods crafted to the particular framework of that study. Procedural criteria, therefore, represent suggested points for consideration rather than rigid measurements of quality.

Deciding what to include when reporting the results of a mixed methods study can be challenging. Too much information may distract your audience from the main purpose of the study, whereas insufficient information will likely damage

### Table 9.1   Checklist for Mixed Methods Reporting

| Criterion | Example |
|---|---|
| *Methodological reasoning* | Rationale for using mixed methods aligns with scope of study. Qualitative and quantitative methods are described. Philosophical/theoretical assumptions are described and appropriately aligned. |
| *Epistemological respect* | Both qualitative and quantitative paradigms are clearly valued and respected. |
| *Literature review* | Citations from mixed methods literature are appropriately applied. |
| *Focus* | Clear statement of what the study is about, which is consistent throughout. |
| *Research questions* | Clearly stated specific mixed methods research question(s). |
| *Mixing methodologies* | Mixing reason(s) clearly stated show why a mixed research study design was needed and used. Link your methodology to your research questions—show how this research design will enable you to answer your questions. |
| *Mixing analysis* | Clear and specific discussion about procedures showing how the data are combined and integrated. |
| *Mixing results* | Evidence of how data are mixed supporting study findings are clearly stated. Use displays (e.g., visuals, graphs, tables, quotes) when presenting your findings. Make sure to integrate your results. |
| *Audience* | Know and write for your audience. |

the credibility and utilization of your work. Mixed methods reporting is particularly challenging given the complexity of combined methods and subsequently needing to report on a large body of mixed results (Creswell & Clark, 2011; Gibson & Brown, 2009; Kajfez & Creamer, 2014; Leech, 2012). The best course of action may well be to err on the side of caution and include sufficient information to ensure adequate coverage of essential elements of your study. Consider the following criteria in Table 9.1 as a list of important considerations that your audience may need to fully understand how the study was conducted.

## 9.3 Case Study: Reporting to Multiple Audiences

This case study demonstrates how visual tools in Dedoose can be used to strengthen conclusions when reporting a study. The visuals can be exported to facilitate the presentation of research findings, and filters are available to drill deeper into findings and see data in additional contexts.

---

**THINK ABOUT, AND ANSWER, THESE QUESTIONS AS YOU READ THE CASE STUDY**

1. What visualization tools will you use in your analysis to help you picture how various data intersect with one another?

2. How do you plan to show a strong audit trail in your analysis?

3. What connections can you capture as you go? For example, how can you show that your findings are connected to your research questions?

---

### Exploration of University Communications on Donor Experience: A Case Study Using Dedoose

#### N. Geoffrey Bartlett & Jeffrey Hoyle

This case study is intended to help the reader better understand how two researchers collaborated using Dedoose. The project is based on research that explored donor–stakeholder relationships with higher education institutions. The application of the Integrated Marketing Communication (IMC) concept, an applied marketing research approach, provided insight into the data. In this case study, we investigate how higher education institutions attempt to influence donor-constructed meaning using the IMC model.

The genesis of the study begins with a desire to understand whether institutions are able to influence how donors create meaning. A key finding by Bartlett (2015) concluded that formal institutional communications did not have significant influence on donors' determination that their donations were effectively used by the institution. From this, we considered Schwandt's (2007) statement that "to claim that we can achieve an understanding means that we also acknowledge the risk that we might misunderstand" (p. 303). In other words, in constructing meaning, we must also acknowledge that our understanding of an occurrence may be incorrect based on the knowledge we possess at the time of meaning making. Schwandt's (2007) assertion of what constitutes construction of meaning is what drew us to better understand communications in higher education fundraising. We therefore set out to better understand how communications are used in higher education fundraising.

## 9.3.1 Setting Up the Project

The case study is based on Bartlett's (2015) study, which found that donors determined the effectiveness of their donation partly by how valued they felt. A key point was that formal communications did not have a significant influence on donors deciding if their donations were being used effectively.

We decided to explore how a marketing perspective could give us further insights. Specifically, we wanted to know how the IMC objectives of *informing*, *persuading*, and *reminding* contribute to our research question: How does the IMC framework provide greater insight into how higher education donors determine the effectiveness of their donations?

Three key objectives of IMC are as follows:

1. Informative advertising, which "develops initial demand for a good, service, organization, person, place, idea, or cause" (Kurtz, 2016, p. 526)

2. Persuasive advertising, which has the goal to "increase demand for existing good, service, organization, person, place, idea, or cause" (Kurtz, 2016, p. 526)

3. Reminder advertising, which "strives to reinforce previous promotional activity by keeping the name of the good, service, organization, person, place, idea, or cause before the public" (Kurtz, 2016, p. 526)

Using the objectives of informing, persuading, and reminding in a consistent manner by higher education institutions when communicating with their donors eliminates an obvious void in the donor communication process. We concluded, after adding the IMC lens to Bartlett's (2015) original study, that formal communications do not have significant influence in the higher education fundraising process.

Deeper understanding of this intersection provides organizations with accrued benefits of improved communication, which improves the overall customer experience (Meyer & Schwager, 2007). Organizations are then better informed where they need to invest resources, both human and financial. This reinvestment leads to improved customer experiences, which will lead to improved customer satisfaction, which ultimately leads to improved meaning making by the customer. Utilizing IMC's framework of informing, persuading, and reminding stakeholders of the experience with an organization builds greater awareness by the customer. This awareness, in turn, allows for a truer interaction between the customer and the organization (Agnihotri, Dingus, Hu, & Krush, 2016; Agnihotri, Rapp, & Trainor, 2009; Clow & Baack, 2016; Kurtz, 2016; Schultz & Block, 2015).

Past research has shown that an individual's perspective and understanding shape one's knowledge (Dewey, 1938). There is agreement on the notion that one's perception mediates understanding, and from that a definition of truth emerges (Noddings, 2007). Bielefeld, Rooney, and Steinberg (2005) expand on this idea of shaping knowledge and conclude that nonprofit professionals are able to motivate a donor by an appeal's message. This influence occurs by focusing on "macro-level economic, political and sociocultural" variables when constructing appeals (p. 139).

The IMC model "is the coordination and integration of all marketing tools, avenues and sources in a company [i.e., organization] into a seamless program designed to maximize the impact on customers and other stakeholders" (Clow & Baack, 2016, p. 5). Historically, IMC emerged after much discussion among scholars and practitioners as a way to coordinate and evaluate the impact of communications by an organization (Hutton, 1996; Kerr & Patti, 2015).

A review of the marketing literature resulted in our discovery that using a marketing perspective in this way illuminates new patterns and themes in the higher education fundraising. We agree with Agnihotri et al. (2009) that the "relationship between information communication and customer satisfaction suggest that information needs of customers should be given a high priority by academicians and practitioners" (p. 482) and conclude that organizations need to invest resources not only in providing technical knowledge but also in training in effective communication skills. Furthermore, in terms of customer satisfaction, providing technology to support communication between organization representatives and customers can benefit the organization (Agnihotri et al., 2009; Agnihotri et al., 2016; Schultz & Block, 2015).

By drawing on both constructivism (Lincoln & Guba, 2013; Patton, 2002; Schwandt, 2007) and IMC (Clow & Baack, 2016; Hutton, 1996; Kerr & Patti, 2015), we are better equipped to understand donor relationships in the higher education philanthropy by illuminating previously unexplored connections between constructivism and IMC. The standard communication model used for this study is adapted from Clow and Baack, 2016 (p. 4) and is illustrated in Figure C9.3-1.

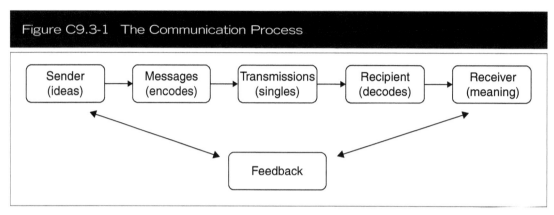

**Figure C9.3-1** The Communication Process

Sender (ideas) → Messages (encodes) → Transmissions (singles) → Recipient (decodes) → Receiver (meaning)

Feedback

*Source:* Adapted from Clow, K. E., and Baack D. (2016). *Integrated Advertising, Promotion, and Marketing Communications.* Cengage.

The IMC strategy begins with the wants or needs of a target audience by sending customer-focused messages. The IMC approach does not begin with an organization's goods or services (Clow & Baack, 2016; Kurtz, 2016). IMC illustrates the interaction of the expressive and receptive nature of the communication process and how it informs a situation/experience. IMC provides a different way to view what is, or is not, happening during the donor communication process as described in the original study by Bartlett (2015).

In conducting our research, we chose to use the REDA tool Dedoose. In the following sections, we not only summarize our research but specifically illustrate how we used Dedoose throughout the process. In the next sections, we will discuss data sources, data management, and data analysis and how Dedoose helped us organize and interpret patterns and themes. We conclude the case study with examples of how we used Dedoose in reporting our findings and finally reflect back on the use of the software.

### 9.3.2 Data Sources

Using Dedoose to view this data, we set out to answer our research questions. Data included site documents, published interviews from Bartlett's (2015) study, field notes, memos, and a review of the literature on constructivism and IMC (see Table C9.3-1, for details). Data analysis involved using both IMC and constructivist frames to better understand how donors construct meaning via their financial contributions.

### 9.3.3 Data Management

The initial challenge in conducting this research was reconfiguring our data into the Dedoose framework. Because we were initially using only a small portion

### Table C9.3-1 Data Collected

| Data Types | Data Sources |
|---|---|
| Interviews | Bartlett's (2015) study |
| Literature review | Constructivism/IMC |
| Site documents | Solicitation examples<br>Acknowledgment examples<br>Recognition examples<br>Other alumni communications |
| Memos | Analytical<br>Method<br>Reflective |
| Field notes | Bartlett's (2015) study |

of Bartlett's (2015) study, we determined what specific data would be most appropriate in answering our research question. We decided that data associated with communications would be uploaded into Dedoose, including interviews, observations, documents, and memos that Bartlett wrote during his research analysis. To organize our data, we chose a file-naming convention to allow us to easily sort our data in Dedoose. We incorporated some of Bartlett's original coding structure and interlaid the IMC framework over it, thereby allowing us to focus primarily on data that related to communications, without excluding other data that may be useful as the analysis process proceeded. The coding structure included adding IMC as a parent code with Informing, Persuading, and Reminding added as child codes. Using Dedoose in this way provided a visual representation of our thinking to better understand what we were observing as we incorporated the IMC lens into the existing data.

Memos became a critical component of this process as we were working independently and geographically separated, as well as primarily asynchronously at our individual schedules, at our own pace. By recording our individual contributions via memos, we tracked how our individual work was contributing to the latest version. More important, we were able to track our evolving understandings as we continued to analyze the data. While this may seem a rather basic idea, it is especially critical when working independently with large amounts of qualitative data.

The initial data uploaded into Dedoose were not in a usable structure, as they were laid out differently than the coding structure used in Bartlett's (2015) study. To proceed, we discussed and organized the data in a way that allowed us to integrate our new approach. We found Dedoose to be user friendly and were able to easily manipulate the layout of our data. We focused on the original codes that discussed communication issues from the original study (Bartlett,

2015) allowing us to create a coding substructure around IMC concepts. Using this substructure, we analyzed our data using the coding structure interwoven with inductive analysis.

### 9.3.4 Analysis Processes

The analysis tools integrated into Dedoose allowed for many unique ways to view data at a deeper level. Dedoose provides numerous ways such as Code Co-Occurrence Table, Code Application by Descriptor Field chart, and the ability to filter data into sets based on descriptors, users, media, and codes that allow for unique ways to view and analyze data. With these tools, we began to see patterns and themes emerge as we viewed Bartlett's original data through the IMC lens. These new patterns and themes allowed us to draw wholly new conclusions as to how institutions can influence meaning making via their communications.

The Dedoose Analyze Workspace offers a wide variety of data visualization tools. We used these tools to expose patterns in the data by looking at coding activity across the IMC functions (Inform, Persuade, and Remind). These charts, tables, and plots are designed to be as informative, intuitive, and transparent as possible. They can be used in numerous combinations and be adapted to address particular research questions. Being able to visualize the data in different ways allowed us to better understand emerging patterns and themes, which in turn helped us develop our findings and provide recommendations. Two tools, in particular, were valuable to our analysis.

The Code Co-Occurrence Table (see Figure C9.3-2) showed us how the code system was used across all project excerpts.

This symmetric, code-by-code matrix presented the frequencies for which all code pairings were applied to the same excerpt and overlapping excerpts. The display exposed both expected and unexpected patterns in which two codes were (or were not) used together. We were able to more clearly view the intersection of IMC with the original study. Specifically, the matrix showed us that the IMC concepts Inform and Persuade were the most often identified IMC functions in the data. This is in line with Bartlett's (2015) original analysis. In Bartlett's study, research participants commented that institutions acknowledged gifts that were made but did not highlight the outcomes to which those gifts contributed. The site document review confirmed this thinking. With the overlay of IMC, we concluded that this continues to be a missing piece in the donor relationship. Institutions do not utilize Informing and Persuading communication tools to illustrate how gifts are used. Therefore, they do not utilize the full spectrum of IMC communication principles to remind donors how their gifts were used. The Code Co-Occurrence Table was critical in discovering this finding.

Another table also was essential in our analysis procedure. The Code Application by Descriptor field chart (see Figure C9.3-3) includes a number of options that can be some of the most useful visualizations for analysis, interpretation, and presentation of research findings. Essentially, this chart represents the number of excerpts that are associated with a particular code separately for each subgroup within a descriptor field.

| Codes | Caller motivation | Caller perceptions | Communication | Donor trust | IMC functions | inform | persuade | remind | broken promise | cause and effect | change | communication | continued support | credibility | donor experience |
|---|---|---|---|---|---|---|---|---|---|---|---|---|---|---|---|
| Caller motivation | | | | | | | | | | | | | | | |
| Caller perceptions | | | | | | | | | | | | | | | |
| Communication | | | | | | | | | | | | | | | |
| Donor trust | | | | | | 1 | | | 2 | | | | | | |
| IMC functions | | | | | | | | | | | | | | | |
| inform | | | | 1 | | | 3 | 2 | 5 | 2 | | 4 | 1 | | |
| persuade | | | | | | 3 | | | | | | | | | |
| remind | | | | 2 | | 2 | | | | | | 7 | 3 | | |
| broken promise | | | | | | 5 | | | | | | 1 | 1 | | |
| cause and effect | | | | | | 2 | | | | | | | | | |
| change | | | | | | | | | | | | | | | |
| communication | | | | | | 4 | | 7 | 1 | | | | 1 | | |
| continued support | | | | | | 1 | | 3 | 1 | | | 1 | | | |

Taken together, these tables provide a critical understanding of the intersections between the original and the new findings. The tables illustrate that certain IMC functions are routinely observed in the data, specifically Inform and Persuade. Data that correspond to the IMC function Remind are not observed as frequently as Inform and Persuade—from this, we conclude that institutions can do a better job of using a variety of communication functions. We found these two tables indispensable in our inductive analysis. By visualizing where the intersections occurred, we were able to draw comparisons between the initial and the current studies.

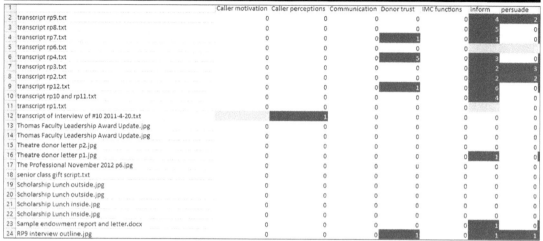

Figure C9.3-3   Code Application by Descriptor Field Chart After Export to Excel

From this point, our analysis takes a more deductive approach, and we conclude that universities routinely do not utilize the whole arsenal of IMC concepts to communicate with donors. This lack of fully communicating with donors limits the institutions' ability to inform donors. Therefore, donors are not given the entire spectrum of information to make informed decisions.

## 9.3.5 Reporting the Project

This case study employs a unique approach to gain a better understanding of communicating with donors in order to contribute to how they make decisions. IMC was used to augment the constructivism approach that resulted in our findings. These findings, which were discovered through the innovative ways to view and analyze data in Dedoose, will be disseminated via peer-reviewed publication.

Using Dedoose was critical for us to complete our research and produce actionable findings. The Code Application by Descriptor field chart and the Code Co-Occurrence Table were especially important in our research. The built-in features of Dedoose simplified the process. We were able to choose from a variety of visualization tools to support our analysis processes without the need to create charts and graphs from scratch.

The Dedoose tables are also important elements to reporting our study. The visuals can be exported to facilitate the presentation of research findings (as illustrated throughout this case study). Filters are available to drill deeper into findings and see data in additional contexts. The visualization tables enabled us to easily picture how various data intersect with one another. As such, this informative visual strengthens our conclusions, allowing for the reader to understand the interpretations we present (Creswell, 2009). The Dedoose options allowed us to illustrate our analysis processes and conclusions in a variety of forms, whether as a table or a word cloud, thereby giving the reader a deeper and richer understanding of our experiences.

## 9.3.6 Looking Back

We found revisiting an existing study was more challenging than first thought. The challenges were basically geographic and perspective. Geographically, the issues revolved around working from different locations separated by a major distance, which were more severe than we anticipated with issues such as time, place, and technology aspects of collaborating on this project being more time-consuming, to working on the project efficiently and effectively. Dedoose was very helpful in allowing to collaborate in real time from different locations. Working on the existing study presented a unique situation in that one of us, Bartlett, was the original author of the study and thus had a different level of familiarity with the study data than Hoyle. Bartlett came to the study with a level of comfort with how the study was conducted, data gathered, and originally analyzed. Hoyle came to the study with a basic understanding of the study and approached it from a marketing perspective, specifically IMC, to explore the original findings reported by Bartlett.

Using Dedoose was a particular challenge for us as neither of us had used the application before. The analysis process, especially, was unfamiliar. In Dedoose, there are two steps to code data. You must first highlight the data of interest and create an "excerpt." You then create a link between the excerpt and a code by coding the excerpt. This seemed an unnecessary first step. However, after using Dedoose to code and analyze the data, it became apparent that this was a useful process, especially in the inductive analysis stage. We were able to set aside data as excerpts that we thought may be important or worth reviewing, without the need to define it at that point. Only after we were well into the analysis process did we recognize the value of creating excerpts.

There are many other tools in Dedoose that may be useful in analyzing data. However, we used the tools that allowed us to look at the data from a previous study in a different or new way. Dedoose allows for data to be filtered into sets based on descriptors, users, media, and codes. This allows for the utilization of the many analytical tools to explore certain data. This encourages the exploration of different aspects of data using the unique visualization tools to slice and dice data. Overall, we found Dedoose to be a beneficial and easy-to-navigate REDA platform. Learning a REDA tool, such as Dedoose, for this project was not an initial draw to contribute to this project. However, after some encouragement and investigation, we discovered that Dedoose was easy to learn and allowed for interesting ways to look at data in unique ways. After weeks of what amounted to trying to use Dedoose by fitting into our existing understanding of REDA foundations, we discovered a new, intuitive, and productive approach to analyzing data. It became exciting to see the patterns and themes appear from the Dedoose tools.

### 9.3.7 Information About the Case Study Authors

**Dr. N. Geoffrey Bartlett** is the assistant vice president for annual giving at the University at Buffalo. He has more than 20 years of fundraising experience in higher education and cultural organizations.

**Dr. Jeffrey Hoyle** is a lecturer of marketing and professional sales in the Department of Marketing in the College of Business Administration at Central Michigan University. Hoyle has more than 15 years of teaching experience combined with 20 years marketing and B2B sales experience in the manufacturing, foodservice, health care, and forest products industries.

# CHAPTER 10

# Sharing Data With a Larger Audience

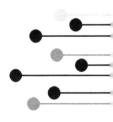

## 10.1 Reaching a Larger Audience

The greater intent of social science research is more than producing a single report to an audience of a few people. Theses and dissertations are broadly shared on searchable databases with the intent of informing decision makers and furthering future research. Scholarly research studies are published with these same goals of enlightening a wide audience of others. Sharing your work through these traditional platforms is recognized as an essential step in the dissemination of knowledge in the social sciences. How might the research community extend and expand the sharing of new knowledge? Some important questions to consider are as follows: What becomes of the raw data that these studies are based on? How might these data be shared?

Rather than relying exclusively on traditional methods of dissemination, we encourage you to share your data with a larger audience. Data sharing offers many benefits, including the transparent democratization of information, access to major data gathering programs, and as a valuable research resource for social science inquiry. A few examples of what data collections may offer include access to government-sponsored surveys, longitudinal studies, census data, business data, narrative case studies, and recorded oral histories. These rich sources of social data can support and strengthen qualitative, quantitative, and mixed methods research.

Practices supporting the sharing of raw data are well established with quantitative studies that report statistical results. Not so with qualitative studies due to the large volume of data and potential human subject protection concerns. The raw data from qualitative studies may raise privacy concerns that potentially expose confidential information, render study participants identifiable, or otherwise violate institutional review board or human research ethics committee approvals and agreements. Nonetheless, this sharing of raw data is of particular interest in qualitative and mixed methods practices.

Foremost in promoting the sharing of social science research is the International Association for Social Science Information Services and Technology (IASSIST). Established in the 1970s, IASSIST is dedicated to (a) advocating access to data; (b) cultivating a community committed to the cultivation, use, and preservation of data; and (c) fostering professional development for data professionals (IASSIST Strategic Plan, 2014). These efforts have promoted and extended data archives in other countries around the world that have become part of the IASSIST. Two examples of national initiatives include one based in the United Kingdom and the other in the United States. Both of these initiatives support ethical practices in publicly sharing qualitative and mixed methods raw data. The U.K. Data Service initiative was founded by the National Social Policy and Social Change Archive at the University of Essex. The U.S. initiative was founded by the Qualitative Data Repository (QDR) at Syracuse University. The following case study explores the role of QDR in the U.S. initiative and discusses the role of Dedoose in these efforts.

## 10.2 Case Study: Sharing Qualitative Social Science Data

Research findings can be shared in many ways primarily in the form of reports, journal articles, and presentations. Here, we discuss the possibilities of sharing data and finished Dedoose projects with larger audiences, such as data repositories around the world, together with the ethical and technical issues involved in such data sharing. As a starting point, remember any ethics application must cover any sharing of your de-identified data such as with a data repository like QDR.

### Sharing and Managing Qualitative Data Using Dedoose

#### Sebastian Karcher, Dessi Kirilova, & Christiane Pagé

The Qualitative Data Repository (QDR, **www.qdr.org**) is an archive dedicated to qualitative data and data underlying multimethod inquiry. QDR is the only repository of its kind in the United States—dedicated specifically to curating and archiving qualitative data and attuned to the requirements and concerns of qualitative researchers, their materials, and their sources. Planning for QDR began in 2007, as discussions about data sharing gained increasing salience in the social sciences. Much of the infrastructure and advice on sharing data, however, focused on quantitative data. QDR was thus founded to fill this gap and provide dedicated guidance and suitable infrastructure for the needs of qualitative and multimethod researchers. With its roots in political science, QDR is now an interdisciplinary and international social science data repository, serving researchers from disciplines as diverse as public health, sociolinguistics, anthropology, and political science.

QDR provides extensive guidance to researchers on key topics such as managing and organizing qualitative data, preparing and formatting data for sharing, working with data based on interaction with human participants, and teaching with and about qualitative data (see qdr.org/guidance). Moreover, the repositories aim to support the particular requirements of qualitative researchers and their data. One example of making data infrastructure work for qualitative research is QDR's Annotation for Transparent Inquiry (ATI) initiative (qdr.org/ati). ATI allows researchers to link specific passages in a published work with source excerpts, notes about their context, and links to the full data sources. In many ways, using annotation and linking to make qualitative research more transparent is rooted in the same practices that underlie REDA software. Such computer-assisted analysis of qualitative and multimethod data is rapidly growing among qualitative researchers. Another area of activity for QDR has thus been to develop guidelines and contribute to technological developments that facilitate the sharing of REDA data. This case study is part of this endeavor, which also includes advice to individual users from a workshop held with developers and practitioners (Karcher & Pagé, 2017) to better understand researchers' needs on both a technical and a practical level.

So why should authors share their qualitative data? And what is it about your REDA project and data that make them particularly good for sharing? Different researchers may share data for different reasons. In many cases, shared data put research on more solid, transparent foundations and make it more credible. Data are also a valuable research output by themselves: As other scholars use and cite them, they enhance the authors' profile. Data sharing also supports those teaching methods, allowing students to learn tools and methods in real-world settings. Shared data can help junior scholars or scholars from low-income economies who may not have the resources to engage in primary data collection. In some cases, researchers share data because they are required by a funder or a journal in which they seek to publish. Finally, where research findings have significant social impact, the dissemination of the data they are built on may be an ethical imperative.

Sharing and exchanging qualitative and multimethods data projects is independent of epistemological or methodological priors. Research transparency is not about positivist versus interpretivist approaches, and it is even less about quantitative versus qualitative methodology. The importance of transparency does not derive from a scientist's goal of replication but from a more fundamental notion that credibility of science is *process dependent:* Its credibility relies on being transparent about the process through which researchers arrive at their conclusions or interpretations (Lupia & Elman, 2014, p. 20). REDA projects lend themselves particularly well to process transparency, because most analysis steps occur in a single environment and can be recorded transparently.

Data sharing can be costly—for example, data collection and preparation in accordance with ethical guidelines, data documentation, and supplemental fees. Good research practices often have a significant impact on minimizing those research costs (see Figure C10.2-1).

REDA analytical attributes coupled with curation and documentation functionalities make them ideal for data sharing; for metadata creation facilitating the processes for how your data can be found, accessed, and searched; and for ensuring their long-term preservation. In effect, data sharing as a REDA user maximizes your return on research documentation and investments, which also enables your data to be citable through the process of assigning them a digital object identifier (DOI). There is a richness and completeness of the research process with REDA,

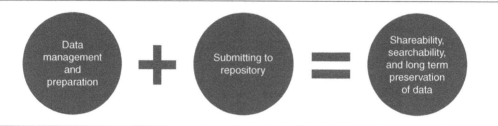

typically beyond what non-computer-aided analysis provides, that intrinsically facilitates and readies the data for sharing. The contemporaneous note taking and documentation involved with REDA often leads those data to be more structured than most other qualitative data. The ability to annotate key decisions in the research process either via memos or by annotating coding labels is another big plus for data sharing. Such memos can even be time-stamped to document the timing of crucial decision(s) in your research process. In this manner, REDA functionalities and attributes readily map onto curation functionality and documentation needs for data sharing.

The additional data visibility and exposure or usage available to REDA researchers often will mean that human participant protections are top of mind. Since the applications add complexity and visibility of data, researchers have often considered additional care by design. Domain repository will benefit from these steps and can help you think through how to legally and ethically share your REDA project. In short, richness and completeness of research process, thanks to applications capabilities, make REDA a great match for data sharing. Data sharing accrues benefits and increases and improves collaboration opportunities. It is championed in the Dedoose design philosophy as it promotes transparency, evaluability, sharing your lessons learned, together with maximizing the use of your contributed data—information. Moreover, in reuse scenarios, data sharing significantly minimizes the effects of data collection.

## 10.2.1 Managing Your Dedoose Project for Sharing

You will find it much easier to share your data, if you consider the possibility of data sharing from the beginning of your project. To make your data widely usable, we recommend sharing it both as a complete Dedoose project (usable by other Dedoose users) and as individual files, usable by anyone regardless of the software (if any) they use. In the following, we present some detailed, step-by-step advice for sharing your REDA project.

## 10.2.1.1 File Naming and Organization

Consider what unit of data is going to be most meaningful for organizing. This may be what you think of as a "case" or any other meaningful unit within your research. Often, these will be geographic units (a city, region, or country), but they could also be groups (political parties, professions), or historical periods. Organize your data around these main units. An important way to help with this organization is to implement a coherent naming convention for your files from the start. Your file naming convention should be driven by the organization of your project, so there is no one-size-fits-all solution.

Some rules of thumb for file naming, however, do exist. Typically, begin a file-name with the name of the main unit you're investigating. We strongly recommend you include the date of when you last edited the file in YYYYMMDD format; this quickly lets you identify the most recent version of a file. To help with organization, also indicate whether a file is data (e.g., an interview transcript) or documentation (e.g., an informed consent form). Other information you may want to consider including is a one-word description of the file's content or an indication that a file needs to remain private or that it is already de-identified. For uniformity, also decide on the use of capital letters in filenames and the delimiter between different components of a filename (hyphen or underscore are the most common). A typical filename following these guidelines would be: Brazil_InterviewA_20170324_ deidentified. Some file naming examples are given in Figure C10.2-2.

### Figure C10.2-2   File Naming Examples

| Type | Title | Added | User | # Ex | Length |
|---|---|---|---|---|---|
| | Argentina_DocumentationA_20190107_deidentified | 01/17/2019 | Support | 1 | 673 |
| | Argentina_DocumentationB_20190106_deidentified | 01/17/2019 | Support | 1 | 398 |
| | Argentina_InterviewA_20190109_deidentified | 01/17/2019 | Support | 1 | 829 |
| | Argentina_InterviewB_20190108_deidentified | 01/17/2019 | Support | 1 | 436 |
| | Bolivia_InterviewA_20190105_deidentified | 01/17/2019 | Support | 1 | 584 |
| | Bolivia_InterviewB_20190104_deidentified | 01/17/2019 | Support | 1 | 681 |
| | Brazil_DocumentationA_20190115_deidentified | 01/17/2019 | Support | 1 | 584 |
| | Brazil_DocumentationB_20190114_deidentified | 01/17/2019 | Support | 1 | 681 |
| | Brazil_InterviewA_20170324_deidentified | 01/17/2019 | Support | 1 | 673 |
| | Brazil_InterviewB_20190116_deidentified | 01/17/2019 | Support | 1 | 398 |
| | Chile_DocumentationA_20190111_deidentified | 01/17/2019 | Support | 1 | 357 |
| | Chile_DocumentationB_20190110_deidentified | 01/17/2019 | Support | 1 | 634 |
| | Chile_InterviewA_20190113_deidentified | 01/17/2019 | Support | 1 | 566 |

### 10.2.1.2 Include File-Level Information

Within individual files, include basic information about their contents, sometimes referred to as metadata or file-level metadata. A common approach is to have a standard header for every file. For example, for interviews, include the date and location of the interview as well as any relevant information about the interview and interviewee following a standard template.

### 10.2.1.3 Keep Track of Sensitive Information

As you collect your data, keep concerns about private and sensitive data in mind. As you add information that may need redacting, use Dedoose tags to highlight it, so you can quickly identify it at a later time. Also consider tagging files that you specifically cannot share (e.g., interviews given "off the record" or signed consent forms). If you include file-level metadata, take care to not include strongly identifying information in the file if the data are very sensitive. For sensitive data, keep a separate, encrypted key that links the code or pseudonym used in the transcript in a secure location. You will typically already have described such procedures in your institutional review board/ethics board application.

### 10.2.1.4 Keep Memos About Analytic Decisions

As you analyze your data, Dedoose will help you make your analytic process transparent. Using best practices, as recommended throughout this book, will make your own life easier, and it will also make your data more shareable and more valuable. In particular, making any coding and analysis decisions explicit in memos will help readers evaluate your conclusions, together with secondary users who can better understand the application of given codes in your data (see Figure C10.2-3).

### 10.2.1.5 Create a "Data Narrative"

We recommend that you include a document dedicated entirely to describing the data—the data narrative that provides a high-level overview over the data project. It begins with a general outline of your research (similar to an abstract or executive summary) to contextualize the data. In the second part, it describes the data in more detail:

a. What sort of data are part of your project? (e.g., interviews, photos, videos, scanned documents)

b. How were the data gathered? Describe, for example, the selection of interviewees and the setting in which interviews were conducted or how particular files in an archive were selected.

c. How were the data processed after they were gathered? (e.g., transcription of interviews, text recognition [OCR] on scans)

**Memos**

Filter by

Search

| Q | Search memos | Q |

Showing 13 of 13

☐ Select All

Date Created

☐ Select a date range.

Memo Groups

Q  Find memo group

| | | |
|---|---|---|
| ☐ Reflection Memos | ✎ | 5 |
| ☐ Assignments | ✎ | 3 |
| ☐ Coding Memos | ✎ | 5 |
| ☐ Milestone Memos | ✎ | 1 |

Linked Items

Q ∨ Select linked item(s).

No Linked items selected

| Desc field decision ☐ | Coding Question 87 ☐ | New Reading by Mother M... ☐ |
|---|---|---|
| why convert a continuous variable..the field name is this and new field is that | not sure about pre write code here | Here are my thoughts about this excerpt and how if fits into the larger context of reading by mother theory amidst all the other reading by mother excerpts. |
| By Support 12/2016 | By Support 03/2016 | By Support 09/2015 |

| Nice Transition ☐ | Week 2 ☐ | Week 1 ☐ |
|---|---|---|
| Dynamic, paced, and good timing...nice David :) | Descriptor data entry please | Start entering interview data and thinking about possibel coding |
| By Support 02/2012 | By Support 02/2012 | By Support 11/2011 |

d. How are the data organized? (see above)

e. How and by whom was coding/analysis conducted?

The data narrative will help other readers better understand your data from the outset, and it can help inform the methods section of your publication. It will also help curators provide better structured metadata that will help make your data more discoverable for others.

## 10.2.1.6 Preparing Your Data for Sharing

Make a copy of your project and delete any information you do not want to share, such as private notes or sensitive information. If you have followed our advice above, you can now use the tags you have created to redact potentially identifying information from transcripts.

De-identifying qualitative transcripts requires great care as you need to remove not only names and addresses ("direct identifiers") but also contextual information that can be used to identify participants to whom you have promised confidentiality ("indirect identifiers").

My father went to [a co-ed high school in South Philadelphia], and then went to [an Ivy League School] on a [sports] scholarship. [Description of his role on the team]. He thought he may have been one of the first Jews to play in the Ivy League.  He played and started his first year, but he [was injured] and lost his scholarship – which is what they did back then. His picture with his team [from the 1930s] is on the wall [at Penn].

Use pseudonyms for individuals. For indirect identifiers such as dates, specific locations, or institutions, use broader categories such as date ranges ("between 1980 and 1985") or a description of the location ("small village in Southern France"). Clearly and consistently, mark places where you have redacted data, for example, using square brackets (see Figure C10.2-4).

Detailed advice on de-identifying qualitative data can be found on QDR (qdr. org/guidance/human-participants/deidentification) and the U.K. Data Archive (ukdataservice.ac.uk/manage-data/legal-ethical/anonymisation/qualitative).

### 10.2.1.7 Exporting Your Data Sharing

At QDR, we recommend your data are shared in two different forms. The first form is the raw full export from Dedoose. Once your data are prepared for sharing, first export the whole project, by clicking on "Export Data," then "Export Project" (see Figure C10.2-5).

Then, create a "human-readable" export, which anyone, regardless of software, can use: Export all relevant files in widely used formats (e.g., RTF, PDF, Excel, as well as widely used video, image, and audio formats). Also, export all relevant memos as RTF or PDF files. See the Dedoose documentation for detailed export instructions.

As of this writing, efforts are underway to provide a standardized format for exchange between different REDA software products (qdasoftware.org). As this exchange format matures and becomes more widely available, we expect it to replace some of these recommendations.

### 10.2.2 Finding a Data Repository

Data repositories provide numerous advantages for sharing data. They provide searchable catalogs that make your data widely findable. They specialize in the long-term storage and preservation of data, so your data will still be accessible 25 years from today. Finally, many data repositories have specialized curators who can help you as you deposit your data.

As you are getting ready to share your data, find a data repository suitable for your purposes. There are several distinctions to consider:

- Some repositories publish data from any scientific discipline and regardless of the origin of the researcher (e.g., Harvard Dataverse,

Figshare, Zenodo). These repositories have large holdings and are typically easy to use, but they will provide little assistance and typically no checks on your data.

- A second group of repositories, "institutional repositories," focuses on data from researchers of a given institution, typically a university. They are interdisciplinary and their expertise given disciplinary data varies considerably, but data librarians at your institution will often be willing to assist you as you deposit data.

- A third group of repositories, often referred to as "domain repositories," specializes in a given discipline, such as social sciences. Such repositories include the U.K. Data Archive, Inter-university Consortium for Political and Social Research, and the QDR.

Depositing with a domain repository lets you benefit from the experience of curators with exactly the sort of data you are depositing. They will curate your data to make it more easily findable, reusable, and (in the case of sensitive data) safe for sharing.

Deposit all exported files with your repository of choice. For many repositories, especially domain repositories, you will already have communicated with a curation specialist at this point, and they may provide additional guidance.

## 10.2.3 Promoting Your Data

Finally, once your data are published, don't forget to promote it! Publications that use secondary analysis of qualitative work are relatively rare, so this is one way in which you can set yourself apart. Remember to include the publication in your CV and promote it via Twitter, your blog, or any other channels you use to disseminate your research. Most data repositories will assign a DOI to your data. The DOI generates a permanent link and should be used in promoting and in citing your data.

QDR welcomes deposits of digital data generated through qualitative and multi-method research in the social sciences, health sciences, applied sciences, and humanities. QDR personnel are available to assist and advise you throughout the data deposit process. The QDR website also includes guidance and resources to help you think through data-related challenges such as protecting human participants, respecting copyright, and others. Further details are available at **https://qdr .syr.edu/deposit**

## 10.2.4 Information About the Case Study Authors

**Sebastian Karcher** is the associate director of the Qualitative Data Repository. He is an expert in scholarly software tools and workflows and the curation of qualitative research data. Sebastian holds a PhD in political science from Northwestern University.

**Dessi Kirilova** is a senior curation specialist at the Qualitative Data Repository. She is particularly interested in educating researchers in good data practices, starting in the research planning stages. Dessi is a PhD candidate in political science at Yale University, where her work focuses on postcommunist foreign policies and national identity formation.

**Christiane Pagé** is the associate director of the Center for Qualitative and Multi-Method Inquiry (CQMI) at Syracuse University. She heads outreach for the CQMI and the Qualitative Data Repository. She is coauthor on numerous CAQDAS projects that look at leadership styles of international NGOs, of global private–public partnerships, and of U.S. Senior Executive Service members.

# 10.3 Changing Reporting Practices: Open Access

Sharing your research findings and data is the last step of the research or evaluation journey. Often, this step is understood as live presentations and publication in academic journals, books, and reports. This view is relatively static; yet, as illustrated in this chapter's case study, data and how you may choose to share them can be of great value to you, to the funding agencies, and to the broader community. Furthermore, as REDA are increasingly employed in the social sciences, there is growing interest in the ability to move among the different technologies. Imagine an agency has invested in a research or evaluation project led by an individual primary investigator who is prominent in a particular area of study. The quality of the data to be gathered, how they will be processed and analyzed, and how they will be disseminated would be high. If so, from a traditional perspective, the funding agency would feel that they received a valuable return for its investment. However, consider if the data gathered and even complete projects were shared with others who then generated other outputs. This, in part, is core to the vision of data/project repositories such as QDR. It is as simple as an academic advisor sharing their data with graduate students who then conduct their thesis or dissertation work without the burden and cost of gathering their own data.

There are many challenges for end users who wish to move from one digital tool to another. Many of these challenges relate to proprietary technology protection, difficulty in exporting what had been done within a particular tool, and the incompatibility of features among the various choices. From its outset, Dedoose

Figure 10.1   List of Digital Tools That Can Be Imported to Dedoose

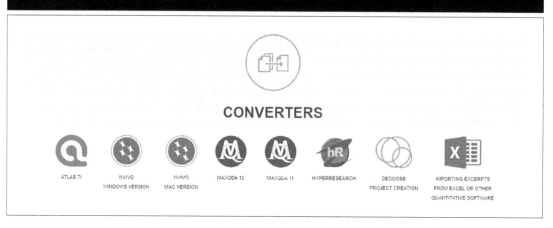

CONVERTERS

ATLAS.TI    NVIVO    NVIVO    MAXQDA 12    MAXQDA 11    HYPERRESEARCH    DEDOOSE    IMPORTING EXCERPTS
         WINDOWS VERSION   MAC VERSION                                   PROJECT CREATION   FROM EXCEL OR OTHER
                                                                                            QUANTITATIVE SOFTWARE

features were intentionally designed to facilitate this sharing and flexibility in how users can proceed. Part of these decisions and design were driven by the simple belief that end users own their data and they should be able to move in and out of Dedoose as easily as possible with their data in formats that can be used elsewhere. This includes the ability to export an entire Dedoose project to XML format, which is fully transparent.

While it has not always been the case, increasingly this vision is shared by others, one example being the open-XML standard being planned and developed by developers of a range of REDA products. Dedoose is at the forefront of this movement as it is currently possible to migrate projects from many of these other products into Dedoose. Dedoose has developed a set of migration tools that enables, as much as possible, to export from other projects and then use the results to populate a Dedoose project. Figure 10.1 shows a list of digital tools that can be imported to Dedoose.

Different REDA offer unique features and may have different infrastructure for projects, so the format needed to migrate your data into Dedoose will vary. Dedoose has outlining steps for setting up a migration file based on your REDA at **https://www.dedoose.com/resources/converters**. Once the export is completed and sent to Dedoose, it will be used to create a Dedoose project for the researcher. The project does not necessarily have to come from another REDA. For example, if you have coded any data locally, placing the excerpts into an Excel file as per the Excel migration Converter steps will allow you to bring all of that coding into Dedoose.

The challenges are that not all REDA products structure a database in the same way and some have features not present in others. The Dedoose developers have built migration tools to read what can be exported from other digital tools and then produce a Dedoose project as close as possible to the original. These tools then allow users of other products to move into Dedoose and capitalize on what Dedoose offers (e.g., collaboration, platform independence, low cost). The open-XML standard being developed is taking a similar approach—that is looking beyond where the tools are incompatible and seeking to find a standard that can be used for all relevant products.

## 10.4 Final Word

The process of designing and implementing a mixed methods study is complex. Analyzing any social science data has always been challenging and is mostly an opaque process to novice researchers. Follow the process in incremental steps. Use Dedoose as a support tool, and always make sure that you, as the researcher, are in charge of the research study design and analysis.

When feeling overwhelmed, take a step back and consider what you have achieved so far, then organize small steps forward to keep your momentum moving forward. A little bit each day, and one day you will be successful in your research and have something to share with your audience.

> Visit **http://www.dedoose.com/** and **http://www.immrglobal.org/** for additional resources, including videos, user guides, FAQs, articles, case studies, and more to help you use Dedoose for your research.

# Closing Remarks

• • • • • • • • • • • • • • • • • • • • • • • • • • • • • • • • • • • • • • • • • • • • • • • • • • • • • • •

This book is a terrific way to engage with mixed methods research using a tool like Dedoose. As one of the founders of Dedoose, it should not be surprising that I am enthusiastic, but I sincerely believe you will appreciate the value of using mixed methods in general and how Dedoose can support this mission.

As a longtime social scientist, I understand we need information in many different forms to do great research, and this is the purpose of Dedoose (**www .dedoose.com**):

> Dedoose is a web-based application that allows you to organize and analyze research data, no matter what form those data take.

The challenges of doing this kind of integration of qualitative and quantitative data are many, and the authors of this book recognize the complexity of integrating multiple levels of data as well as the remarkable value and strengths of doing so. Generally, mixed methods research can be used to capitalize on the strengths of various research methods, where the researcher hopes to acquire a better and more comprehensive understanding of that intrinsic complexity faced when exploring the context of any natural phenomena.

One of our most important purposes in research is to get as close as we can to understanding the topics we have chosen to study. Becoming "closer" suggests using as many ways of learning about the things we are trying to understand as we can. Closer also suggests, to most of us, the idea of gathering more intimate, more fine-grained kinds of information, so we are better able to grasp the experiences and the intentions, the meaning systems, the local rationality that drives many of our actions in life, and the narratives that provide the evidence to help us understand our social and cultural world. But getting closer to full, holistic understanding also suggests using methods to be more certain of what we are trying to understand, to strive for validation of findings, and to generate evidence that is believable and credible to a wide range of people. To help us better understand the world, then, we need to get closer to that world in systematic ways as well as ways that creatively explore and discover new things about the world with an openness to the richness and surprises that research can reveal.

Getting as close as we can to the phenomena we want to understand in our research using both qualitative and quantitative approaches can help us achieve powerful outcomes, and we are more likely to discover findings that matter. Research findings matter in many ways, including to influence policy or practice. Our findings also matter more when they can add to the *evidence base* for how people and communities behave, think, and feel, particularly how *international and cross-cultural* evidence matters for our understanding of work done only in Euro-American contexts. Our findings matter when we can account for the *mechanisms* that produce the outcomes we are studying and when they *contribute to theories and conceptual frameworks* for the topics we are studying, and they can matter more when they help *integrate work across the social sciences* by speaking to different disciplines through the use of multiple methods. Last but not least, findings matter through the production of evidence and understandings that, it is hoped, *improve the well-being* of those we study and their communities. One way to achieve these goals is through engaging and participating with the community as part of the research—that is, seeing their world through their experiences. Using integrated qualitative and quantitative methods can help produce findings that matter in all these ways. This is a strong claim, no doubt, but there is evidence for this throughout this book, particularly the terrific case studies that exemplify this kind of research using Dedoose and other software.

There are many reasons to consider integrating qualitative and quantitative methods. Perhaps the most important is that *the world that we study is definitely not linear, additive, and decontextualized*, and so we need a suite of complementary methods that, as best as we can, capture more of the holistic, contextual world we are trying to understand. Of course, for very good analytical reasons, we can model the world *as if it were* linear, additive, and decontextualized. However, we should always remain aware that these models are incomplete and that there are other methods and levels of analysis that exist to help us understand the nonlinear, nonadditive, and contextualized nature of the world we are studying. All methods have strengths and limitations, so the goal is to complement the strengths of one method with the strengths of others. Another essential reason is that there is a very high likelihood that the data and results obtained will produce stronger, richer, and more *believable* findings that will really matter, be more useful, and be better prepared to be taken up for policy and practice purposes.

To be clear, the claim is not that mixed methods are always required. Many studies use only a single method, only qualitative or quantitative measures, or only a single sample for many reasons, and these can be very strong studies that produce findings that matter. Of course, many samples, funding levels, and designs make mixed methods difficult or impossible. However, would including more methods or subsamples and voices in these studies not have made the work even stronger? This is why the aspirational goal, a gold standard to be hoped for, would be for most studies to use mixed methods to get closer to holistic understandings, even when it is not always feasible to do so all the time. The epistemological assumption underlying the use of mixed methods is that in scientific endeavors the world can be represented through both numbers and words and that numbers and words should be given equal status in social science. Behaviors or contexts that are relevant for social science research are not inherently qualitative or quantitative; rather, it is the methods of representation through which behaviors or contexts are recorded in research that matter. For more narrowly focused studies, say a single research study or two on a particular topic, single-method designs may be best with respect to time constraints, money, researcher expertise, and other reasons. However, for a larger *program* of research, mixed methods seem much more needed.

Expertise in particular quantitative or qualitative methods is important and desirable, as is disciplinary and topical specialization, both often essential for research training. Once established, wherever indicated and possible, specialization by one person must be partnered with the use of other, complementary methods where others are expert. Otherwise, there is the risk of *methodocentrism*, the privileging of one kind of datum, method, research design, or sampling strategy over others simply because it is the one you or your discipline or group already know and favor. The term *methodocentrism* alerts us to not simply favoring certain methods based on personal identity or ideology, or just due to convention, familiarity, or claims of inherent superiority. Instead, a more open and pluralistic view considers methods as tools for representing the world in diverse ways.

Dedoose is a terrific tool to start a research program along a mixed methods path, and it is also very useful to use Dedoose to do qualitative research alone. Simply upload your interview transcripts, videos, photos, or text samples from Internet searches and then organize and store them by categories. You and your team are then prepared to read them and comment, do further qualitative and pattern analyses, and capitalize on the qualitative data in your research. Dedoose is set up for shared teams to read, comment on, and find patterns in qualitative data. Next steps to doing mixed methods? Add survey and other data to your study, code or otherwise transform some of the qualitative data, do some statistical analyses of these new data, and compare with your qualitative findings. You will have added a lot of value to your study, your findings will matter more, and you will be closer to a fuller and richer understanding of your topic.

Mixed methods research is growing in importance and acceptance, but it is far from the default practice as yet in the social and behavioral sciences. These methods may be recognized as valuable in principle but not in practice in terms of disciplinary research training, funding, publishing, and so forth. So it is important, at least to me, to not only practice mixed methods work and use tools such as Dedoose to do so but also *identify* and claim standing as a mixed methods person and an expert user of Dedoose. Often, we hear researchers say that they are a "qualitative person" or a "quantitative person" or announce that they exclusively use a particular qualitative or quantitative piece of software. The role of a mixed methods specialist as a scholarly and professional identity is growing, as is our self-construal as an interdisciplinary researcher who is proud of training in, using, and understanding mixed methods in the social sciences. This is now and should be in the future a comparative advantage for hiring, funding, publishing, and career advancement. I am also confident that mixed methods researchers will be better able to produce findings that matter, and Dedoose was specifically conceived of and developed to support such goals.

*Thomas S. Weisner, PhD*

**Tom Weisner** is professor emeritus of anthropology in the Departments of Psychiatry and Anthropology at the University of California, Los Angeles. His research and teaching interests are in culture and human development, families and children at risk, children with disabilities and their families, and mixed methods. He has done fieldwork in Kenya; Hawaii; Milwaukee, Wisconsin; and Los Angeles, California. His publications and further information are available at **www.tweisner.com.**

## RELATED READINGS

Weisner, T. S. (2016). Findings that matter: Commentary. In C. Hay (Ed.), *Methods that matter: Integrating mixed methods for more effective social science research* (pp. 393–408). Chicago, IL: University of Chicago Press.

Weisner, T. S. (2018). Culture, context, and the integration of qualitative and quantitative methods in the study of human development. In M. Gelfand, C. Y. Chiu, & Y. Y. Hong (Eds.), *Advances in culture and psychology* (Vol. 7, pp. 153–216). New York, NY: Oxford University Press. doi:10.1093/oso/9780190879228.003.0004

Weisner, T. S., & Duncan, G. (2014). The world isn't linear or additive or decontextualized: Pluralism and mixed methods in understanding the effects of anti-poverty programs on children and parenting. In E. T. Gershoff, R. A. Mistry, & D. A. Crosby (Eds.), *Societal contexts of child development: Pathways of influence and implications for practice and policy* (pp. 124–138). New York, NY: Oxford University Press.

Yoshikawa, H., Weisner, T. S., Kalil, A., & Way, N. (2008). Mixing qualitative and quantitative research in developmental science: Uses and methodological choices. *Developmental Psychology, 44*(2), 344–354.

# References

Agnihotri, R., Dingus, R., Hu, M., & Krush, M. (2016). Social media: Influencing customer satisfaction in B2B sales. *Industrial Marketing Management, 53,* 172–180.

Agnihotri, R., Rapp, A., & Trainor, K. (2009). Understanding the role of information communication in the buyer seller exchange process: Antecedents and outcomes. *Journal of Business & Industrial Marketing, 24*(7), 474–486. doi:10.1108/08858620910986712

Anderson, R. C., Guerreiro, M., & Smith, J. (2016). Are all biases bad? Collaborative grounded theory in developmental evaluation of education policy. *Journal of MultiDisciplinary Evaluation, 12*(27), 44–57.

Anfara, V. A., Jr., Brown, K. M., & Mangione, T. L. (2002). Qualitative analysis on stage: Making the research process more public. *Educational Researcher, 31*(7), 28–38.

Anjali, M. K., & Babu Anto, P. (2014). Ambiguities in natural language processing. *International Journal of Innovative Research in Computer and Communication Engineering, 2*(5), 392–394.

Ayres, L., Kavanaugh, K., & Knafl, K. A. (2003). Within-case and across-case approaches to qualitative data analysis. *Qualitative Health Research, 13*(6), 871–883.

Barbour, R. S. (2001). Checklists for improving rigour in qualitative research: A case of the tail wagging the dog? *British Medical Journal, 5*(322), 115–117.

Bartlett, N. G. (2015). *Exploring donor-defined effectiveness within higher education philanthropy* (Unpublished doctoral dissertation). Central Michigan University, Mount Pleasant, MI.

Bazeley, P. (2013). *Qualitative data analysis.* Thousand Oaks, CA: SAGE.

Bazeley, P. (2017). *Integrating analyses in mixed methods research.* London, UK: SAGE.

Belgrave, L. L., & Smith, K. J. (1995). Negotiated validity in collaborative ethnography. *Qualitative Inquiry, 1*(1), 69–86.

Bernard, H. R. (2013). *Social research methods: Qualitative and quantitative approaches.* Thousand Oaks, CA: SAGE.

Bernard, H. R., Wutich, A., & Ryan, G. W. (2017). Introduction to text: Qualitative data analysis. In H. R. Bernard & G. W. Ryan (Eds.), *Analyzing qualitative data* (2nd ed., pp. 3–16). Thousand Oaks, CA: SAGE.

Bernheimer, L., Weisner, T. S., & Lowe, T. (2003). Impacts of children with troubles on working poor families: Mixed-methods and experimental evidence. *Mental Retardation, 41*(6), 403–419.

Bielefeld, W., Rooney, P., & Steinberg, K. (2005). How do need, capacity, geography, and politics influence giving? In A. C. Brooks (Ed.), *Gifts of time and money: The role of charity in America's communities* (pp. 127–158). Lanham, MD: Rowman & Littlefield.

Blank, G. (2008). Online research methods and social theory. In N. Fielding, R. M. Lee, & G. Blank (Eds.), *The SAGE handbook of online research methods and social theory* (pp. 537–550). Thousand Oaks, CA: SAGE.

Blei, D. M., Ng, A. Y., & Jordan, M. I. (2003). Latent Dirichlet allocation. *Journal of Machine Learning Research, 3,* 993–1022.

Blismas, N. G., & Dainty, A. R. J. (2003). Computer-aided qualitative data analysis: Panacea or paradox? *Building Research & Information, 31*(6), 455–463.

Braun, V., & Clarke, V. (2006). Using thematic analysis in psychology. *Qualitative Research in Psychology, 3,* 77–102.

Broer, C., Moerman, G., Wester, J. C., Malamud, L. R., Schmidt, L., Stoopendaal, A., Kruiderink, N., . . . Sjolie, H. (2016). Open online research: Developing software and method for collaborative interpretation. *Forum: Qualitative Social Research Sozialforshcung/Forum: Qualitative Social Research, 17*(3), 2. Retrieved from http://www.qualitative-research.net/index.php/fqs/article/view/2388/4039

Brown, R. A., Kennedy, D. P., Tucker, J. S., Golinelli, D., & Wenzel, S. L. (2013). Monogamy on the street: A mixed methods study of homeless men. *Journal of Mixed Methods Research, 7*(4), 328–346. Retrieved from http://mmr.sagepub.com/content/7/4/328.abstract

Brown, R. A., Kennedy, D. P., Tucker, J. S., Wenzel, S., Golinelli, D., Wertheimer, S., & Ryan, G. (2012). Sex and relationships on the street: How homeless men judge partner risk on skid row. *AIDS and Behavior, 16*(3), 774–784. doi:10.1007/s10461-011-9965-3

Bryman, A. (2006). Integrating quantitative and qualitative research: How is it done? *Qualitative Research, 6*(1), 97–113.

Cambria, E., & White, B. (2014). Jumping NLP curves: A review of natural language processing research. *IEEE Computational Intelligence Magazine, 9*(2), 48–57.

Caracelli, V. J., & Greene, J. C. (1993). Data analysis strategies for mixed-method evaluation designs. *Educational Evaluation and Policy Analysis, 15*(2), 195–207.

Caruth, G. D. (2013). Demystifying mixed methods research design: A review of the literature. *Mevlana International Journal of Education, 3*(2), 112–122.

Centers for Disease Control and Prevention. (2015). *2015 sexually transmitted diseases treatment guidelines: Special populations.* Retrieved from http://www.cdc.gov/std/tg2015/specialpops.htm

Centers for Disease Control and Prevention. (2016). *Diagnoses of HIV infection among adolescents and young adults in the United States and 6 dependent areas 2010–2014* (HIV Surveillance Supplemental Report). Retrieved from http://www.cdc.gov/hiv/library/reports/surveillance/

Charmaz, K. (2014). *Constructing grounded theory* (2nd ed.). Thousand Oaks, CA: SAGE.

Cisneros Puebla, C. A., Davidson, J., & Faux, R. (Eds.). (2012). Qualitative computing: Diverse worlds and research practices. *Forum Qualitative Sozialforschung/Forum: Qualitative Social Research, 13*(2). Retrieved from http://www.qualitative-research.net/index.php/fqs/issue/view/40

Clow, K., & Baack, D. (2016). *Integrated advertising, promotion, and marketing communications* (7th ed.). Boston, MA: Pearson.

Coffey, A., Holbrook, B., & Atkinson, P. (1996). Qualitative data analysis: Technologies and representations. *Sociological Research Online 1*(1), 1–12.

Cohen, J. (1988). *Statistical power analysis for the behavioral sciences.* New York, NY: Academic Press.

Corbin, J., & Strauss, A. (2015). *Basics of qualitative research: Techniques and procedures for developing grounded theory* (4th ed.). Thousand Oaks, CA: SAGE.

Creswell, J. W. (2009). *Research design: Quantitative, qualitative, and mixed methods approaches* (3rd ed.). Thousand Oaks, CA: SAGE.

Creswell, J. W. (2017). *Research design: Qualitative, quantitative, and mixed methods approaches* (5th ed.). Thousand Oaks, CA: SAGE.

Creswell, J. W., & Clark, V. L. P. (2011). *Designing and conducting mixed methods research* (2nd ed.). Thousand Oaks, CA: SAGE.

Creswell, J. W., & Poth, C. N. (2017). *Qualitative inquiry and research design choosing among five approaches* (4th ed.). Thousand Oaks, CA: SAGE.

Creswell, J. W., & Tashakkori, A. (2007). Developing publishable mixed methods manuscripts. *Journal of Mixed Methods Research, 1*(2), 107–111.

Crook, C. (1994). *Computers and the collaborative experience of learning.* London, UK: Routledge.

Davidson, J., & di Gregorio, S. (2012). Qualitative research and technology: In the midst of a revolution. In N. K. Denzin & Y. S. Lincoln (Eds.), *Collecting and interpreting qualitative material* (4th ed., pp. 481–516). Thousand Oaks, CA: SAGE.

Davis, F. D. (1986). *A technology acceptance model for empirically testing new end-user information systems: Theory and results.* Cambridge: Sloan School of Management, MIT.

Davis, F. D. (1989). Perceived usefulness, perceived ease of use, and user acceptance of information technology. *MIS Quarterly, 13*(3), 319–340.

Day, C., Sammons, P., & Gu, Q. (2008). Combining qualitative and quantitative methodologies in research on teachers' lives, work and effectiveness: From integration to synergy. *Educational Researcher, 37*(6), 330–342.

Dedoose. (2017). *User guide.* Retrieved from http://dedoose.com/userguide

Denzin, N. K., & Lincoln, Y. S. (2013). *Strategies of qualitative inquiry* (4th ed.). Thousand Oaks, CA: SAGE.

Denzin, N. K., & Lincoln, Y. S. (2017). *The SAGE handbook of qualitative research* (5th ed.). Thousand Oaks, CA: SAGE.

Dewey, J. (1938). *Experience and education* (Touchstone ed.). New York, NY: Simon & Schuster.

Dey, I. (1993). *Qualitative data analysis: A user-friendly guide for social scientists.* London, UK: Routledge Kegan Paul.

di Gregorio, S. (2010). Using web 2.0 tools for qualitative analysis: An exploration. In R. H. Sprague, Jr. (Ed.), *Proceedings of the 43rd Hawaii International Conference on System Sciences,* 1–10. Piscataway, NJ: Institute of Electrical and Electronic Engineers. doi:10.1109/HICSS.2010.432

di Gregorio, S., & Davidson, J. (2008). *Qualitative research design for software users.* Berkshire, UK: Open University Press.

DuBois, L. Z., Macapagal, K. R., Rivera, Z., Prescott, T. L., Ybarra, M. L., & Mustanski, B. (2015). To have sex or not to have sex? An online focus group study of sexual decision making among sexually experienced and inexperienced gay and bisexual adolescent men. *Archives of Sexual Behavior, 44*(7), 2027–2040. doi:10.1007/s10508-015-0521-5

Erickson, F. (2007, May). *Specifying "usually" and "some": Using simple descriptive statistics in qualitative inquiry.* Paper presented at the 2007 Congress of Qualitative Inquiry, Urbana, IL.

Erickson, F. (2012). Comments on causality in qualitative inquiry. *Qualitative Inquiry, 18*(8), 686–688.

Evers, J. C., Mruck, K., Silver, C., & Peeters, B. (Eds.). (2011). The KWALON experiment: Discussions on qualitative data analysis software by developers and users. *Forum Qualitative Sozialforschung/Forum: Qualitative Social Research, 12*(1). Retrieved from http://www.qualitative-research.net/index.php/fqs/issue/view/36

Fairclough, N. (2000). *New Labour, New Language.* London, UK: Routledge.

Finlay, L. (2002). "Outing" the researcher: The provenance, process, and practice of reflexivity. *Qualitative Health Research, 12*(4), 531–545.

Fisher, C. B., Arbeit, M. R., Dumont, M. S., Macapagal, K., & Mustanski, B. (2016). Self-consent for HIV prevention research involving sexual and gender minority youth: Reducing barriers through evidence-based ethics. *Journal of Empirical Research on Human Research Ethics, 11*(1), 3–14. doi:10.1177/1556264616633963

Futch Ehrlich, V. A., Deutsch, N. L., Fox, C. V., Johnson, H. E., & Varga, S. M. (2016). Leveraging relational assets for adolescent development: A qualitative investigation of youth–adult "connection" positive youth development. *Qualitative Psychology, 3*(1), 59–78.

Geldhof, G. J., Bowers, E. P., Boyd, M. J., Mueller, M. K., Napolitano, C. M., Schmid, K. L., . . . Lerner, R. M. (2014). Creation of short and very short measures of the Five Cs of positive youth development. *Journal of Research on Adolescence, 24,* 163–176. doi:10.1111/jora.12039

Gerstl-Pepin, C. I., & Gunzenhauser, M. G. (2002). Collaborative team ethnography and the paradoxes of interpretation. *Qualitative Studies in Education, 15*(2), 137–154.

Gibbs, G. R., Friese, S., & Mangabeira, W. C. (2002). The use of new technology in qualitative research. Introduction to Issue 3(2) of FQS. *Forum Qualitative Sozialforschung/Forum: Qualitative Social Research, 3*(2), Art. 8. Retrieved from http://nbn-resolving.de/urn:nbn:de:0114-fqs020287

Gibson, W., & Brown, A. (2009). *Working with qualitative data.* Thousand Oaks, CA: SAGE.

Gilbert, L. S. (2000, April). *From print to pixels: Practitioners' reflections on the use of qualitative data analysis software.* Paper presented at the meeting of the American Educational Research Association, New Orleans, LA.

Gilbert, L., Jackson, K., & di Gregorio, S. (2014). Tools for analyzing qualitative data: The history and relevance of qualitative data analysis software. In J. M. Spector, M. David Merrill, J. Elen, & M. J. Bishop (Eds.), *Handbook of research on educational communications and technology* (4th ed., pp. 221–236). New York, NY: Springer.

Glaser, B. G. (1999). Keynote address from the fourth annual qualitative health research conference: The future of grounded theory. *Qualitative Health Research, 9*(6), 836–845.

Glaser, B. G. (2002). Conceptualization: On theory and theorizing using grounded theory. *International Journal of Qualitative Methods, 1*(2), 23–38.

Glaser, B. G. (2010). The future of grounded theory. *Grounded Theory Review, 2*(9), 1–14.

Glaser, B. G., & Strauss, A. L. (1967). *Discovery of grounded theory: Strategies for qualitative research.* Hawthorne, NY: Aldine de Gruyter.

Greene, G. J., Andrews, R., Kuper, L., & Mustanski, B. (2014). Intimacy, monogamy, and condom problems drive unprotected sex among young men in serious relationships with other men: A mixed methods dyadic study. *Archives of Sexual Behavior, 43,* 73–87. doi:10.1007/s10508-013-0210-1

Guest, G., MacQueen, K. M., & Namey, E. E. (2012a). *Applied thematic analysis.* Thousand Oaks, CA: SAGE.

Guest, G., MacQueen, K. M., & Namey, E. E. (2012b). Data reduction techniques. In G. Guest, K. M. MacQueen, & E. E. Namey (Eds.), *Applied thematic analysis* (pp. 129–160). Thousand Oaks, CA: SAGE.

Hay, M. C., & Furst, D. E. (2016). The responsibilities of daily life may interfere with adherence to medications in patients with rheumatoid arthritis (RA) and systemic sclerosis (SSc). *Journal of Clinical Rheumatology, 22*(7), 392.

Hayes, R. D., Sherbourne, C. D., & Mazel, R. M. (1993). The RAND 36-Item Health Survey 1.0. *Health Economics, 2,* 217–227.

Hechtman, L., Swanson, J. M., Sibley, M. H., Stehli, A., Owens, E. B., Mitchell, J. T., . . . MTA Cooperative Group. (2016). Functional adult outcomes 16 years after childhood diagnosis of attention-deficit/hyperactivity disorder: MTA results. *Journal of the American Academy of Child & Adolescent Psychiatry, 55*(11), 945–952, e942. doi:10.1016/j.jaac.2016.07.774

Hesse-Biber, S. N. (2010a). *Mixed methods research: Merging theory with practice.* New York, NY: Guilford Press.

Hesse-Biber, S. (2010b). Qualitative approaches to mixed methods practice. *Qualitative Inquiry, 16*(6), 455–668.

Hill, C. E., Knox, S., Thompson, B. J., Williams, E. N., Hess, S. A., & Ladany, N. (2005). Consensual qualitative research: An update. *Journal of Counseling Psychology, 52*(2), 196–205. doi:10.1037/0022-0167.52.2.196

Hirsch, B. J., Deutsch. N. L., & DuBois, D. L. (2011). *After-school centers and youth development: Case studies of success and failure.* New York, NY: Cambridge University Press.

Hofer, B. K., & Bendixen, L. D. (2012). Personal epistemology: Theory, research, and future directions. In K. R. Harris, S. Graham, T. Urdan, C. B. McCormick, G. M. Sinatra, & J. Sweller (Eds.), *APA educational psychology handbook: Vol. 1. Theories, constructs, and critical issues* (pp. 227–256). Washington, DC: American Psychological Association. doi:10.1037/13273-009

Huston, A. C., Duncan, G. J., McLoyd, V. C., Crosby, D. A., Ripke, M. N., Weisner, T. S., & Eldred, C. A. (2005). Impacts on children of a policy to promote employment and reduce poverty for low-income parents: New Hope after 5 years. *Developmental Psychology, 41*(6), 902–918.

Hutton, J. (1996). Integrated marketing communications and the evolution of marketing thought. *Journal of Business Research, 37,* 155–162.

IBM. (2013). *IBM SPSS statistics for Windows: Version 22.0.* Armonk, NY: Author.

International Association for Social Science Information Services and Technology. (2014). *Democratizing data: The IASSIST strategic plan for 2010–2014.* Retrieved from https://iassistdata.org/about/strategic-plan

Janz, N. (2015). Bringing the gold standard into the classroom: Replication in university teaching. *International Studies Perspectives.* doi:10.1111/insp.12104

Jehn, K. A., & Doucet, L. (1996). Developing categories from interview data: Text analysis and multidimensional scaling—Part 1. *Cultural Anthropology Methods Journal, 8*(2), 15–16.

Jehn, K. A., & Doucet, L. (1997). Developing categories for interview data: Consequences of different coding and analysis strategies in understanding text—Part 2. *Cultural Anthropology Methods Journal, 9*(1), 1–7.

Jensen, P. S., Yuki, K., Murray, D., Mitchell, J. T., Weisner, T., Hinshaw, S., . . . Wells, K. (2018). Turning points in the lives of youth of with/without ADHD: Are they linked to changes in substance use? *Journal of Attention Disorders, 22*(9 Suppl.), 38S–48S. doi:10.1177/1087054717700977

Johnson, R. B., & Christensen, L. (2017). *Educational research: Quantitative, qualitative, and mixed approaches* (6th ed.). Thousand Oaks, CA: SAGE.

Jonassen, D. H. (1997). Instructional design models for well-structured and ill-structured problem-solving learning outcomes. *Educational Technology Research & Development, 45*(1), 65–94.

Josselson, R. (2011). Narrative research: Conducting, deconstructing, and reconstructing story. In F. J. Wertz, K. Charmaz, L. M. McMullen, R. Josselson, R. Anderson, &

E. McSpadden (Eds.), *Five ways of doing qualitative analysis: Phenomenological psychology, grounded theory, discourse analysis, narrative research, and intuitive inquiry* (pp. 224–242). New York, NY: Guilford Press.

Kaczynski, D., Miller, E., & Kelly, M. A. (2014). *Ensuring quality and rigor: A few lessons learned from a national evaluation study* (in companion website to L. Richards, *Handling qualitative data*, 3rd ed.). London, UK: SAGE. Retrieved from https://study.sagepub.com/richards3e/student-resources/methods-in-practice/youth-offender-program-evaluation

Kaczynski, D., Salmona, M., & Smith, T. (2014). Qualitative research in finance. *Australian Journal of Management, 39*(1), 127–135.

Kajfez, R., & Creamer, E. (2014, June). *A mixed methods analysis and evaluation of the mixed methods research literature in engineering education.* Paper presented at the ASEE Annual Conference and Exposition, Indianapolis, IN.

Karcher, S., & Pagé, C. (2017). Workshop Report: CAQDAS Projects and Digital Repositories' Best Practices. *D-Lib Magazine, 23*(3/4). doi:10.1045/march2017-karcher

Kennedy, D. P., Brown, R. A., Golinelli, D., Wenzel, S. L., Tucker, J. S., & Wertheimer, S. R. (2012). Masculinity and HIV risk among homeless men in Los Angeles. *Psychology of Men & Masculinity, 14*(2), 156–167.

Kerr, G., & Patti, C. (2015). Strategic IMC: From abstract concept to marketing management tool. *Journal of Marketing Communications, 21*(5), 317–339.

Kurtz, D. (2016). *Contemporary marketing* (17th ed.). Boston, MA: Cengage Learning.

Leech, N. L. (2012). Writing mixed research reports. *American Behavioral Scientist, 56*(6), 866–881.

Lieber, E. (2016). Collaborative research on emergent literacy: Capturing complex mixed methods data and tools for their use. In M. C. Hay (Ed.), *Methods that matter: Integrating mixed methods for more effective social science research* (pp. 185–209). Chicago, IL: University of Chicago Press.

Lieber, E., Weisner, T. S., & Presley, M. (2003). EthnoNotes: An Internet-based field note management tool. *Field Methods, 15*(4), 405–425.

Lincoln, Y. S., & Guba, E. G. (1985). *Naturalistic inquiry.* Newbury Park, CA: SAGE.

Lincoln, Y. S., & Guba, E. G. (2013). *The constructivists credo.* Walnut Creek, CA: Left Coast Press.

Loseke, D. R. (2017). *Methodological thinking: Basic principles of social research design* (2nd ed.). Thousand Oaks, CA: SAGE.

Lowe, E., Weisner, T., Geis, S., & Huston, A. (2005). Child care instability and the effort to sustain a working daily routine: Evidence from the New Hope Ethnographic Study of Low-Income Families. In C. Cooper, C. Garcia-Coll, T. Bartko, H. Davis, & C. Chatman (Eds.), *Developmental pathways through middle childhood: Rethinking contexts and diversity as resources* (pp. 121–144). Mahwah, NJ: Erlbaum.

Lupia, A., & Elman, C. (2014). Openness in political science: Data access and research transparency. *PS: Political Science & Politics, 47*(1), 19–42. doi:10.1017/S1049096513001716

Macapagal, K., Coventry, R., Arbeit, M. R., Fisher, C. B., & Mustanski, B. (2016). "I won't out myself just to do a survey": Sexual and gender minority adolescents' perspectives on the risks and benefits of sex research. *Archives of Sexual Behavior, 46*(5), 1393–1409. doi:10.1007/s10508-016-0784-5

Magee, J. C., Bigelow, L., Dehaan, S., & Mustanski, B. S. (2012). Sexual health information seeking online: A mixed-methods study among lesbian, gay, bisexual, and transgender young people. *Health Education and Behavior, 39,* 276–289. doi:10.1177/1090198111401384

Marshall, C., & Rossman, G. B. (2015). *Designing qualitative research* (6th ed.). Thousand Oaks, CA: SAGE.

Martelo, M. L. (2011). Use of bibliographic systems and concept maps: Innovative tools to complete a literature review. *Research in the Schools, 18*(1), 62–70.

Mauthner, N. S., & Doucet, A. (2003). Reflexive accounts and accounts of reflexivity in qualitative data analysis. *Sociology, 37*(3), 413–431.

Maxwell, J. A. (2010). Using numbers in qualitative research. *Qualitative Inquiry, 16*(6), 475–482.

Maxwell, J. A. (2013). *Qualitative research design: An interactive approach.* Thousand Oaks, CA: SAGE.

McKenny, S., & Reeves, T. (2012). *Conducting educational design research.* New York, NY: Routledge.

Mertens, D. M. (2017). *Mixed methods design in evaluation.* Thousand Oaks, CA: SAGE.

Meyer, C., & Schwager, M. (2007). Understanding customer experience. *Harvard Business Review, 85*(2). Retrieved from https://hbr.org/2007/02/understanding-customer-experience

Michler, E. G. (1979). Meaning in context: Is there any other kind? *Harvard Educational Review, 49*(1), 1–19.

Miles, M. B., & Huberman, A. M. (1984). Drawing valid meaning from qualitative data: Toward a shared craft. *Educational Research, 13*(5), 20–30.

Miles, M. B., & Huberman, A. M. (1994). *Qualitative data analysis* (2nd ed.). Thousand Oaks, CA: SAGE.

Miles, M. B., Huberman, A. M., & Saldana, J. (2014). *Qualitative data analysis: A methods sourcebook.* Thousand Oaks, CA: SAGE.

Miller, G. A. (1956). The magical number seven, plus or minus two: Some limits on our capacity for processing information. *Psychological Review, 63*(2), 81–97.

Mitchell, J. T., Howard, A. L., Belendiuk, K. A., Kennedy, T. M., Stehli, A., Swanson, J. M., . . . Molina, B. S. G. (2019). Cigarette smoking progression among young adults diagnosed with ADHD in childhood: A 16-year longitudinal study of children with and without ADHD. *Nicotine and Tobacco Research. 21*(5), 638–647.

Mitchell, J. T., Weisner, T. S., Jensen, P. S., Murray, D. W., Molina, B. S., Arnold, E. L., . . . Nguyen, J. L. (2017). How substance users with ADHD perceive the relationship between substance use and emotional functioning. *Journal of Attention Disorders, 22*(9 Suppl.), 49S–60S. doi:10.1177/1087054716685842

Molina, B. S., Flory, K., Hinshaw, S. P., Greiner, A. R., Arnold, L. E., Swanson, J. M., . . . Wigal, T. (2007). Delinquent behavior and emerging substance use in the MTA at 36 months: Prevalence, course, and treatment effects. *Journal of the American Academy of Child & Adolescent Psychiatry, 46*(8), 1028–1040. doi:10.1097/chi.0b013e3180686d96

Molina, B. S., Hinshaw, S. P., Eugene Arnold, L., Swanson, J. M., Pelham, W. E., Hechtman, L., . . . Marcus, S. (2013). Adolescent substance use in the multimodal treatment study of Attention-Deficit/Hyperactivity Disorder (ADHD) (MTA) as a function of childhood ADHD, random assignment to childhood treatments, and subsequent medication. *Journal of the American Academy of Child & Adolescent Psychiatry, 52*(3), 250–263. doi:10.1016/j.jaac.2012.12.014

Molina, B. S. G., Howard, A. L., Swanson, J. M., Stehli, A., Mitchell, J. T., Kennedy, T. M., . . . Hoza, B. (2018). Substance use through adolescence into early adulthood after childhood-diagnosed ADHD: Findings from the MTA longitudinal study. *Journal of Child Psychology and Psychiatry, 59*(6), 692–702. doi:10.1111/jcpp.12855

Moravcsik, A. (2014). Transparency: The revolution in qualitative research. *PS, Political Science & Politics, 47*(1), 48–53.

Moss, P. A., Phillips, D. C., Erickson, F. D., Floden, R. E., Lather, P. A., & Schneider, B. L. (2009). Learning from our differences: A dialogue across perspectives on quality in education research. *Educational Researcher, 38*(7), 501–517.

Moylan, C. A., Derr, A. S., & Lindhorst, T. (2015). Increasingly mobile: How new technologies can enhance qualitative research. *Qualitative Social Work, 14*(1), 36–47.

Mulhall, A. (2003). In the field: Notes on observation in qualitative research. *Journal of Advanced Nursing, 41*(3), 306–313.

Mustanski, B., Coventry, R., Macapagal, K., Arbeit, M. R., & Fisher, C. B. (2017). Sexual and gender minority adolescents' views on HIV research participation and parental permission: A mixed-methods study. *Perspectives on Sexual and Reproductive Health, 49*(2), 111–121. doi:10.1363/psrh.12027

Mustanski, B., Lyons, T., & Garcia, S. C. (2011). Internet use and sexual health of young men who have sex with men: A mixed-methods study. *Archives of Sexual Behavior, 40*(2), 289–300. doi:10.1007/s10508-009-9596-1

Mustanski, B., Macapagal, K., Thomann, M., Feinstein, B. A., Newcomb, M. E., Motley, D., & Fisher, C. B. (2018). Parents' perspectives about adolescent boys' involvement in biomedical HIV prevention research. *Archives of Sexual Behavior, 47*(7), 1923–1935.

Namey, E. E., Guest, G., Thairu, L., & Johnson, L. (2008). Data reduction techniques for large qualitative data sets. In G. Guest & K. MacQueen (Eds.), *Handbook for team-based qualitative research* (pp. 137–161). Lanham, MD: AltaMira Press.

Nicassio, P., Wallston, K. A., Callahan, L. F., Herbert, M., & Pincus, T. (1985). The measurement of helplessness in rheumatoid arthritis. *Journal of Rheumatology, 12,* 462–467.

Noddings, N. (2007). *Philosophy of education* (2nd ed.). Boulder, CO: Westview Press.

O'Cathain, A., Murphy, E., & Nicholl, J. (2008a). The quality of mixed methods studies in health services research. *Journal of Health Services Research and Policy, 13*(2), 92–98.

O'Cathain, A., Murphy, E., & Nicholl, J. (2008b). Multidisciplinary, interdisciplinary, or dysfunctional? Team working in mixed-methods research. *Qualitative Health Research, 18*(11), 1574–1585.

Onwuegbuzie, A., & Leech, N. (2005). Taking the "Q" out of research: Teaching research methodology courses without the divide between quantitative and qualitative paradigms. *Quality & Quantity, 39*(3), 267–296.

Onwuegbuzie, A. J., Slate, J. R., Leech, N. L., & Collins, K. M. T. (2009). Mixed data analysis: Advanced integration techniques. *International Journal of Multiple Research Approaches, 3,* 13–33.

Onwuegbuzie, A. J., & Teddlie, C. (2003). A framework for analyzing data in mixed methods research. In A. Tashakkori & C. Teddlie (Eds.), *Handbook of mixed methods in social and behavioral research* (pp. 351–383). Thousand Oaks, CA: SAGE.

O'Reilly, M., & Kiyimba, N. (2015). *Advanced qualitative research: A guide to using theory.* Thousand Oaks, CA: SAGE.

Parasuraman, A. (2000). Technology readiness index (TRI): A multiple-item scale to measure readiness to embrace new technologies. *Journal of Service Research, 2*(4), 307–320.

Parasuraman, A., & Colby, C. L. (2015). An updated and streamlined technology readiness index: TRI 2.0. *Journal of Service Research, 18*(1), 59–74.

Patton, M. Q. (2015). *Qualitative research and evaluation methods* (4th ed.). Thousand Oaks, CA: SAGE.

Phillips, J., & Springer, F. (1992). *Extended National Youth Sports Program 1991–1992 evaluation highlights, Part Two: Individual Protective Factors Index (IPFI) and risk assessment study* (Report prepared for the National Collegiate Athletic Association). Sacramento, CA: EMT Associates.

Poulis, S., & Dasgupta, S. (2017). *Learning with feature feedback: From theory to practice.* Paper presented at the Proceedings of the 20th International Conference on Artificial Intelligence and Statistics (AISTATS), Fort Lauderdale, FL.

Richards, L. (2015). *Handling qualitative data: A practical guide* (3rd ed.). London, UK: SAGE.

Richards, L., & Richards, T. (1991). Computing in qualitative analysis: A healthy development? *Qualitative Health Research, 1*(2), 234–262.

Rogers, E. (1962). *Diffusion of innovations* (1st ed.). Glencoe, IL: Free Press.

Rogers, E. (2003). *Diffusion of innovations* (5th ed.). New York, NY: Simon & Schuster.

Ryan, G. (1993). Using WordPerfect macros to handle fieldnotes I: Coding. *Field Methods, 5*(1), 10–11.

Ryan, G. W., & Bernard, H. R. (2003). Techniques to identify themes. *Field Methods, 15*(1), 85–109.

Saldana, J. (2013). *The coding manual for qualitative researchers* (2nd ed.). Thousand Oaks, CA: SAGE.

Salmona, M., & Kaczynski, D. (2016). Don't blame the software: Using qualitative data analysis software successfully in doctoral research. *Forum Qualitative Sozialforschung/Forum: Qualitative Social Research, 17*(3), 11. Retrieved from http://nbn-resolving.de/urn:nbn:de:0114 -fqs1603117

Salmona, M., Kaczynski, D., & Smith, T. (2015). Qualitative theory in finance: Theory into practice. *Australian Journal of Management, 40*(3), 403–413.

Schiffman, S. S. (1991). Instructional systems design: Five views of the field. In G. J. Anglin (Ed.), *Instructional technology: Past, present, and future* (pp. 102–116). Englewood, CO: Libraries Unlimited.

Schram, T. H. (2006). *Conceptualizing and proposing qualitative inquiry* (2nd ed.). Upper Saddle River, NJ: Pearson Merrill Prentice Hall.

Schultz, D., & Block, M. (2015). Beyond brand loyalty: Brand sustainability. *Journal of Marketing Communications, 21*(5), 340–355.

Schwandt, T. (2007). *The SAGE dictionary of qualitative inquiry* (3rd ed.). Los Angeles, CA: SAGE.

Schwandt, T. A. (2015). *Dictionary of qualitative inquiry* (4th ed.). Thousand Oaks, CA: SAGE.

Shoemaker, A. L. (1980). Construct validity of area specific self-esteem: The Hare Self-Esteem Scale. *Educational and Psychological Measurement, 40*(2), 495–501.

Silver, C., & Lewins, A. (2014). *Using software in qualitative research: A step-by-step guide.* London, UK: SAGE.

Silver, C., & Woolf, N. H. (2015). From guided instruction to facilitation of learning: The development of Five-level QDA as a CAQDAS pedagogy that explicates the practices of expert users. *International Journal of Social Research Methodology, 18*(5), 527–543.

Somekh, B., & Lewin, C. (2012). *Theory and methods in social research* (2nd ed.). Thousand Oaks, CA: SAGE.

Spiro, R. J., Coulson, R. L., Feltovich, P. J., & Anderson, D. (1988). Cognitive flexibility theory: Advanced knowledge acquisition in ill-structured domains. In V. Patel (Ed.), *Proceedings of the 10th annual conference of the Cognitive Science Society.* Hillsdale, NJ: Erlbaum.

St. John, W., & Johnson, P. (2000). The pros and cons of data analysis software for qualitative research. *Journal of Nursing Scholarship, 32*(4), 393–397.

Sternberg, R. J. (2014). Expertise in complex problem solving: A comparison of alternative conceptions. In P. A. Frensch & J. Funke (Eds.), *Complex problem solving: The European perspective* (pp. 295–321). New York, NY: Psychology Press.

Swanson, J. M., Arnold, L. E., Jensen, P. S., Hinshaw, S. P., Hechtman, L. T., Pelham, W. E., . . . Stehli, A. (2018). Long-term outcomes in the multimodal treatment study of children with ADHD (the MTA). In T. Banaschewski, D. Coghill, & A. Zuddas (Eds.), *Oxford textbook of attention deficit hyperactivity disorder* (pp. 315–332). Oxford, UK: Oxford University Press.

Swanson, J. M., Wigal, T., Jensen, P. S., Mitchell, J. T., Weisner, T. S., Murray, D., . . . Stehli, A. (2018). The qualitative interview study of persistent and nonpersistent substance use in the MTA: Sample characteristics, frequent use, and reasons for use. *Journal of Attention Disorders, 22*(9 Suppl.), 21S–37S. doi:10.1177/1087054717714058

Tashakkori, A., & Teddlie, C. (2003). The past and future of mixed methods research: From data triangulation to mixed model designs. In A. Tashakkori & C. Teddlie (Eds.), *Handbook of mixed methods in social and behavioral research* (pp. 671–702). Thousand Oaks, CA: SAGE.

Tashakkori, A., & Teddlie, C. (2013). *Foundations of mixed methods research.* Thousand Oaks, CA: SAGE.

*Technology Readiness Index 2.0.* (2014). Rockbridge Associates. Retrieved from https://rockresearch.com/technology-readiness-index-primer/

Tuckman, B. W. (1965). Development sequence in small groups. *Psychological Bulletin, 63*(6), 384–399.

Tuckman, B. W., & Jensen, M. A. C. (1977). Stages of small-group development revisited. *Group & Organization Management, 2*(4), 419–427.

Underwood, M., Satterthwait, L. D., & Bartlett, H. P. (2010). Reflexivity and minimization of the impact of age–cohort differences between researcher and research participants. *Qualitative Health Research, 20*(11), 1585–1595.

Vaux, A. (1988). *Social support: Theory, research, and intervention.* New York, NY: Praeger.

Venkatesh, V., Brown, S. A., & Bala, H. (2013). Bridging the qualitative–quantitative divide: Guidelines for conducting mixed methods research in information systems. *MIS Quarterly, 37*(1), 21–54.

Waimann, C. A., Marengo, M. F., de Achaval, S., Cox, V. L., Garcia-Gonzalez, A., Reveille, J. D., . . . Suarez-Almazor, M. E. (2013). Electronic monitoring of oral therapies in ethnically diverse and economically disadvantaged patients with rheumatoid arthritis: Consequences of low adherence. *Arthritis & Rheumatism, 65*(6), 1421–1429.

Wald, H. S., Davis, S. W., Reis, S. P., Monroe, A. D., & Borkan, J. M. (2009). Reflecting on reflections: Enhancement of medical education curriculum with structured field notes and guided feedback. *Academic Medicine, 84*(7), 830–837.

Wei, M., Russell, D. W., Mallinckrodt, B., & Vogel, D. L. (2007). The Experiences in Close Relationship Scale (ECR)-Short Form: Reliability, validity, and factor structure. *Journal of Personality Assessment, 88,* 187–204.

Weisner, T. W. (1996). Why ethnography should be the most important method in the study of human development. In R. Jessor, A. Colby, & R. A. Shweder (Eds.), *Ethnography and human development: Context and meaning in social inquiry* (pp. 305–324). Chicago, IL: University of Chicago Press.

Weisner, T. S. (1997). The ecocultural project of human development: Why ethnography and its findings matter. *Ethos, 25*(2), 177–190.

Weisner, T. S. (2002). Ecocultural understanding of children's developmental pathways. *Human Development, 45*(4), 275–281.

Weisner, T. S. (2014). Why qualitative and ethnographic methods are essential for understanding family life. In S. M. McHale, P. Amato, & A. Booth (Eds.), *Emerging methods in family research: Approaches to measuring families* (pp. 163–178). Dordrecht, Netherlands: Springer.

Weisner, T. S., & Duncan, G. (2014). The world isn't linear or additive or decontextualized: Pluralism and mixed methods in understanding the effects of anti-poverty programs in children and parenting. In E. T. Gershoff, R. S. Mistry, & D. A. Crosby (Eds.), *Societal contexts of child development: Pathways of influence and implications for practice and policy* (pp. 124–138). New York, NY: Oxford University Press.

Weisner, T. S., Murray, D. W., Jensen, P. S., Mitchell, J. T., Swanson, J. M., Hinshaw, S. P., . . . Stehli, A. (2018). Follow-up of young adults with ADHD in the MTA: Design and methods for qualitative interviews. *Journal of Attention Disorders, 22*(9 Suppl.), 10S–20S. doi:10.1177/1087054717713639

Weller, S. C. (2007). Cultural consensus theory: Applications and frequently asked questions. *Field Methods, 19*(4), 339–368. Retrieved from http://fmx.sagepub.com/cgi/content/abstract/19/4/339

Welsh, E. (2002). Dealing with data: Using NVivo in the qualitative data analysis process. *Forum Qualitative Sozialforschung/Forum: Qualitative Social Research, 3*(2), Art. 26. Retrieved from http://nbn-resolving.de/urn:nbn:de:0114-fqs0202260

Wickham, M., & Woods, M. (2005). Reflecting on the strategic use of CAQDAS to manage and report on the qualitative research process. *Qualitative Report, 10*(4), 687–702.

Wills, T. A., & Shinar, O. (2000). Measuring perceived and received social support. In S. Cohen., L. G. Underwood., & B. H. Gottlieb (Eds.), *Social support measurement and intervention: A guide for health and social scientists* (pp. 86–135). Oxford, UK: Oxford University Press.

Wong, D., & Baker, C. (1988). Pain in Children: Comparison of assessment scales. *Pediatric Nursing, 14,* 9–17.

Woolf, N. H., & Silver, C. (2018). *Qualitative analysis using ATLAS.ti, MAXQDA, and NVivo: The Five-Level QDA method.* New York, NY: Routledge.

Yoshikawa, H., Weisner, T. S., Kalil, A., & Way, N. (2008). Mixing qualitative and quantitative research in developmental science: Uses and methodological choices. *Developmental Psychology, 44*(2), 344–354.

Yu, M. V. B., Deutsch, N. L., Futch Ehrlich, V., Arbeit, M., Johnson, H. E., & Melton, T. (2019). "It's like all of his attention is on you": A mixed methods examination of attachment, supportive nonparental youth–adult relationships, and self-esteem during adolescence. *Journal of Community Psychology, 47*(2), 414–434. doi:10.1002/jcop.22129

# Index

www.ingramcontent.com/pod-product-compliance
Ingram Content Group UK Ltd.
Pitfield, Milton Keynes, MK11 3LW, UK
UKHW051846070225
454829UK00007B/270